GRAHAM GREENE: A CRITICAL STUDY

Encyclopaedia of World Great Novelists Series

GRAHAM GREENE

A Critical Study

Edited by

Robert Hudson

Edwin Arnold

ANMOL PUBLICATIONS PVT. LTD.

NEW DELHI - 110 002 (INDIA)

ANMOL PUBLICATIONS PVT. LTD.
4374/4B, Ansari Road, Daryaganj
New Delhi - 110 002
Ph.: 23261597, 23278000
Visit us at: www.anmolpublications.com

Graham Greene: A Critical Study

First Published, 2005

ISBN 81-261-2066-5

PRINTED IN INDIA

Published by J.L. Kumar for Anmol Publications Pvt. Ltd., New Delhi - 110 002 and Printed at Mehra Offset Press, Delhi.

Contents

Preface

English novelist, short-story writer, playwright and journalist, whose novels treat moral issues in the context of political settings. Greene is one of the most widely read novelist of the 20th-century, a superb storyteller. Adventure and suspense are constant elements in his novels and many of his books have been made into successful films. Although Greene was a candidate for the Nobel Prize for Literature several times, he never received the award.

Graham Greene was born in Berkhamsted, Hertfordshire, as the son of Charles Greene and Marion Raymond Greene, a first cousin of the author Robert Louis Stevenson. Greene's father had a poor academic record but became the headmaster of Berkhamsted School, following Dr. Thomas Fry. Charles Greene had a brilliant intellect. Originally he had intended to become a barrister. However, he found that he had liking for teaching and he decided to stay at Berkhamsted. Often his history lessons were less lessons than comments on the crack-up of Liberalism. Greene was educated at Berkhamstead School and Balliol College, Oxford. He had a natural talent for writing, and during his three years at Balliol, he published more than sixty poems, stories, articles and reviews, most of which appeared in the student magazine *Oxford Outlook* and in the *Weekly Westminster Gazette*. As a writer Greene was very prolific and versatile. He wrote five dramas and screenplays for several films based on his novels. Greene's first published book was *Babbling April* (1925), a collection of poetry. It was followed by two novels in the style of Joseph Conrad.

The Confidential Agent (1939) is a problematic work. The war was too evidently still in progress." Greene's religious convictions did not become overtly apparent in his fiction until *The Brighton Rock* (1938), which depicted a teenage gangster Pinkie with a kind of demonic spirituality. Religious themes were explicit in the novels *The Power and the Glory* (1940), *The Heart of the Matter* (1948), which Greene characterized as "a success in the great vulgar sense of that term," and *The End of the Affair* (1951), which established Greene's international reputation. *The Quiet American* (1955), which was about American involvement in Indochina. *Our Main in Havanna* (1958) was born after a journey to Cuba, but Greene had the story sketched already much earlier. On one trip he asked a taxi driver to buy him a little cocaine and got boracic powder. The novel was made into a film in 1959, directed by Carol Reed. During the filming Greene met Ernest Hemingway, and was invited to his house for drinks. *The Comedians* (1966) depicted Papa Doc Duvalier's repressive rule in Haiti, and *The Honorary Consul* (1973) was a hostage drama set in Paraguay. *The Human Factor* (1978) stayed on the *New York Times* bestseller list for six months. *Travels with my Aunt* (1969), which was filmed by George Cukor, took the reader on journey round the world with an odd couple, a retired short-sighted bank manager and his temperamental Aunt Augusta, whose two big front teeth gives her "a vital Neanderthal air."

This book gives a vivid account of his life events and critique of his literary works by various commentators on him. Certainly this will be useful and informative for students, researchers and teachers besides the general readers.

—Editors

1

Graham Greene: An Overview

'With the death of James, the religious sense was lost to the English novel, and with the religious sense went the sense of the importance of the human act.' Graham Greene, an English novelist considered by many to be among the most gifted now writing, says this while speaking of François Mauriac; he goes on to add that Mauriac's 'first importance to an English reader, therefore, is that he belongs to the company of the great traditional novelists: he is a writer for whom the visible world has not ceased to exist, whose characters have the solidity and importance of men with souls to save or lose, and a writer who claims the traditional and essential right of a novelist, to comment, to express his views'. The words are significant: Greene's own development as a novelist has revealed above all an attempt to restore these two qualities—religious sense and the sense of the importance of the human act—to the English novel; to give back to it that extra dimension which places characters against the background of a world in which they are seen through the eyes of God. However unimportant they may seem in the world of the senses—for he often chooses to portray the weak, the failures—they have an overwhelming importance in another world. Indeed, perhaps through their very weakness and sense of failure they have an especial love for God which makes them the 'heroes' of Greene's books: 'it is the love for God that mainly survives because in his eyes they can imagine themselves always drab, seedy, unsuccessful, and therefore worthy of notice.' Greene's preoccupation with the seedy and the sordid—'seediness has a very deep appeal,' he writes in *Journey Without Maps*—springs from this: 'it seems to satisfy, temporarily, the sense of nostalgia for something lost; it seems to represent a stage further back'.

'In all writers there occurs a moment of crystallization when the dominant theme is plainly expressed, when the private universe becomes visible even to the least sensitive reader.' The words are Greene's. The dominant theme was stated, tentatively, in his first novel, and appeared again and again throughout his work, becoming crystallized with his acceptance—he was not converted, he says, since his was an intellectual conviction and not an emotional one—of the Roman Catholic faith. This was the turning point in his career: from then on the conflict between good and evil that takes place daily within a man's soul tended to become more and more specialized within the terms of Greene's own faith.

One is struck, when reading the earlier books, by the invariable presence of the element of pursuit: the pursuit of a criminal by the police, a traitor by those whom he has betrayed, a victim by his persecutors. It symbolized the pursuit of man's soul, his inner self, by God; he was hunted down in his search for a peace that often was found only in death. Later, the religious theme became more explicit: God was the pursuer from whom there could be no escape, even when despair dictated a way out that looked, from the Catholic point of view, like damnation. Caught between pain and pain, tormented by pity, afraid of damnation, Greene's characters are often the victims only of their own unforgettable love for God.

Yet with all this, his development as a novelist has not entirely pleased either his fellow Catholics or his non-Catholic readers. For many Catholics he has sailed too near the wind of the things that lead to damnation: he has exposed 'all the beauty and the horror of the flesh'. In *Brighton Rock*, his first specifically Catholic novel, he was on safe ground: the conflict between good and evil, damnation and salvation, was clearly defined. But in his later novels there was a mingling of good and evil, strength and weakness in his central characters; moreover his concern with adultery and physical love has disturbed some of his Catholic critics. On the other hand, to non-Catholics his sense of sin has been distasteful; his preoccupation with evil and with squalor has seemed over-emphatic, almost gloating; much of the suffering he emphasizes has appeared pointless and artistically unjustified. The struggle that he analyses in his later books between salvation and damnation is often unnecessarily tortuous; the final miracles explicitly treated of in *The End of the Affair*, and hinted at in earlier novels, have been regarded as stretching things too far.

The answer is that Greene's view-point and the working out of his themes demanded just such conclusions. He had to carry to their absolute ends both what he believes to be the human capacity for love, pity, fear and, above all, despair, and God's capacity for mercy. Whether such conclusions are always technically and artistically successful is a different matter.

Violence again characterizes many of his novels. These are 'thrillers', with murder, suicide and betrayal as their ingredients. He has, too, a feeling for cruelty which is only made bearable by his compassion. Partly the violence of which he writes is symbolical of the struggles going on all the time within men's souls; partly it is the expression of the brutality and violence of our world. 'Today our world seems peculiarly susceptible to brutality. There is a touch of nostalgia in the pleasure we take in gangster novels, in characters who have so agreeably simplified their emotions that they have begun living again at a level below the cerebral . . . when one sees to what unhappiness, to what peril of extinction centuries of cerebration have brought us, one sometimes has a curiosity to discover if one can from what we have come, to recall at which point we went astray.'

The Man Within, Greene's first novel, was published in 1929. Here the theme of pursuit is expressed in clear-cut terms: 'A sense of overwhelming desolation swept over him, a wonder whether he would ever know peace from pursuit . . .' The hero, if hero he can be called, betrayed his fellow smugglers to the excisemen; he takes refuge from his avengers in a girl's house and she persuades him to give evidence in court against his accomplices. The pursuit is both actual and symbolic: in the words of Sir Thomas Browne: 'There's another man within me that's angry with me.' Andrews is a coward; he has some groping sense of peace in his love for the girl, seeing in her a love for God which he does not possess. In her death he is able to find himself, to identify himself with that 'stern unresting critic' which was the 'man within'.

The same tradition of historical adventure story is followed in two other books—*The Name of Action* and *Rumour at Nightfail*—both of which were afterwards suppressed by the author. None of the three can be called a distinguished novel—they are oddly obscure, and the characters are pasteboard—but it can be said that in them Greene was stating the themes that he was afterwards to work out with success.

Perhaps they are insufficiently integrated because all this time Greene was working as a journalist. This is evident in some of his traits of style: tricks of observation—a half-eaten sausage-roll in a saucer, the cigarette ash on the trousers-little crudities and sensationalisms, an occasional overpithiness. They are faults that have tended to fall away from him over the years, but they are still detectable here and there.

Greene's reputation was established by his fourth novel, *Stamboul Train*. He called it 'an entertainment'—a name which he has given to six of his books by way of distinguishing them from his more serious works. It was written in a hurry, he said later, 'because one desperately wanted the money'. This fact is perhaps evident in the book, which lacks cohesion, but both as a thriller and as a foretaste of what he can do in the way of characterization, it is excellent.

It's a Battlefield is a bitter and ironic novel which mirrored a good deal of political unrest in the country when it was published in 1934. A Communist bus-driver has wounded a policeman during a political riot because he thought that the policeman was going to strike his wife; the policeman has died and the bus-driver has been sentenced to death for murder. At the time that the book opens his appeal has failed and it remains to be seen whether the Home Secretary will grant him a reprieve. The title of the book is taken from Kinglake's well-known work, *Eothen*.

In so far as the battlefield presented itself to the bare eyesight of men, it had no entirety, no length, no breadth, no depth, no size, no shape, and was made up of nothing except small numberless circlets commensurate with such ranges of vision as the mist might allow at each spot. . . . In such conditions, each separate gathering of English soldiery went on fighting its own little battle in happy and advantageous ignorance of the general state of the action; nay, even very often in ignorance that any great conflict was raging.

There is a deadly irony about the little battles that are being fought here, while all the time one is conscious of the 'general state of the action' behind them: the newly appointed Commissioner of Police afraid of retirement and loneliness, preoccupied with the Paddington murder and the Streatham Common rape, eyed with suspicion by his subordinates, hounded by the bus-driver's brother who longs to do something to justify his manhood and who sleeps with his brother's wife as much out of pity as lust; the pathetic journalist; the idealistic Frenchman; the reprieve which depends for its granting on the political situation. The final irony comes when it is granted, for the bus-driver's brother has died of shock after an accident believing that he has failed, and the prison chaplain has resigned as a protest against the horror of keeping a young man in prison for eighteen years. The pity of it is that in this book Greene has been defeated by his own ends: like *Stamboul Train* it is too diffuse; too many characters spoil the total impact.

The novel which followed, *England Made Me*, is possibly Greene's most ambitious book; it is not, however, his most successful because in it he has aimed at something which he has only imperfectly achieved. For the first and last time in his work he uses the stream of consciousness technique. Artistically the book is a failure: it, also, is too diffuse; moreover, somewhere he loses control of his raw material and the final effect is one of dissatisfaction. Nevertheless, in feeling the book is deeper than anything he had written hitherto, and the bitterness and irony here have a subtler edge; for all its imperfections, it has great interest for his admirers.

At this time, Greene made a journey through the Republic of Liberia, through areas where in living memory no white man had been seen, where no proper maps were available, and where tropical diseases were rampant. It was a strange and often terrifying journey: one feels that his reasons for making it were something like those that sent the hero of *The Name of Action* on an unconsidered adventure to Trier: 'His only hope of escape from a life of which he had grown inexpressibly tired, a life without meaning, without risk and without beauty.' At any rate, in the forests of Africa he discovered in himself a passionate interest in living. 'I had always assumed before, as a matter of course, that death was desirable,' he writes in *Journey Without Maps*, the book which was the fruit of his 350-mile journey. Like 'the revolver in the corner cupboard' with which as a boy he played a game of chance, and about which he writes in an essay in *The Lost Childhood*, Africa was an escape from the intolerable burden of ennui.

Thus, *Journey Without Maps* is interesting chiefly for its subject matter and for the vivid descriptions that Greene gives of people and places. But it is interesting, too, for what it tells one about its author: the way in which Africa seemed familiar to him, like something to which one gropes back under psychoanalysis; the fascination that the seediness of the civilization of the coast exercised over his mind, the sense of disappointment when the journey was finished and he could go back to civilization as we know it. Later, during the war he was to return to the British colony of Sierra Leone for the Foreign Office, where he found the raw material for his best book, *The Heart of the Matter*.

Diverging now to "entertainment', as he called it, he next gave his readers *A Gun for Sale*; although in bare content a thriller, this contains a psychological study as arresting as any that he presents in his novels.

'Murder didn't mean much to Raven. It was just a new job.' Raven has been hired as an assassin by a firm of armament manufacturers to kill the head of a European state; he is to be paid two hundred pounds for his work and as far as he is concerned that will be the end of the matter: the repercussions do not interest him. But the two hundred pounds is reported to the police as stolen money and Raven is on the run, while in Europe war is threatening. His path is crossed by a girl, the actress with who inspector in charge of the case is in love; Raven intends to make use of her and then to kill her. But because of her compassion—as he sees it—she is spared, and for the first time in his life he gives someone his trust, in telling her everything. For her his story means the avoidance of war: she believes him and sticks by him in order to prove it, but in the end she is driven to betray him, as he has always been betrayed. For Raven has a hare-lip, 'like a badge of class. It revealed the poverty of parents who couldn't afford a surgeon.' All his life he had been conscious of his own ugliness, of the repulsion that he inspired in others; this, and the father hanged in Wandsworth prison and the mother with her throat cut had conditioned his life.

Raven foreshadows Pinkie, the boy gangster in Brighton Rock, but whereas Pinkie, being a Catholic, is fully aware of the nature of his own wickedness, Raven is amoral: he regards the whole structure of religion as so much claptrap, associating it with a that he had been taught in the institution in which he was brought up:

> In a religious shop by the Catholic Cathedral he found himself facing again the images that angered him in the Soho café: the plaster mother and child, the wise men and the shepherds. They were arranged in a cavern of brown paper among the books of devotion, the little pious scraps of St. Theresa. 'The Holy Family': he pressed his face against the glass with a kind of horrified anger that that tale still went on. 'Because there was no room for them in the inn'; he remembered how they sat in rows on the benches waiting for Christmas dinner, while the thin precise voice read

> on about Caesar Augustus and how everyone went up to his own city to be taxed. Nobody was beaten on Christmas Day: all punishments were saved for Boxing Day. Love, Charity, Patience, Humility: he was educated: he knew all about those virtues; he'd seen what they were worth. They twisted everything: even that story in there, it was historical, it had happened, but they twisted it to their own purposes. They made him a God because they could feel fine about it all, they didn't have to consider themselves responsible for the raw deal they'd given him. He'd consented, hadn't he? That was the argument, because he could have called down 'a legion of angels' if he'd wanted to escape hanging there. On your life he could, he thought with bitter lack of faith, just as easily as his own father taking the drop at Wandsworth could have saved himself when the trap opened. He stood there with his face against the glass waiting for somebody to deny that reasoning, staring at the swaddled child with a horrified tenderness, 'the little bastard', because he was educated and knew what the child was in for, the damned Jews and the double-crossing Judas and only one man to draw a knife on his side when the soldiers came for him in the garden.

But in death his bitterness is somehow transformed: 'the only problem when you were once born was to get out of life more neatly and expeditiously than you had entered it. For the first time the idea of his mother's suicide came to him without bitterness, as he fixed his aim at the long reluctant last and Saunders shot him in the back through the opening door. Death came to him in the form of unbearable pain. It was as if he had to deliver this pain as a woman delivers a child, and he sobbed and moaned in the effort. At last it came out of him and he followed his only child into the darkness.'

There is much companion in *A Gun for Sale*: compassion which makes the reader feel tenderness and sympathy for Raven. But there is irony and bitterness, too, in the terrible picture it presents of society: the Midland manufacturing town; the armaments king who says that a murderer ought not to be allowed to benefit from his crime while calmly planning to start a war through the death of a boyhood friend; the seedy, half-comic, half-tragic life backstage of the local repertory theatre, in the straggling rows of decaying houses, in the local medical school.

The first positive indication of Greene's conversion to the Roman Catholic faith was Brighton Rock, published in 1938. Hitherto, the conflict within his characters had been a general one: from now on it tends to become increasingly specialized. Pinkie, the boy gangster, with his 'face of starved intensity', is a Catholic. So, too, is Rose, the girl he marries in order to prevent her from going to the police. Pinkie is wicked, but he is aware of his own wickedness, half in love with the idea of Hell: at the back of his mind is the thought of repentance, 'of making peace, of going home, and his heart weakened with a faint nostalgia for the tiny dark confessional box, the priest's voice, and the people waiting under the statue, before the bright lights burning down in the pink glasses, to be made safe from eternal pain. Later, damnation came to him as something he could accept: 'He had a sense that he would never be scared again: running down from the track he had been afraid, afraid of pain an more afraid of damnation—of the sudden and unshriven death. Now it was as if he was damned already and there was nothing more to fear ever again.'

Like Raven, Pinkie has been conditioned by his upbringing. His horror of sex as an act of darkness springs from the tiny room in which on every Saturday night he had watched from his single bed his parents performing the 'exercise'. On one of the few occasions when he is articulate for any length of time he describes the death of a young girl on the railway line, her head severed: she was going to have her second baby; when her first was born any of a dozen youths might have been its father.

Rose is good, and she, too, knows the nature of her sin when she marries Pinkie in a registry office. But she will risk damnation for him, out of love and a blind trust in the mercy of God. Ida Arnold, who suspects Pinkie and works to convict him of murder, is the good pagan:

> No real sense of danger could lodge behind those large vivacious eyes. Nothing could ever make her believe that one day she too would be where the worms . . . her mind couldn't take that track; she could go only a short way before the switch automatically shifted and set her vibrating down the accustomed line, the seasonticket line marked by desirable residences and advertisements for cruises and small fenced boskages for rural love.

There is an intense pathos about Fred Hale, Pinkie's victim, with his fear and his weak heart and varicose veins and bad liver; about Spicer, the man who gets scared after the murder and is conveniently killed by a falling bannister; above all, about Rose, who could bear anything so long as she thought Pinkie loved her, but for whom the full horror of realization was to come.

Brighton Rock made a successful film, because it has a film technique in much of its writing. But it is repetitive, often, in its ideas: Pinkie's horror of sex, for instance, is overdone. Also, there is a certain priggishness, a certain Catholic partisanship, which detracts from its worth.

In the spring of 1938 Greene was commissioned to visit part of Mexico in order to write a book about the religious situation at a time of persecution. The Lawless

Roads is, therefore, not an ordinary travel book, but specifically a book about religion, and despite the charm of many of his personal descriptions—of American travellers, old settlers, Germans, Indians—it is chiefly for his attitude to the religious problem that the book is interesting. Also, it was on his journey that he found the material for his very fine novel, The Power and the Glory.

The Church in many parts of Mexico had been persecuted and religious services forbidden, but everywhere people continued to honour the God that they were not allowed publicly to worship. As a Catholic, Greene's attitude was not unnaturally clear:

> I went into the Templo del Carmen, as the dark dropped, for benediction. To a stranger like myself it was like going home—a language I could understand—'*Ora pro nobis*'. The Virgin sat on an extraordinary silver cloud like a cabbage with the Infant in her arms above the altar; all along the walls horrifying statues with musty purple robes stood in glass coffins; and yet it was home. One knew what was going on. Old men came plodding in dungarees and bare feet, tired out with work, and again I thought: how could one grudge them the gaudy splendour of the giltwork, the incense, the distant immaculate figure upon the cloud? The candles were lit, and suddenly little electric lights sprayed out all round the Virgin's head. Even if it were all untrue and there was no God, surely life was happier with the enormous supernatural promise than with the petty social fulfilment, the tiny pension and the machine-made furniture.

The way in which the poor squeezed the last drop of mortification out of their already terribly hard lives, convinced Greene of the vital need these people felt for their religion: for the gilt and incense and ceremony. He hated Mexico, but at times it seemed as if there were worse places. 'Here were idolatry and oppression, starvation and casual violence, but you lived under the shadow of religion—of God or the Devil.' On the other side there was nothing-'just the drugstore and the Coca-Cola, the hamburger, the graceless sinless empty chromium world'.

The Power and the Glory was Greene's best novel to date when it was published in 1940, being at once more concentrated and economical in its effects than anything he had written previously. For the first time he had succeeded comletely in relating his characters and story to form a coerent, taut whole.

It is set in the primitive landscape of the Mexico of The *Lawless Roads* (reading the two books one can find many parallels in the writing), during a time of political strife and religious persecution in the nineteen-twenties. All the priests have fled or been shot or have made their submission to authority by marrying. (There is a brilliant study of old Padre José, who has married a great mountain of flesh in the form of a nagging wife.) One priest has eluded capture and is being harried by his pursuers throughout the state with a price on his head. He is a bad priest—'a whisky priest'-with a child of his own whom he cannot help but love. He longs for the peace of confession, but here he is, condemned to go round making 'God knew what martyrs' when he feels that he himself is 'without grace enough to die'.

When the book opens, he is about to escape, but he gives up the chance in order to visit a woman who is reputed to be sick. He is a priest and there is nothing he can do except go on. The English child who gives him shelter asks him why he does not renounce his faith:

> 'He said: "It's impossible. There's no way. I'm a priest. It's out of my power."

> 'The child listened intently. She said: "Like a birthmark."'

Again he is about to escape when he is called to the deathbed of an American gangster. He knows that it is a trick, that he will be betrayed by the half-caste who has followed him, waiting for just such an occasion, but he cannot refuse to go. It is his duty to give the man absolution. The irony is that the gangster refuses to make his confession: his last thought before he dies is for the priest's safety. But he is taken and shot. As Greene wrote of his actual counterpart, in *The Lawless Roads*: 'He was little loss, poor man, but who can judge what terror and hardship and isolation have excused him in the eyes of God?' At any rate, in a characteristic final scene he suggests that the whisky priest's prayer: 'Oh, God, send them someone more worthwhile to suffer for'—had been answered. A boy who has witnessed the death of the priest before the firing-squad has gone to bed when he hears an insistent knocking at the door. Wearily, he gets up, knowing that his father is out and that it is his duty to answer the knocking:

> Slowly he made his way across the patio towards the outer door. Suppose it was the lieutenant come back to revenge himself for the spittle . . . He unlocked the heavy iron door and swung it open. A stranger stood in the street: a tall pale thin man with a rather sour mouth, who carried a small suitcase. He named the boy's mother and asked if this were the senora's house. Yes, the boy said, but she was asleep. He began to shut the door, but a pointed shoe got in the way.
>
> The stranger said: 'I have only just landed. I came up the river tonight. I thought perhaps . . . I have an introduction for the senora from a great friend of hers.'

> 'She is asleep,' the boy repeated. 'If you would let me come in,' the man said with an odd frightened smile, and suddenly lowering his face he said to the boy: 'I am a priest.'
>
> 'You?' the boy exclaimed.
>
> 'Yes,' he said gently. 'My name is Father—.' But the boy had already swung the door open and put his lips to his hand before the other could give himself a name.

The Power and the Glory is a considerable advance on Brighton Rock because in it good and evil, weakness and strength, are more truly mingled in the central character of the priest than they are in the separate characters of Pinkie and Rose. The rest of the characterization, too, is brilliant: Mrs. Fellowes, the Englishwoman to whom even to speak of life is to remind her with terror of death; the young-old child, her daughter; Mr. Tench, the seedy English dentist with his stomach pains; the half-caste who betrays the priest.

Shortly before the publication of *The Power and the Glory*, Greene published a grim little 'entertainment', *The Confidential Agent*. It is not up to the standard of his other entertainments: written on the eve of war it is a thriller with pursuit, fear and desperation as its ingredients, but with the underlying horror of the ruthlessness of war in which human life is expendable.

Another entertainment followed *The Power and the Glory*, set in wartime London, *The Ministry of Fear*. This, too, is a secret service thriller, but with, as in *A Gun for Sale*, a psychological import. The chief character is a man pursued by pity and terror. He has a few years before killed his wife out of pity for her, dying slowly in agony from a long illness. He has been tried for murder, but acquitted, and since then has longed to receive in some way the punishment that he has felt to be his due. Accidentally he is involved with a ring of enemy agents and has to flee from a murder which he has not committed: a murder staged to frighten him. In a bomb explosion he loses his memory: its gradual return and his dawning realization that he is a murderer are beautifully treated, though the process by which he finds salvation is a little obscure.

Compassion runs as a strong thread through all Greene's work: in *The Heart of the Matter* he carries the character of Rowe in *The Ministry of Fear* to its terrifyingly logical conclusion. Scobie in *The Heart of the Matter* is truly three-dimensional in a way that no other character had been in Greene's work to date. He is a Catholic, converted when he married his pious Catholic wife. As Deputy Commissioner of Police in a West African district he is above all a just man, incorruptible: this, perhaps, is the reason why he is passed over for promotion. A man so treated is expected to retire, but retirement to him is worse than death (an echo of the Commissioner of Police in It's a Battlefield): 'the thought of retirement set his nerves twitching and straining: he always prayed that death would come first.' But it is his wife whose feelings are most outraged by the news of his failure, and it is the pity which he feels for her as she lies under her mosquitonet like 'a joint of meat under a meat-cover'—even that image is quickly hustled away by pity—that sets in train a course of events which is to lead to disaster. Louise wants to get away to South Africa for a holiday: she hates the society in which she is condemned to live, knowing that everyone laughs at her. Scobie promises her that she shall go, although he knows that he has not got the money for her passage:

> No man could guarantee love for ever, but he had sworn fourteen years ago, at Ealing, silently during

> the horrible little elegant ceremony among the lace and candles, that he would at least always see to it that she was happy . . . He would still have made the promise even if he could have foreseen all that would come of it. He had always been prepared to accept the responsibility for his actions, and he had always been half aware too, from the time he made his terrible private vow that she should be happy, how far this action might carry him. Despair is the price one pays for setting oneself an impossible aim. It is, one is told, the unforgivable sin, but it is a sin the corrupt or evil man never practises. He always has hope. He never reaches the freezing-point of knowing absolute failure. Only the man of goodwill carries always in his heart this capacity for damnation.

This, as far as Scobie goes, is the heart of the matter. He is a good man, but his fatal weakness is that he cannot bear to hurt those whom he loves. Pity for Louise, a passion more intense than love, drives him to borrow money from a Syrian trader in order to send her to South Africa. While she is away he falls in love with a nineteen-year-old widow who is brought to the colony as a survivor from a torpedoed ship. Here again, it is pity from which his love springs: pity for this child hovering between life and death, still clutching the stamp album that her father gave her on her fourteenth birthday. Scobie's own child had died, but he had been spared witnessing her death: what follows is in a way an expiation for the guilt that he has secretly felt for this. Out of pity as much as love (another echo of *It's a Battlefield*) he begins an affair with Helen Rolt and an indiscretion involves him further and further with the Syrian: the incorruptible man sees himself caught up in corruption. Unexpectedly Louise, who has heard about the affair which Scobie imagines he is so well concealing, returns. She asks him to go with her to Holy Communion, well knowing that he cannot do so in a state of mortal sin.

Scobie cannot hurt her by refusing, but at the same time he cannot hurt Helen by giving her up, and he is too honest to promise in confession to do something that he knows he cannot. In this matter the priest fails to help him, and with the knowledge of damnation in his heart he receives Communion. (There is a wonderful description of his feelings as he approaches the Sacrament.)

Caught between pity and pity, and knowing that he cannot continue to wound God—'striking God when he's down'—he methodically plans his suicide in such a way that neither Louise nor Helen will know that he took his own life.

The Heart of the Matter can be called a study in despair, despair as the Roman Catholic Church knows it, but it does not end there. There is Scobie's last cry: 'Dear God, I love . . .'; there is the last chapter when Louise, who has had it suggested to her by the special agent from London who is in love with her, realizes that Scobie killed himself and goes to see the priest:

> 'He was a bad Catholic.'
>
> 'That's the silliest phrase in common use,' Father Rank said.
>
> 'And at the end this—horror. He must have known that he was damning himself.'
>
> 'Yes, he knew that all right. He never had any trust in mercy-except for other people.'
>
> 'It's no good even praying . . .'
>
> Father Rank clapped the cover of the diary to and said, furiously, 'For goodness sake, Mrs. Scobie, don't imagine you—or I—know a thing about God's mercy.'

> 'The Church says . . .'
>
> 'I know the Church says. The Church knows all the rules. But it doesn't know what goes on in a single human heart.'
>
> 'You think there's some hope then?' she wearily asked.
>
> 'Are you so bitter against him?'
>
> 'I haven't any bitterness left.'
>
> 'And do you think God's likely to be more bitter than a woman?' he said with harsh insistence, but she winced away from the arguments of hope.
>
> 'Oh, why, why did he have to make such a mess of things?'
>
> Father Rank said, 'it may seem an odd thing to say—when a man's as wrong as he was—but I think, from what I saw of him, that he really loved God.'
>
> She had denied just now that she felt any bitterness, but a little more of it drained out now like tears from exhausted ducts. 'He certainly loved no one else,' she said.
>
> 'And you may be in the right of it there, too,' Father Rank replied.

The Heart of the Matter is Greene's best book because of its tautness, economy and evenness of style. Only here and there is a jarring note struck: Scobie's imaginings about his daughter, had she lived, for instance:

> He thought: If my child had lived, she too would have been conscriptable, flung into some grim dormitory, to find her own way. After the Atlantic, the A.T.S. or the W.A.A.F., the blustering sergeant with the big bust, the cook-house and the potato peelings, the Lesbian officer, with the thin lips and the tidy gold hair, and the men waiting on the Common outside the camp, among the gorse bushes . . .

The effect of the heat is beautifully done, although here again he tends to use the same image more than once, which immediately weakens its power, as it did in Brighton Rock: here, it is the blotting-paper put under the wrist while writing to absorb the sweat. The characterization is excellent, not only in the case of Scobie, but also in that of Helen, Louise, the priest conscious of his inadequacy, the pathetic Harris, the brash Wilson.

But it is also Greene's best book because in it he has full and finally developed the themes that have run through all his novels: the pity, fear, love and despair; the search of a man for salvation. He has, too, carried to its conclusion the implications of his own faith—the love and mercy and mystery of God.

After The Heart of the Matter, *The End of the Affair* reads like a disappointing postscript. It is written mainly in the first person of a middle-aged novelist who has had an affair with the wife of a civil servant: two years before the book opens she has ended their relationship without ever giving him a reason. Casually meeting her husband, the 'I' of the book sets out on a diabolical quest to find out what his exmistress is doing, in the course of which he stumbles on the truth in her diary. She has given him up because she had believed him dead in an air-raid and had prayed for a miracle: if he was returned to life she had vowed to leave him. The diary, which forms part of the novel, is something of a *tour de force*: it describes her painful awareness of God, her struggle to escape from him, to find a reason to break her vow. When her lover discovers that she still cares for him, he goes to her house to persuade her to return. But she is ill, and the next thing he hears is that she is dead. Although he learns that she had wanted to become a Catholic, he persuades her husband to have her cremated: later he discovers that as a child she had been baptized into the Catholic Church. There follows what can only be described as a series of miracles.

Despite the brilliance of the diary, *The End of the Affair* is an artistic failure. The first person technique makes for a lack of detachment that prevents the reader from ever seeing the story in perspective. At times it is embarrassingly personal. The time sequences, moving from past to present, are unnecessarily hard to follow. The miracles, even if they are perfectly logical in the terms of Greene's faith, fail to be an organic part of the book and simply strike a false note, as though they have been tacked on. It is for these reasons that the book must be regarded as a stumble in Greene's progress.

Greene's only work for the theatre, *The Living Room*, is a further development of the themes of despair and the problem of the Catholic in relation to an impossible physical love. It is, too, a terrible indictment of the pious Catholic, just as the character of Louise Scobie was, though for her one could feel pity. Rose is the daughter of a Catholic mother and a non-Catholic father who begins an affair with a middle-aged psychiatrist who is her trustee, on the night after her mother's funeral. She comes to stay with her two great-aunts and her great-uncle, a crippled priest, whose failure to provide the right words of comfort at the right time has much in common with Father Rank's. The conflict which develops for Rose when she finds herself caught between the pain of giving up her lover and the pain of hurting his wife leads in the end to a despair akin to Scobie's, and she takes her own life, a childish prayer on her lips.

The significance of the title of the play is contained in the fact that the two old women are so afraid of death that they will not use any room in which someone has died—so that they are now left with a bedroom, next to a lavatory, as a living room. In this room Rose dies, and it is a mark of God's forgiveness that her death so reassures and comforts the elder of the two women that, so far from not wishing to sleep in the room in which she died, she voluntarily chooses to do so: 'There'd be no better room for me to asleep in for ever than the room where Rose died.'

The failure of both priest and psychiatrist leaves room only for the mercy of God; but whereas in *The Heart of the Matter* Greene succeeds in conveying the meaning and purpose of Scobie's action, in the case of *The Living Room* one is left with a sense of waste.

A short novel which appeared in 1955, *Loser Take All*, amply justified its designation of 'entertainment'; written with a professional ease that approaches slickness, it is highly diverting but makes no claim to be considered among Greene's important books.

The remainder of his writings consists of a number of short stories, articles and essays; work for the films, and some stories for children. His short stories are sidelines to his work written to be read, but only to be seen. The Basement Room, the story from which the film, The Fallen Idol, was made, is interesting 'in its use of a technique that he also used tentatively with one character in *A Gun for Sale*—a sort of God's-eye view into the future. The small boy in *The Basement Room* is to witness something that he will carry with him until the day he dies. 'He would never forget that scene. In a week he had forgotten it, but it conditioned his career, the long austerity of his life.' *The End of the Party* is a grim little story which uses the idea of the peculiar relationship existing between twins that he used also in *England Made Me*. His essays and articles have recently been published in a volume called *The Lost Childhood*: his critical work is fresh and stimulating, and throws much light on his own work as a novelist.

Fear, pity, violence, pursuit and the endless, restless quality of man's search for salvation and of God's love for man, are the recurring themes of Greene's novels. These have been interpreted outstanding technical ability; everything he writes is readable. Acute observation, a style which maintains, without obscurity, a high level of intensity, a sensitivity to atmosphere (especially to certain aspects of modern English life which he was among the first to capture in print, so that his readers often say of a character or a place, 'Just like something in Graham Greene!'): these are among his assets. Some find his continual emphasis on squalor and 'seediness', his slightly adolescent nostalgie de la boue, his almost ridiculous addiction to describing such subjects as lavatories, indigestion and the less appealing side of sexual adventure, an irritating drawback to enjoyment of his work. Certainly these are overdone; possibly they give his books a spurious attraction to some readers: however, his sincerity is never in question. It will be interesting to see how in the future he will use and develop his remarkable gifts; and it is a sign of his originality and versatility that no easy prediction of the course he will follow is possible.

FINDING HIS WAY

If Greene had not written his provocative novels, he might today be known for some of the most penetrating commentary on the art of fiction.[1] His criticism is exceptional because he is willing to be unconventional, sometimes eccentric, in his literary perspectives. Ultimately trusting his intuition, he has succeeded in writing a number of essays in which he tracks down the daemon which compels some people to create fiction. Because they often arrive quickly at what Greene feels are the supreme truths about an author's art, these essays are particularly accessible to the general reader of fiction. As for the discerning readers of Greene's fiction, they will discover that these speculations are frequently self-revealing.

In this indirect fashion Greene is often his best critic. This is especially true, of course, when he is writing of those authors with whom he shares certain compulsions. Thus some of his most brilliant and self-revealing speculations are on such obsessive writers as Dickens, Mauriac, and de la Mare. But it is in his essays on Henry James that he is most obviously writing with this double vision. There, indeed, much of what he writes about James is perhaps more conspicuously true of himself than of his subject. It is certainly as true of Greene as of James that he had a "ruling fantasy which drove him to write," that this fantasy was inspired by a "sense of evil religious in its intensity," and that, believing in the supernatural, he "saw evil as an equal force with good." It is also clear that, no less than James, he had a private vision which "has left a series of novels . . . of one moral piece."[2]

Novelists may be notorious for being less than perfectly reliable when they turn their critical attention directly on their own work. But Greene writes as accurately about his own achievements as anybody.[3] He is, for instance, certainly right when he advances several lines from Browning *"Bishop Bloughram's Apology"* as an epigraph for all of his novels:

> Our interest's on the dangerous edge of things.
> The honest thief, the tender murder,

The supersitious artheist, demi-rep
That loves and saves her soul in new French books—

We watch while these in equilibrium keep
The giddy line midway.[4]

These lines summarize Greene's vision perfectly. The characters who populate his exotic world come readily to mind, and so does his technique of suspending them between immaterial territories.

The guiding vision of a novelist, Greene believes, is perceived by him once and for all early in his youth. In his own case, Greene first beheld his creative prospect in a number of primary dreams about amoral power. The first dream which haunted him was about "something outside that has got to come in." Later the figures of power assumed various disturbing shapes: "a troop of black skinned girls who carried poison flowers which it was death to touch; an old Arab; a half-caste; armed men with shaven heads and narrow eyes and the appearance of Tibetans out of a travel book; a Chinese detective." These adumbrate his later dreams of positive evil, represented by "the man with gold teeth and rubber surgical gloves; the old woman with ringworm; the man with his throat cut dragging himself across the carpet to the bed."[5]

These shocking dreams made the young Greene perceive evil as something frightfully real. But it was his later experience of public school which convinced him of the reality of hell. There, he remembers, he became aware of fear and hate, a kind of lawlessness—appalling cruelties could be practiced without a second though; one met for the first time characters, adult and adolescent, who bore about them the genuine quality of evil. There was Collifax, who practiced torments with dividers; Mr. Cranden with three grim chins, a dusty gown, a kind of demoniac sensuality; from these heights evil declined towards Parlow, whose desk was filled with minute photographs-advertisements of art photos. Hell lay about them. . . .[6]

This terrifying world existed behind a door which separated the school from home and the study of the schoolmaster, who happened to be Greene's father. Because of this double life, Greene developed an anxiety about dislocation which is often expressed in his fiction. More important, the "horror and the fascination" of the school caused him to look for and to find faith. As he recalls it, he escaped surrepitiously for an hour at a time: unknown to frontier guards, one stood on the wrong side of the border looking back—one should have been listening to Mendelssohn, but instead one heard the rabbit restlessly cropping near the croquet hoops. It was an hour of release—and also an hour of prayer. One became aware of God with an intensity . . . And so faith came to one—shapelessly, without dogma, a presence above a croquet lawn, something associated with violence, cruelty, evil across the way. One began to believe in heaven because one believed in hell...[7]

This conviction of hell on earth was re-inforced by his childhood reading. At first the works of Rider Haggard haunted him most profoundly. In fact, Haggard's exploration of the ordeal of entrapment influenced his imagination permanently. But later, when he was fourteen years old, Greene read a novel which determined his future. From the moment he picked up Marjorie Bowen's *The Viper of Milan*, he wanted to become a writer. As he remembers it:

> All the other possible futures slid away . . . Imitation after imitation of Miss Bowen's magnificent novel went into exercise-books . . . It was as if I had been supplied once and for all with a subject.[8]

According to Greene, Miss Bowen's novel also provided him with a creative pattern which Catholicism would later explain to him in different terms: "perfect evil walking the world where perfect good can never walk again, and only the pendulum ensures that after all in the end justice is done."[9] Greene's recollections once more bear out the facts, for evil is an omnipresent subject in his fictional world where human nature is continuously in conflict with itself and divine forces.

Greene became a Catholic when he was 22 years of age, but it was not the ultimate turning point in his life that it might appear to be. Catholicism may have provided him with the metaphysical justification for his tormenting belief that human nature was "not black and white but black and grey."[10] Now he also became persuaded of a strange bond between hell on earth and heaven. It is, nevertheless, important to point out that his beliefs had not yet been truly challenged by an essential experience of despair.

He had courted self-destruction when he was 17 years old and imagined himself to be hopelessly in love with his sister's governess. Yet he gambled with Russian roulette not because of a conviction that life was abominable but because of a deep boredom with it at that time.[11] Out of this period of suicidal fantasies Greene emerged, as he says, "irrevocably in love with failure." He also was left with a relish for testing himself against the limits of personal endurance. This allure of the ordeal ultimately led him to take a journey to Africa when he was 31 years old, and it was then that Greene's vision achieved full maturity.[12]

While on this journey his disillusionment with what modern man had made of his childhood was confirmed. His nostalgia for the primitive, he now became convinced, was for "the finer taste, the finer pleasure, the finer terror on which one might have built." But if Greene's pessimism about his age deepened on one hand, on the other he had an experience which revived his interest in life. He had been more attracted to death than to life before. When during his journey he discovered a "passionate interest in living," however, he recalls it like a conversation.[13] Because of this new feeling for life, Greene's bleak vision of life is finally tempered by effectual love.

Since Greene writes from deep memories and fixations, the fiction he has written after his trip to Africa reflects this new faith in life. Prior to that journey his novels carry such a heavy burden of pessimism that one tends to believe only in the evil they describe. When they attempt to be affirmitive about life, they aren't very convincing and instead incline toward rather awkward melodrama. After his African experience, however, Greene's novels often succeed in capturing the true complexity of the human spectacle, consisting of suffering and betrayal but also of glory and self-sacrifice.

In a way, Greene has been writing about his spiritual journey ever since. His fictional world still retains much of its disturbing gloom. Certainly his books are still pervaded by the issues of guilt, revenge, betrayal, pursuit, and failure. Indeed, these subjects often recur with such intensity that they add up to a shattering vision of hell on earth. At such time one might be inclined to agree with the view of one critic that "a terror of what experience can do to the individual, a terror at a predetermined corruption, is the motive force that drives Greene as a novelist."[14] Such an assessment, however, would ultimately be imprecise. Especially after his African trip, Greene began to explore the possibilities of salvation, and this search has continued in his novels in various forms for the rest of his career.

Early Novels

Greene first published novel, *The Man Within* (1929), focuses on the character of Andrews, a young man on the run. The story, somewhat vaguely set in the early part of the 19th century, opens with the fugitive desperately making his way across the foggy Sussex Downs. He has betrayed to the law a gang of smugglers, of which he himself was a member and which was once led by his father, now by Carlyon, a man whom he has worshipped. Carlyon and three other members of the gang have escaped the authorities, and Andrews is sure they are bent on revenge and in close pursuit. At first, it might appear that he is simply running out of physical fear. However, it quickly becomes apparent that he is at the same time trying to escape his moral conscience and the haunting influence of his dead father. Thus, when he finds refuge with a courageous young woman in her cottage, he doesn't really feel safer. Instead, his panic increases because, through the woman's spiritual force, he is made to confront his tormented, divided self. What's more, he feels himself falling in love with her. As a consequence, he gives in to her suggestion that he go to the assizes held in Lewes and testify in person against the smugglers who were caught. But in Lewes, Andrews fails badly, for he not only betrays Elizabeth by giving in to the temptations of a seductive, corrupt young woman; he also proves to be so inept as a witness for the prosecution that the smugglers are freed. Now, spurred on by the fear of what the smugglers might try to do to him and the girl, who, they know, has helped him, he hurries back to Elizabeth's cottage. Finding her still safe, he declares his love, and she reciprocates. But the happiness of the lovers doesn't last long. Soon thereafter Elizabeth dies protecting her man from his pursuers and Andrews surrenders himself to the law as her murderer and, as a further act of atonement, appears to contemplate suicide.

Even such a brief summary of the story indicates that Greene is already dealing with many themes which would continue to fascinate him. Most obviously, there are those of betrayal, pursuit, revenge, atonement, and sacrificial love. In addition, he works in his concerns with the nature and impact of innocence, pity, responsibility, sex, childhood experiences, death, personal fragmentation, and religious belief. This is a very ambitious list of topics for any novel, much less a first one by a young writer. Eventually Greene would become a brilliant exponent of all these concerns. In this book, however, he largely fails, mainly because he has not yet discovered a way in which to mesh all the subjects together by means of an organic style and a controlling theme.

Moreover, as Greene himself came to realize, it was a book which in some ways represented a false start. In time, he would learn to write thoroughly contemporary works inspired by his own emotions and experiences. But in this novel he was obviously working under the heavy influence of several of his favorite writers, notably Robert Louis Stevenson, Henry James, Joseph Conrad, and the metaphysical poets. As a result, *The Man Within* is, as Greene says, a "very young and very sentimental" book which now seems to him "like the book of a complete stranger."[15] In other words, Greene now realizes just how overwrought, schematic, repetitive, and romantically self-indulgent it actually is. Of course, as he suggests, the underlying problem was that of youthful inexperience. He had simply not yet learned to balance in his writing certain personal and artistic elements—romanticism and realism, melodrama and irony, belief and despair.

Unfortunately, before Greene discovered what his literary path should be, he drifted through a period of misdirection. Mislead by the very encouraging reviews which *The Man Within* received,[16] and still working under the influence of other writers, especially that of Conrad, he went on to publish two books which took him even further away from the kind of novels he would eventually perfect.

The year after he published *The Man Within* he brought out *The Name of Action* (1930). This is a story which centers on a young man's entanglement in a Ruritanian revolution. The following year he published *Rumour at Nightfall* (1931). Another adventure story set in the past, it deals with the Carlist Rebellion set in Spain, a place about which Greene at that time incidentally knew next to nothing. Today it's easy to see why both of these novels were bound to be commercial and critical failures. In a manner of speaking, these highly derivative novels simply had too little of Greene himself in them. Hence it's understandable why Greene subsequently dismissed them as mere juvenilia and has decided to exclude them from the Uniform Edition of his works.

In his fourth book, *Stamboul Train* (1932),[17] Greene at last decided to try his hand at telling a story set in contemporary times. The resulting difference was nothing less than amazing. Certainly, no one could deny that there is an exciting story. One might even say that several exciting stories are recounted. In this book, Greene has gathered a number of interesting characters and put them aboard a train running from Ostend to Istanbul. During the course of the journey, we focus on the stories of a young female dancer, a Jewish merchant, a lesbian journalist, a professional criminal, and a Communist revolutionary. In addition, we meet a number of vividly drawn minor figures.[18] At first the connections between the various characters aren't very clear. But as the train continues on its way, their stories begin to intertwine, so that by the end of the trip the multiple plot takes on an impression of purposeful unity. And this impression is strengthened by the fact that Greene has by now learned a great deal about the relationship between style and subject matter.

While Greene was working on his earliest novels, he was learning some of the most valuable lessons about writing fiction from his careful study of one book in particular, Percy Lubbock's *The Craft of Fiction.* Most notably, he learned the importance of point-of-view. However, one thing that Lubbock's book couldn't teach him was actually very crucial to him. This was how to write in such a way that serious matters were carried along by a surface of physical action.

Largely because in *Stamboul Train* Greene has discovered how to convey this kind of excitement, it's his first distinctive book. At last, as he recalls, he had reached the point where, looking back at his previous efforts, he could see for himself where he had gone wrong and what he must try to do instead:

> Excitement is simple: excitement is a situation, a single event. It mustn't be wrapped up in thoughts, similes, metaphors. A simile is a form of reflection, but excitement is of the moment when there is no time to reflect. Action can only be expressed by a subject, a verb and an object, perhaps a rhythm—little else. Even an adjective slows the pace or tranquilizes the nerve . . . But I was too concerned with "the point of view" to be aware of simpler problems, to know that the sort of novel I was trying to write, unlike a poem, was not made with words but with movement, action, character. Discrimination in one's words is certainly required, but not love of one's words—that is a form of self-love, a fatal love which leads a young writer to the excesses of Charles Morgan and Lawrence Durrell, and, looking back to this period of my life, I can see that I was in danger of taking their road. I was only saved by failure.[19]

Because of the failure of his previous novels, Greene was in such a terrible financial plight that, for the first and only time in his life, he consciously set out to write a book which would be so popular that it might ultimately be made into a film.[20] This plan, in turn, seems to have influenced his style in a significant way. It's remarkable how cinematic his style now became. More precisely, he employs a variety of techniques usually favored by expressionistic filmmakers. Among these are superimposition, colliding images, dissolves, montage, suggestive reflections, parallel editing, tight framing, extreme angles of vision, and purposeful light and shadow. All this is done, it should be emphasized, with such skill that its cumulative effect resembles the sensual, direct impact of a great film.[21]

Mixed in with these components is one more stylistic advance which bears pointing out. This is the way Greene lays out key scenes.[22] These scenes might come at any time, but they stand out because of the import they carry. Usually, they center on Greene's primary thematic concerns, and these concerns are brought out through an exchange of dialogue. To intensify the climate of exchange, Greene tends to place two or three characters in close quarters where, under the urgency of events, they are prone to express their views by means of indirect confessions.

In the key scenes of *Stamboul Train*, a few of the same concerns which had already been introduced in Greene's first novels appear. Some new themes also appear, such as those of pity and modern politics. It's important to note, however, that the theme of sacrificial and redemptive love which was so prominent in *The Man Within* has been replaced by a pervasive disillusion. Most of the characters are seen to be morally hollow and emotionally dry. One or two may have a capacity for love or sacrifice. But they are pictured as the most helpless of victims. Thus Coral Musker, the younger dancer who is the one character exhibiting any real capacity for personal affection and loyalty, winds up in the suffocating clutches of the lesbian journalist. And Dr. Czinner, the idealistic revolutionary, dies of a gun shot wound in a shed. He had hoped to change the chaotic world where "the poor were starved and the rich were not happier for it . . . the thief might be punished or rewarded with titles . . . wheat was burned in Canada and coffee in Brazil, and the poor in his own country had no money for bread and froze to death in unheated rooms."[23] But after his martyrdom, we see that his dream and sacrifice were totally futile.[24]

The death of Dr. Czinner is both the most riveting and the most worrisome thing about this novel. Many of the characters are treated like caricatures, and thus they can be ultimately dismissed as mere objects of satiric contempt. Dr. Czinner, on the other hand, is fleshed out sufficiently to take on real life. The result is that we begin to care for him as we can't for the other characters. Yet, at the end, he is shown to have led just as meaningless an existence as the rest. As a consequence, one might come away from this novel with the feeling that it's been a rousing story, but that there was nothing behind it except a profound disillusionment bordering on nihilism.

A Political Phase

The pervading sense of futility is even stronger in Greene next book, *It's a Battlefield* (1934). With it, Greene entered a phase during which he wrote three troubling novels with specific political frameworks. The events of the first one are set off by the death of a policeman. This was an accident, since the Communist bus driver who killed him was just trying to defend his wife when a riot broke out at Hyde Park. Nevertheless, the driver is sentenced to death. The government, however, is nervous about carrying out the sentence because it is afraid of political repercussions. Thus it hesitates about what course to take, and while it does, the effect this situation has on the people directly or indirectly involved is brought out. Needless to say, justice isn't served in the end. Instead, the book leaves the impression that injustice is the unavoidable condition of the contemporary world.

This continues to be Greene's most unpopular book, and it's easy to see why. As if the subject of pervasive injustice weren't bleak enough, Greene adds such related themes as the perversion of love and the anguish of isolation. Moreover, as far as technique is concerned, he becomes so bold that he winds up with some confusing extravagancies. Having used a cinematic style with great success in *Stamboul Train*, he was bound to continue in this vein. Unfortunately, he now takes the idea of identifying the point-of-view with a ubiquitous camera eye so far that the story is sometimes too fragmented. Overlapping this problem is his experimentation with the stream-of-consciousness technique. There are occasions when he manages to use this method with great success, especially toward the end of the story when he attempts to link thought and action. At other times, though, he uses it so crudely that it's somewhat distracting.

It's indisputable, however, that in this novel Greene made important advances on several other fronts. He had taken the risk of populating a novel with many apparently unrelated people in his previous book, but there he used the simple device of the train to bring them together. This time he has taken just as many characters and set them adrift in London. But they are ultimately all joined together through several devices Greene had now mastered. The most significant of these are the employment of a circular, highly integrated plot structure; the use of vivid metaphors, similes, synecdoches, oxymorons, and other figures of speech to link the abstract with the concrete; the repetition of words which express the main themes; and the introduction of authorial comments.

As far as the latter point is concerned, it should be pointed out that Greene was something of a maverick.[25] While this novel was being written, modernism was a powerful new movement, and such former traditions as authorial comments in a novel were supposed to be on the way out. Greene, however, believed in the idea that behind a novel must stand the omniscient mind. When he set out to apply this idea, though, he wished to do it in a more subtle way than had usually been done in the past. The method he came up with was to bring out his views through the actions and thoughts of his characters, but in such an unobtrusive way that, barely revealing there has been a transitional shift, he makes us accept the words as those of one of his characters while at the same time making us feel the power of the greater expressiveness and wisdom which emanates from an authorial voice.[26] Because Greene uses this technique with very great skill, *It's a Battlefield* acquires a depth and thematic resonance it wouldn't otherwise have. At the same time it should be added that in this book the authorial voice expresses nothing but despair.[27]

The tone of despair in *England Made Me* (1935)[28] doesn't at first appear as strong as it was in *It's a Battlefield*. Yet this is only a temporary illusion due primarily to two factors. Greene now employs more deflecting irony than was his previous habit, and he places the political scene behind a story of love. This story, however, is hardly an ordinary love story. It involves a brother and sister and their confused feelings of incestuous love. As their story unfolds, we begin to see that in this novel Greene is exploring abnormal psychology because it's something which fascinates him. Yet at the same time we begin to understand that the incestuous, doomed love story is in a way a reflection of the times. It's the 1930's, and these are the years of incestuous corruption in international business, of depression in Europe, and, even though no direct mention is made of this in the novel, of the rise of Hitler.[29]

Consequently, a person like the brother, who is characterized as being too innocent, has no real chance. He is doomed to die a victim of someone like the financial tycoon for whom his sister works and whose mistress she had become. He simply had no real chance in a world where, as his sister says at the end of the book, everybody steals while "giving nothing back" and where there is no such thing as "brotherhood in our boat. Only who can cut the biggest dash and who can swim."[30]

In several ways this is Greene's most successful novel up to this point. The counterpoints between love and betrayal, greed and politics are effectively drawn. The two main levels of the plot are clearly integrated. The setting is brilliantly wrought.[31] The movement and pacing of the story are charged with great energy.[32] And, unlike in the past, the multiple shifts between points-of-view almost invariably are brought off without any confusion.

Nevertheless, Greene was now fast approaching an impasse in his art. Since *Stamboul Train* he had steadily improved upon his stylistic techniques. But the same couldn't be said for his creation of protagonists. However vividly drawn, they tended to have the flatness of caricatures instead of the depth of fully realized characters. Evidently sensing this, Greene tried the extensive use of interior monologue in *England Made Me* to get inside his major characters. The results, at best, were only partially successful.[33] The combination of this self-conscious literary technique and Greene's instinctively sensual, direct, and subjective approach just wouldn't go together very well. There are times, in fact, when this combination takes away from the impact of the story because it seems as if Greene is straining too much to make this point with style. Fortunately, Greene learned from this unhappy experiment, and thus he more or less abandoned the use of interior monologue as a primary means of character development in his future novels. Instead, he would begin to write stories which tended to center on a protagonist who is developed by means of reflective minor characters, plot line, dialogue, figurative language, and such additional refined means as dreams.

Before Greene published his next novel, *A Gun for Sale* (1936),[34] he took the crucial trip to Africa during which he made the discovery that he actually had a love for life. As a result, his fiction began to take on a different quality. *A Gun for Sale* is in most ways still typical of what had gone before. As far as style is concerned, there are no real departures from past practices. The startling use of surrealism may be noted, but this is more a refinement than a change in Greene's technique. With respect to themes, several of those which had always concerned Greene are found in this book. He is still exploring such matters as betrayal, greed, injustice, violence, and political exploitation. However, when it comes to the central character and the effect he leaves on the story, there is an important difference. Unlike in the previous stories, the actions of the protagonist in *A Gun for Sale* ultimately give a certain meaning to his life and even hope to some of those who are affected by him.

At the beginning of this story, the protagonist, Raven, is pictured as a completely cold-blooded person who has no qualms at all about murdering an idealistic minister for pay. But once he is betrayed by his employers, and he sets out to revenge himself while at the same time running from the law, he starts to look more sympathetic. We begin to see him not only as a malevolent criminal but also as a victim, and finally as a kind of instrument of social justice. During the course of the double chase, we discover that there are things about his past which help to explain his violent behavior. Also, after he involves a girl in his desperate actions, we begin to see that he has a capacity to be emotionally influenced by other people. Finally, when he catches up to those who have betrayed him and kills them, before being shot himself, he becomes a kind of judicial scourge. For in killing them, he has saved society from people who were trying to force a war so that their armaments industry would thrive.

If one looks forward two years to the publication of *Brighton Rock*, it seems as if *A Gun for Sale* might have been a kind of preliminary study for it. There are a number of correspondences between the two books. The most striking of these is that Raven and Pinkie Brown, the protagonist of the later book, have so much in common as far as their past and present ways of life are concerned.[35] There is one big difference between them, though. Raven is running from his past and from the law. These forces are also after Pinkie. But the most powerful force which is in pursuit of him is that of religious salvation. Because of the injection of this extra dimension, *Brighton Rock* will turn out to be without a doubt a more distinguished book than anything Greene had written before.

Another Direction

It might be said that with the publication of *A Gun for Sale* Greene ended his formative period. He had now developed a highly distinctive style, and though he would continue to try to sharpen it, he wouldn't change it in any significant way. As for subject matter, he had by now introduced a number of themes which he would continue to investigate in an obsessive manner. Of these concerns, politics began to dominate. It's tempting, consequently, to speculate what would have happened if he had left it at that, if, that is, *A Gun for Sale* had turned out to be not the end but a continuing part of a phase. Would Greene today be remembered primarily as a writer of political thrillers set in the 1930's, a member of the Auden generation overshadowed by the poets of that time? It's not unlikely.

If Greene's reputation as a distinct and major writer is now assured, it's because after *A Gun for Sale* he would begin to write books which are directed toward salvation. Starting with *Brighton Rock,* he would write a series of so-called Catholic novels in which he explores the means of theological salvation. He tries a variety of angles, but they actually come down to a basic scheme. The focus is on protagonists who, at the beginning of their stories, are living in states of anxiety and decadence. Then, as their stories unfold, they begin to find their way to at least a glimpse of the redeeming light of God. More specifically, these novels end with the suggestion that grace has been the ultimate means of salvation, not primarily because the characters have been spiritually responsive, but because of the haunting mercy of God. The persistent and mysterious action of grace in the Catholic novels is what most clearly sets them apart from those that follow.

Beginning with the appearance of *The Quiet American* in 1955, Greene major novels start to take on a secular slant. Like their religious counterparts, the protagonists in these later novels all appear to be doomed at first, and like them they manage to find their way to at least a glimmer of the possibility of salvation. But now this process leads to earthly and personal salvation. To get them to this end, Greene prefers to employ a basic pattern which, again, is similar to what is found in the Catholic novels. In his most recent novel he will try something a bit different, perhaps. Until then, his method in general is to start out by describing moribund men living in festering isolation and psychic dissolution, then follow them closely as they manage to escape, for however fleeting a moment, their private egoistical hells by learning to become imaginatively engaged with other human beings. The patterns of their regeneration are all complex, but on the whole it can be said that they take emotional and spiritual journeys which purge them and lead them toward a clearer self-understanding and a fuller and more compassionate vision of life.

THE CATHOLIC NOVELS

When Greene set out to write *Brighton Rock* (1938), his intention was to come up with a plain detective novel, not the theological thriller it turned out to be.[36] Although he had been a practicing Catholic for several years, he had up to this point kept his religion and profession clearly separated. Then two events shook Greene out of this position—the assault against religion by the socialists in Mexico and the attack by Franco against Republican Spain. Now Greene had to admit that, given the nature of the present world, it was no longer possible, at least not for him, to place religion and contemporary existence in different compartments. This discovery impelled him, in turn, to involve himself in the examination of how faith can affect action.[37] From then on, Greene would always be concerned with this subject to some extent in his major works. But it's especially prominent in the Catholic tetralogy which began with *Brighton Rock*.

Because this concern took over fully only after Greene had already started *Brighton Rock*, the book is slightly disjointed at one point.[38] The first of the seven parts of the story seems to be written in the vein of the pure detective novel Greene had originally in mind. Then the story shifts toward the theological perspective, and keeps to it relentlessly until the end. This shift, it should be emphasized, is not so pronounced as to call attention to itself. Nevertheless, there is a likelihood that, at least on a subliminal level, it brought on some of the uneasiness which can be discerned in the first reviews which met the book. At least in most of these reviews, it's apparent that the commentators didn't quite know what to make of the religious subject once it entered the story, and as a result they by and large directed their attention toward the melodrama of undeniably a sensational story.

The story is set in motion when Pinkie Brown, a seventeen year old hoodlum, and his gang decide to kill Fred Hale because the latter's act of betrayal has led to the death of Kite, the previous leader of the mob. Trying to escape the killers, Hale attaches himself to Ida Arnold, a big-hearted sex figure who specializes in fun. But when she excuses herself momentarily to relieve herself of too much ale and to have a quick wash, the gang murders Hale. When Ida later reads in the newspapers about the mysterious circumstances surrounding Hale's death, she decides to investigate. As she begins closing in on Pinkie, he murders a nervous member of the gang and marries a young girl who knows too much about the true facts of Hale's violent death in order to avoid the possibility of her testifying against him in court. Driven into a panic by an accumulation of menacing circumstances, he decides that Rose must go, too. He thinks of a way to trick her into committing suicide; however, before he can succeed, Ida and her retinue arrive in time to save Rose. And Pinkie falls to a ghastly death over a cliff as he runs screaming from them.

All this, of course, is just the surface of the story. Underneath the melodrama, the dominant concern is profoundly religious. As the book starts to unfold, it becomes apparent that the major struggle is not between the forces of society and crime but between good and evil. This may be an age-old subject. What distinguishes this book from any number of other, more pious ones is that this struggle takes place primarily within a character who seems to take the risk of willingly damning himself despite his Catholic conscience. Not too long after the appearance of the novel, these issues began to replace the story's melodramatic qualities as the focus of critical attention. Nevertheless, even after all these years, Greene's first major novel remains his most widely misread.

This, ironically, is in large part the fault of Greene himself. Sometime after the publication of *Brighton Rock*, Greene made a careless remark to the effect that the novel was about a character who was bound for hell. He later tried to qualify this view by adding that what he "really meant was that . . . *Brighton Rock* is written in such a way that people could plausibly imagine that Pinkie went to hell, and then I cast doubt upon it in the ending."[39] Unfortunately, by then his earlier remark had, it appears, been accepted as the absolute truth by too many people.

The most influential of these was doubtless Evelyn Waugh. Evidently accepting Greene's earlier comment as simple fact, he came to the conclusion that *Brighton Rock* "challenged the soft modern mood by creating a completely damnable youth. Pinkie . . . is the ideal examinee for entry to Hell. He gets a pure alpha on every paper."[40] And this view has, more or less, persisted until this day.

Looking at the structure of the action of *Brighton Rock*, one would tend to agree that Pinkie seems clearly destined for damnation. He appears to progress steadily in the maliciousness and cruelty of his acts. Evidence can even be found that he perverts one by one the seven sacraments in the seven sections of the book.[41] Hence there are critics who have concluded that he is a sort of "juvenile Satan."[42] And there are many critics who agree with the one who finds that Pinkie progressively "descends in stature throughout the work, until at the end he is damned for all eternity."[43]

If there is an apparent structure of damnation, however, there runs counter to it a subtle but impressive pattern of salvation. For one thing, Greene persuades us often enough that we should take into consideration as an extenuating circumstance the background of Pinkie. This is not to say that Greene is writing a sociological tract about the deterministic influence of the past in creating juvenile delinquency, but that natural environment is one of the factors to be considered when trying to evaluate the fate of a human being. Therefore, it is significant that Pinkie has lived in squalor and degradation for all of his life. As a child he lived in the slums with parents whose only apparent moments of escape from an existence of grinding poverty consisted of the sexual ritual on Saturday nights, performed in the same room where the boy had to sleep. Not surprisingly, Pinkie became desperate to escape the horror of his surroundings. As a result he was deeply grateful when Kite rescued him and made him a member of the mob. When Kite, who becomes a father figure to the boy, is murdered, Pinkie seeks consoling revenge while at the same time trying to perpetuate the memory of the man who had given him a new life by retaining his sad and violent habits. What he has also retained throughout his mobster years is a memory, however faint at times, of his Catholic upbringing. Within him there always exists the fearful realization that he is on the road to hell but that there remains an omnipresent possibility of theological salvation.

This intense religious conviction is something that sets him apart from a host of characters with whom we are forced to compare him. It is part of Greene's scheme to imply through the device of contrast that Pinkie has qualities which make him at least as worthy of our fair estimation as the persons surrounding him. A descriptive passage is particularly revealing of Greene's intent in this connection:

> A negro wearing a bright striped tie sat on a bench in the Pavilion garden and smoked a cigar. Some children played touch wood from seat to seat, and he called out to them hilariously, holding his cigar at arm's length with an air of pride and caution, his great teeth gleaming like an advertisement. They stopped playing and stared at him, backing

> slowly. He called out to them again in their own tongue, the words hollow and unformed and childish like theirs, and they eyed him uneasily and backed further away . . . A band came up the pavement . . ., a blind band playing drums and trumpets, walking in the gutter, feeling the kerb with the edge of their shoes, in Indian file. You heard the music a long way off, persisting through the rumble of the crowd, the shots of exhaust pipes, and the grinding of the buses starting uphill for the racecourse.[44]

The absurd medley that is heard is the music of a spere where too many persons are, unlike Pinkie, blind to their direction. And the suspicious hilarity of the gaudy, alien man insinuates the truth about such people as Colleoni, the successful businessman-crook who was earlier depicted as one who "clinked very gently as he moved" in a plush ambience consisting of mechanical young men and their "small tinted creatures, who rang like expensive glass when they were touched but who conveyed an impression of being as sharp and tough as tin" (*BR*, p. 73). Later we see Sylvie, the moll of the recently dead Spicer, who "literally ran . . . towards the dark car-park and the game" less because she was excited by the reluctant advances of Pinkie than because of her love for a Lancia (*BR*, p. 166). Such people have very little to lose—perhaps a bit of money or time. Pinkie, on the other hand, is always intensely aware that he has a soul at stake.

It is especially this point that should be kept in mind when Pinkie is compaed to Ida, who at first appears to be a generous earth goddess wishing only to comfort and please her admirers. Her big, friendly breasts promise security and warmth; but they have actually destroyed many an adventurer with their false promises. She is a siren, alluring and powerful in the flesh but hollow in spirit. We are told that she "wasn't religious. She didn't believe in heaven or hell, only in ghosts, ouja boards, tables which rapped and little inept voices speaking plaintively of flowers" (*BR*, p. 40). Her philosophy and creed consisted of a remorseless mathematical formula: "An eye for an eye . . . And vengeance and reward—they both were fun" (*BR*, p. 42). She stalks Pinkie not because she cares about what he did to Hale or what he might do to Rose. The hunt itself, not the people concerned, is what matters to her.

Ida's remorseless pursuit of Pinkie accentuates the progress of despair that her prey undergoes. As he travels along his violent road, Pinkie yearns for the end, but he can't stop because he is driven by pressures beyond his control. While he is driven from crime to crime, his hunger for peace increases in proportion to his growing panic. He starts out with the death of Hale because, as he sees it then, there exists an incumbent need for exact revenge. But the way of violence does not become easier with each act. He experiences, instead, an ever growing panic that things are getting out of hand, emphasized by his repeated references to the refrain from the *Agnus Dei* calling for peace. Finally forced into the position at the end where he has evidently no way out but through more slaguhter, he screams with horror: "My God, have I got to have a massacre?" (*BR*, p. 303).

The high emotion of these climactic words indicates how far Pinkie has come in the way of human feeling. In the early pages of the book he is pictured as thoroughly, even supernaturally, evil. He is described in serpentine terms, with a flickering tongue and venom coursing through his veins. His eyes are ancient and icy, as of those in whom "human feeling has died" (*BR*, p. 5). His face has a "starved intensity, a kind of hideous and unnatural pride" (*BR*, p. 4). This infernal pride is the source of his murderous strength, for it allows him to be totally unconcerned about anyone else. Other people mean nothing to him because his "imagination hadn't awoken . . . He couldn't see through other people's eyes, or feel with their nerves" (*BR*, p. 52). However, in the central section of the novel there is a reversal scene of sorts, for here Pinkie, facing the imminent possibility of his own death, goes through a process of humiliation and humility during which we see him weep, try to pray, and even think momentarily of confession and giving a holy statue to the church by way of atonement for his past.

It is of course true that Pinkie does not in reality fully repent just yet, nor does he feel lasting remorse, since he rationalizes that there was no time for such resolutions while he was on the run. Nevertheless, the experiences of this crisis will leave a lasting effect on him. After these moments when he is forced to fully face his own character and fate, he will be capable of being shocked by his own cruelty in pushing the blind band out of his way on one occasion. Also, after this crisis Pinkie has moments when he has a strong sense of nostalgia for an imagined innocence of the past and a yearning for his own annihilation. And it's remarkable how he begins to feel a need to understand other people. When he goes to see his lawyer at his wretched home, he is shaken by a new experience. Pinkie "had never known Prewitt like this before: it was a frightening and an entrancing exhibition. A man was coming alive before his eyes: he could see the nerves set to work in the agonised flesh, thought bloom in the transparent brain" (*BR*, p. 262). He had come to see Prewitt because of his immense self-concern; but when he leaves, he is thinking of the lawyer's life of putrefaction. Even more significant, though is the development of some affection for Rose.

What really matters in Greene's world is whether or not his characters experience a change of heart; and this happens to Pinkie, however slow and reluctant the process, most clearly in his relations with Rose. At first he only looks on her with intense hatred as another obstacle to safety from the law. After the reversal scene, however, he begins to experience certain feelings for Rose that are new and surprising to him. It's clear that he will grow ever more desperate to destroy her, since she represents not only a dangerous witness but also the marriage trap. Yet concurrently she sparks a hint of imaginative sympathy in him. He is touched by her loyalty to him when he goes to her for aid after being cut up and nearly bleeding to death at the race track. The pure hatred that he had felt for Rose when she remined him of Nelson Place becomes a faint feeling of longing for her and what she represented when he sees her face up to Ida in his behalf and an obscure sense of humility when she thereafter swears her eternal fidelity to him. When he goes to her parents to bargain for their daughter's hand, he feels a touch of pity for Rose because of her inability to escape the trap of poverty. After the sad marriage, he is ready to defend her against Cubitt's innocent yet painful marriage humor to such an extent that he startles himself: "An extraordinary indignation jerked in the Boy's brain and fingers. It was almost as if someone he loved had been insulted" (*BR*, p. 184). During their wretched honeymoon he can experience the beginnings of tenderness, and instead of the anticipated revulsion he reacts with faint sensation of fondness when they consummate their marriage.

It is true that all too soon Pinkie begins to plan to get rid of Rose once and for all; but this is possibly because he now fears that these growing feelings of affection will drain him of his venomous strength. He is clearly perplexed and frightened by the discovery that he was becoming involved in someone else's character and fate. Understandably, when the time comes to go through with the plan for the death of Rose, his feelings undergo an intensity which illustrates the agonizing paradox of the situation. He must be rid of her; yet he knows that she had somehow broken his habit of hate: "It was quite true—he hadn't hated her; he hadn't even hated the act. There had been a kind of pleasure, a kind of a pride, a kind of—

something else" (*BR*, p. 299). This is the closest indication that Pinkie has at least a rudimentary experience of love.

One does not, however, have to prove that Pinkie actually goes beyond these stirrings of love for Rose in the metaphysical framework of this book. It is obvious that Rose loves Pinkie—in fact to such an extent that she flirts with suicide, the worst imaginable sin to her since she is also a Catholic, to show her readiness to do anything for him. Since Rose, like Greene's later heroine in *The End of the Affair*, is a repository of sacred love, she becomes a powerful factor in the process of salvation. Having followed the example of Christ's redemptive suffering, she contains within her mysterious powers of forgiveness. She is the clearest and most compelling representative of what Greene imagines as the omnipresent and appalling force of grace.

Significantly enough, the story begins on Whitsun, which celebrates the descent of the Holy Spirit. Then we are reminded of the presence of grace through several reappearing images and symbols. The recurring rhythmic pressure of the wind, tide, and rain act as unobtrusive symbols of the nature of grace. The frequent wail of music functions as a painful reminder to Pinkie of his primary season of peace, specifically when he was a choirboy. Subtly imposed is a montage sequence of an old man and a seagull which suggests God's complex and protean mercy. In a key passage grace is, by implication, pictured as immensely patient and gentle and capable of disturbing consequences:

> An old man went stooping down the shore, very slowly, turning the stones, picking among the dry seaweed for cigarette ends, scraps of food. The gulls which stood like candles down the beach rose and cried under the promenade. The old man found a boot and stowed it in his sack and a gull dropped from the parade and swept through the iron nave

> of the Palace Pier, white and purposeful in the obscurity: half-vulture and half-dove (*BR*, p. 161).

Grace, like the old man, patiently picks among the rubble of humanity for anything that might be redeemed. And, like the gull, it is purposeful in a mysterious way, both a bird of prey and of peace. This paradoxical nature of grace is what we see when it is pictured at the moment of its greatest pressure, when it tempts Pinkie as he drives toward the planned death of Rose:

> An enormous emotion beat on him; it was like something trying to get in; the pressure of gigantic wings against the glass. Dona nobis pacem. He withstood it, with all the bitter force of the school bench, the cement playground, the St. Pancras waiting-room, Dallow's and Judy's secret lust, and the cold unhappy moment on the pier. If the glass broke, if the beast—whatever it was—got in, God knows what it would do. He had a sense of huge havoc-the confession, the penance and the sacrament—and awful distraction, and he drove blind into the rain (*BR*, p. 300).

Pinkie withstands its force here. Yet whether this means that God's grace ever gives up on him is a different question because, as the priest at the end tells Rose in words which can serve as the coda of this and Greene's other Catholic novels, "You can't conceive, my child, nor can I or anyone the . . . appalling . . . strangeness of the mercy of God" (*BR*, p. 308).

Consequently, when we see Pinkie during his last moments on earth, it is not at all certain that he is about to enter hell. Rather than being pictured as an infernal figure, he finally appears like a child, "badgered, confused, betrayed"; and he is not expanded with Satanic pride but shrinks "into a schoolboy flying in panic and pain, scrambling over a fence, running on" (*BR*, p. 304). His agony is hellish as the vitriol steams on his face and, fetus like, he folds in terrible pain. In the context of the total picture of his life, however, it's clear that these are the last in a long series of agonies on earth, a life which has certainly been an utter hell for him, thus actually cancelling out the need for another one. Therefore, when Pinkie seems to be "withdrawn suddenly by a hand out of any existence—past or present," he is significantly "whipped away into zero-nothing" (*BR*, p. 304), perhaps that restful vacancy which he had yearned for so intensely, if God has as much mercy as Greene imagines and as a writer he was always inclined to reveal.

Brighton Rock is the clearest example of what was becoming one of Greene's habitual schemes. This was to begin a book by focusing on a protagonist who initially strikes us as very unsympathetic, and then to force our attitudes to undergo a fundamental change. Because of Greene's penchant for the harsh delineation of the flaws in his characters, this process of adjustment can be exceedingly reluctant on our part. Yet it's obvious that Greene actually wants us to undergo a real struggle. Without it, he seems to imply, our sympathetic understanding is bound to be shallow, incomplete, or merely sentimental. Moreover, without such a process of engagement, the stories wouldn't be effective on a level which is most important to Greene—to reveal something essential of the reader to himself. The challenge to do this happens to be most extreme in the case of Pinkie Brown. But it is apparent throughout Greene's major work, and it certainly has considerable intensity in his next Catholic novel, *The Power and the Glory*.

Before Greene brought out *The Power and the Glory* in 1940, he published two more books. One, *The Confidential Agent* (1939), was in fact written at the same that *The Power and the Glory* was taking shape. It's obvious where Greene's main effort went. *The Power and the Glory* turned out to be the most accomplished of the Catholic tetralogy, and to many people Greene's masterpiece. *The Confidential Agent*, on the other hand, was in several ways Greene's least satisfactory book since his first ones.

The trouble is not with the story, for it's undeniably gripping. Using a thriller pattern, Greene focuses on an agent from a foreign government who has come to England to negotiate a coal contract. His mission is desperately urgent because the coal is needed to continue a civil war struggle back home. As soon as he lands in England, however, serious problems begin to beset him. The most ironic is that his government doesn't really have confidence in him. But, even aside from that, treachery follows him like a disease wherever he goes. That is, with one important exception. There is a girl who manages to inspire a measure of trust and love in him through her example. As a consequence, although he fails to fulfill his political mission, he begins to regain his capacity for human emotions at the end.

If Greene's primary attention hadn't been elsewhere, *The Confidential Agent* might have turned out to be one of his better efforts. Nowhere else is he smoother or more consistent in applying certain techniques. The employment of a circular structure, a deliberate point-of-view, and an impressionistic atmosphere are thoroughly commendable. Also, the presentation of such themes as the importance of trust and the contagion of war is effectively direct. On the other hand, Greene hardly bothers to get below the surface of his characters. And this, in turn, is due to what appears to be the major problem with the book. It's written in a curiously detached way.[45] At one point in the story, Greene has his protagonist think that he "was damned like a creative writer to sympathy" for "other people's pain, their lives, their individual despairs."[46] In his most successful novels, Greene undergoes just this kind of wrenching passion, but it's missing in *The Confidential Agent*.

The other book which was published in 1939, *The Lawless Roads*,[47] was Greene's second travel book. Unlike *Journey Without a Map*, this travel book gives us little insight into the paradoxical mind of the writer. It was a commissioned book on the religious persecution going on in Mexico in the spring of 1938, and this is what Greene set out to describe with a reporter's eye. While he was observing the political and physical conditions around him, however, the novelist in him was sometimes at least subconsciously at work. As a result, he sprinkled his account with the depiction of a number of interesting characters he met during his trip. Several of these characters, in turn, found their way into the pages of *The Power and the Glory*. And one who didn't actually provide Greene with the subject for his next novel by recounting a story a "whiskey" priest who had been so drunk during a baptism that he insisted on christening a boy Brigitta.[48]

The Power and the Glory

In a sense, *The Power and the Glory* (1940) is a kind of sequel to *Brighton Rock*, since it also may fall under the heading of an eschatological thriller. However, there is at the same time a fundamental difference which should be pointed out at the start. If there is any doubt that Pinkie goes to hell, there is none that the priest in *The Power and the Glory* is destined for heaven. At the conclusion of this novel we are left with the peculiar feeling that we have been following the progress of a saint. We do, in fact, have in this book a strikingly contemporary hagiography. The priest's painful way to sainthood has been marked with fear, betrayal, and temptations especially typical of modern society. When we first see him, he is trying to escape the terrors of a political state. But gradually we come to see clearly with and through him that, as far as Greene was concerned, our mundane existence is naturally infernal, and that the only way to truly find peace is by means of a guiding vision of heaven.

The man-made political hell which appears to be abandoned by God is Mexico of the 1930's, where the government had decided to stamp out Catholicism and to erect in its place socialism and atheism as guiding principles. God's power appears to be impotent against the new politics that demand of the priests who have not already fled either betrayal of the church or execution. When the story opens, it seems that the government has indeed been highly successful in its campaign since the church buildings stand empty of worshippers and the priesthood has all but disappeared. Only one priest seems to be left, and he looks to be merely a grotesque parody of his vocation because he has a terrible weakness for the various sins of the flesh and he appears to be inept at performing his duties. Yet because he has remained, the atheistic state, vividly emobied by a lieutenant, feels compelled to hunt him down. The priest manages to continue to evade the lieutenant and his men for some time, even though they come face to face twice. And after his prolonged flight the priest even succeeds in crossing the border to a more tolerant state where he can find sanctuary. He is lured back across the border, however, in order to give confession to a dying gangster, even though he knows full well that a trap laid by the state is surely waiting for him. After he is indeed captured, little time expires before the morning of his execution. As he faces his death and looks back on his life, he feels that he has been a terrible disappointment to God. And when he does not succeed in being given confession by another frightened priest, it appears to him that damnation is his due. From a doctrinal point of view, the priest dies in a state of eternal damnation. However, as the structure and texture of the story show, salvation does not depend on formulas or even deeds, but on faith and ultimately on God's mercy.

To emphasize the thrust of his story, Greene took some calculated risks. This time he was writing a novel initially controlled both by a preconceived theme and genre. In order to work within these narrow bounds, he had to devise a strategy which would turn the constriction to his advantage. What he came up with was almost the perfect solution. While using the thriller pattern as a basic structural pattern, he cast the moral burden of the priest into a parable and populated the story with stark, flat characters who would take on life mainly by the way they contrasted with each other and, additionally, by the way the brilliantly depicted setting reflected upon them. This scheme is so fully under the control of Greene that sometimes the novel suffers from a kind of rigidity. Nevertheless, there is no denying that what the story loses in spontaneity it more than makes up in intensity, and that this intensity is of a rare kind. No one, not even Dostoevsky, could have written a more hypnotic, feverish book about guilt, love, and redemption.

Not surprisingly, there are various ways in which one might trace the priest's arduous journey from corruption to redemption, for in Greene's Catholic novels the *way* to God is what is aesthetically interesting to him. The surface story, of course, suggests an intricate thriller in which the hunt motif operates in revealing the thematic design. Our first view of the priest tells us that he is a fugitive trying to escape from the pursuing forces of the political state; but then we discover with him that he is even more intensely pursued by the power of grace. When the priest encounters most directly the persistent nature of grace, that is, when he finds out that he is compelled to re-cross the border even though it will surely mean his capture, he surrenders to God once and for all and accepts his destiny. At the same time, now no longer the quarry of either the state or God, he becomes the spiritual hunter of the lieutenant who begins to feel haunted after he has several discussions with the priest. Thus there is a crisscross pattern to be discovered in a book filled with cross motifs and images. Naturally the Christian cross dominates this story of a priest whose way parallels and meets at many points the path of Christ to his crucifixion.[49] From another angle one can discover Danteian circles.[50] Or one can find the parabolic curve of a Greek tragedy.[51] In fact, there seem to be as many patterns to be found as there are angles of observation. Still, if such patterns exist in the story, the basic way to measure the tortuous progress of the priest is to recognize that he carries his spiritual fidelity like a temptation among various contrasting characters.

In other words, during his pilgrimage the priest meets a succession of people who serve to signify to him and to us the various sides of his nature and whose chronological accumulation suggests the distance he already has and has yet to travel. Accordingly, the first person that we see him with is one who feels abandoned and has hopes of escape. His name, Tench, comes near to spelling out the aroma of his occupation and his condition. He is a dentist who dreams of leaving this festering land, whose physical and spiritual condition is made concrete by the ever-present scavengers and by the rotting teeth, which are the source of Tench's income and his view of human corruption. While he literally spends his life gazing into the depths of human decay, he dreams of escape. But, unlike the priest, he is more concerned with saving his pesos than his soul. Following the brief encounter during which each has dwelled on his entrapment, Tench gazes after the boat which pulls away from his wretched town with romanticized feelings of huge despair. But the priest, who had hoped to get on the boat only to be drawn back into the interior by a personal and, one suspects, heavenly summons, realizes in his disappointment as he prays to be caught that there can be no escape for him since he is still a servant of his people and of God.

Coral, a young girl of 13 years who is a willing slave of her hypochondriac mother and childish father, represents the priest's next significant encounter. Although, as she informs the priest, she is an atheist who lost her religious faith at age 10, she possesses an immense sense of responsibility for those who seem to need her. Similar to the developing feelings of the priest, she was "ready to accept any responsibility . . . without a second thought. It was her life."[52] Wher the priest is later forced to go back to the village where, in a moment of despair, he had lain with a woman, he is once more confronted by his experience of lust in the person of Maria and by the issue of his momentary despair in the form of Brigida, his child. When he sees his daughter for the first time in six years, he feels as if he were "seeing his own mortal sin look back at him, without contrition" (*PAG*, p. 77). He agonizes over the conviction that she was fated for corruption upon discovering that the "world was in her heart already, like the small spot of decay in a fruit" (*PAG*, p. 95). And so, shaken by a certainty that she was without protection, he offers a fearfully unselfish prayer: "O God, give my any kind of death—without contrition, in a state of sin—only save this child" (*PAG*, p. 95). It is while he thinks of her in these sacrificial terms that he approaches the discovery of the nature of God's love—that is, that "one must love every soul as if it were one's own child" (*PAG*, p. 96). Being human, he feels his love "tethered and aching" for Brigida (*PAG*, p. 96); yet he is ultimately powerless to offer her sanctuary. Nevertheless, he has come to the point where he can imagine the radiance of divine love.

The maturation of his Christian understanding of divine love is illustrated during his next significant encounter, which is with a mestizo who, he soon realizes, will be his Judas. Instead of reacting with hatred and self-pity, he looks at himself closely and sees that he, too, has had the capacity for evil—not only to betray but also to feed on ambition, pride, lust, greed, and love of authority. No one should be beyond charitable thoughts, he thinks, for "Christ had died for this man too" (*PAG*, p. 117). When the priest looks at a man now, he can think of what is central to his faith, the "convincing mystery—that we were made in God's image. God was the parent, but He was also the policeman, the criminal, the priest, the maniac, and the judge. Something resembling God dangled from the gibbet or went into odd attitudes before the bullets in a prison yard or contorted itself like a camel in the attitude of sex" (*PAG*, p. 119). At this point his extraordinary vision of love is complete, and he can feel charity for any sinner he meets thereafter.

Because he has been going through a process of purgation, he is ready for an apocalypse which serves to dramatize his spiritual progress. That experience takes place during a night in a jail cell, where he finds himself among prisoners who function to represent both his past sins and mankind in general. When he is made to enter, he asks, "Who are these people?" However, before he leaves he knows that they are intimately related to him through the ties of sin and that they are to be pitied, not hated, since hate "was just a failure of imagination" (*PAG*, p. 157). That they are in jail only serves to symbolize the nature of this life to him, for this place was really "very like the world: overcrowded with lust and crime and unhappy love, it stank to heaven; but . . . after all it was possible to find peace there, when you knew for certain that the time was short" (*PAG*, p. 149). Ironically, because he is passed off by the police as a mere derelict who has been caught with some illegal spirits, he will be dismissed the next morning. But though he escapes this time, he will thereafter be drawn back to the memory of this night when he experienced an extraordinary feeling of fellowship for and identification with a communion of sinners. The place is filled with carnality, wrath, false pride, and various other sins; but he can now discover beauty even here, as he tells the pious woman complaining about the sounds of lust in a corner:

> Such a lot of beauty. Saints talk about the beauty of suffering. Well, we are not saints, you and I. Suffering to us is just ugly. Stench and crowding and pain. *That* is beautiful in that corner—to them. It needs a lot of learning to see things with a saint's eye: a saint gets a subtle taste for beauty and can look down on poor ignorant palates like theirs. But we can't afford to (*PAG*, pp. 155-156).

His overwhelming humility makes him giggle when it is suggested that he was a martyr, but we can see that he has the feelings of a saint although he cannot realize it.

After this night his immense humility, not his self-concern, is what actually forces him to continue to try to escape the civil authorities by fleeing to another state.[53] He believes that he is not good enough to stay because he sees himself as a continuing insult to God if he remains as a representative of the church. In time he finally does manage to cross the border and finds a place of refuge with the Lehrs. This is what he dreamed of at the beginning of the novel. Yet although the Lehrs live in a material paradise, he finds that their life cannot satisfy him. Lehr, too, is an exile who has successfully escaped civil oppression, and he now seems content with his major concern—being "cunning in the defence of the good life" (*PAG*, p. 192). However, as his German name suggests, his life, which is based on hedonistic satisfaction, is not edenic but quite empty. He and his sister lead lives of dignified order, but the ritual of their existence, like the index of the Gideon bible in their home, follows an absurd formula. Thus the priest finds himself suddenly possessed by a strange sense of nostalgia for the night in the cell. When the Judas figure materializes abruptly to lure him back across the border, his reaction is less shock than a kind of dumb relief. He had, after all, previously felt the temptation of self-sacrifice in a number of ways. One also recalls that he has been particularly drawn by the summons of children, who, it becomes apparent in the course of the book, come to symbolize both his lost innocence and the agency of grace. And although he could not then clearly define it as such, he had felt the growing force of grace through a series of epiphanies as he had approached the border from the other direction. Now the reappearance of the Judas figure to tempt him back was a clear indication that God, more than the lieutenant, was the hunter. Thus, even if he knows that capture awaits him, he "felt quite cheerful; he had never really believed in this peace. He had dreamed of it so often on the other side that now it meant no more to him than a dream [and] it was time he woke up" (*PAG*, p. 216). He goes back with the conviction that God's territory is the only sanctuary.

The lieutenant who waits for him in ambush is a secular counterpart of the priest. He is a mystic too, but "what he had experienced was vacancy—a complete certainty in the existence of a dying, cooling world, of human beings who had evolved from animals for no purpose at all" (*PAG*, p. 23). He can admire the quality of loyalty in the priest, but he can see no real meaning behind it. And as he tells the priest on the way back to the city and the execution, it seems that the priest's God is not even grateful for good service; to him it appears that in the case of the priest God has cruelly rewarded loyalty with punishment. But the priest's answer summarizes his willing acceptance of his fate and his awe of the mystery of God's grace:

> I don't know a thing about the mercy of God: I don't know how awful the human heart looks to Him. But I do know this—that if there's ever been a single man in this state damned, then I'll be damned too . . . I wouldn't want it to be any different. I just want justice, that's all (*PAG*, p. 240).

The lieutenant, like the priest, dedicates his life to justice; but because his idealistic hope depends ultimately on imperfect men, it is, the novel tells us, doomed.

As the priest confronts his fate on the morning of his execution, he has doubts about whether he is even hell-worthy. We can see, however, that he is now clearly favored by God's grace. It is true that he has traveled a bizarre, convoluted road to sainthood—through the wilderness of human failure and the entanglements of his own heart. Yet there is no doubt that his final thoughts about his failures are deeply ironic for we can see that the priest has attained what he had no hope for: "He knew now that at the end there was only one thing that counted—to be a saint" (*PAG*, p. 253).

When Greene published his next book, *The Ministry of Fear* (1943), it might have seemed for a time that what can now be called his Catholic phase had ended. After all, this novel was conspicuously secular in nature,[54] and it was the only book Greene published for some eight years with the exception of a collection of short stories which were characterized more by psychological than religious concerns.[55] But when *The Heart of the Matter* finally appeared in 1948, it became evident in retrospect that *The Ministry of Fear* had been a kind of warm-up for the following novel.

In *The Ministry of Fear* Greene illustrates that with the onset of World War II there was no longer any doubt that "thrillers are like life."[56] The protagonist, Arthur Rowe, learns this fact while on the run from various dangers. Another of Greene's hunted men, he is most obviously threatened by the blitz of London and by some spies who have infested his country. More indirectly, and more significantly, he is also threatened by the assaults of contending emotions. The mainspring of his emotional terror goes back to an act of euthanasia. He had poisoned his dying wife, thinking to spare her from more pain. Since then, however, he has been haunted by severe remorse and doubts about his act. These feelings have grown to such an extent that at the beginning of the story his life seems paralyzed with guilt. Then, accidentally, he is thrust into a melodrama of political and moral confrontation, and this starts him on his way toward a kind of rebirth. By the end of what is orchestrated like a mixture of spy thriller and Jacobean revenge play, Rowe is still a somewhat haunted man. Yet he is emotionally alive again, having reached the point where he can love again, and, conversely, having learned what the paradoxical reflection between love and pity is. He has learned that pity is allied with cruelty and destruction, and that it may indeed be the "worst passion of all" (*MOF*, p. 206). At the same time, he has become convinced that the ministry of fear was "as large as life to which all who loved belonged. If one loved one feared" (*MOF*, p. 267).

This lesson represents the crux of *The Ministry of Fear*. Still, one can object that the novel suffers because the issues of pity and love don't arise naturally enough out of the drama. At times the impression is quite distinct that these thoughts are superimposed on the story, and this has the ultimate effect of undermining Rowe's believability as an exponent of the dangers of confusing love with pity. Fortunately, Rowe's story didn't represent Greene's last word on this subject. In his next novel, he created a protagonist who is again torn by these emotional factors. But this character's agony is depicted with much greater success.

The Heart of the Matter

If Rowe and Scobie, the protagonist of *The Heart of the Matter* (1948), have certain emotional preoccupations in common, they are at the same time very different. The essential difference, not surprisingly, is the fact that Scobie is a serious Catholic whose religion affects all of his emotions in a decisive way. Therefore, soon after the story gets under way, it becomes apparent that Rowe serves as his predecessor only in a thematic way. As far as his disposition is concerned, Scobie has much more in common with the whiskey priest. This does not mean that he is also headed for sainthood. Yet he does turn out to be a martyr of sorts, and a person of inviolable motives, despite the fact that he appears willingly to head toward his own damnation by committing suicide. At least as Scobie prepares for his death he is convinced that he is ensuring his doom. And clearly according to Catholic doctrine he dies in a state of mortal sin. Scobie's act is, however, not one of theological defiance but of deeply felt human self-sacrifice and compassion. Consequently, there remains the clear possibility of salvation, because, as the novel argues, God's love is profoundly receptive, especially when love is invoked.

Scobie's motives behind his act of hopelessness are what ultimately count. He does not commit the unforgiveable sin, as church doctrine calls it and he believes it to be, because his despair is less religious than psychological. He advances to his fate with the inevitability of a protagonist in a Greek tragedy.[57] As he finds himself being whirled in an ever-growing circle of despair,[58] to him there seems finally no way out except through self-destruction. To remain, he has decided, would mean that he would have to live with overwhelming feelings of guilt, cause immense unhappiness to the two women in his life, and bring outrageous pain to God.

What has driven Scobie to his unbearable impasse is a sinister quality that can devour one from within—pity. His heart goes out to all suffering humanity, but because pity feeds on pride rather than on humility, he is in danger of turning malignant with this dangerous emotion. Having the illusion of a virtue, pity is in reality what Auden describes as "that corrupt parody of love and compassion which is so insidious and deadly for sensitive natures."[59] In a novel the form of which is based on the eternal subject of triangular love, that emotion in its pure state is remarkably elusive. Although Scobie is hopelessly tied to his wife Louise and to his young mistress Helen, it is pity which is the link that matters for him, and it is pity that leads to his ultimate betrayal of them. And on the allegorical plane of the novel, where another triangle exists, Scobie is drawn to both Yusef, who comes to personify the infernal temptations, and to God by this same corrupt form of love. As in a morality play, the real drama will take place within the soul of the protagonist, with an evil genius pulling in one direction and God in the other. Divine love, however, proves powerful enough to embrace a debased kind of affection and to transform it into a higher form.

After fifteen years of marriage to Louise, it is a wretched victim of time Scobie sees when he looks at her, not a partner in life. She has been ravaged by the sudden death of an only child, by the hard life of a policeman's wife in an African colony, by the subtle decay of marriage, and by the thousand little defeats of her years. Life has been continuously disappointing to her, and this has weakened her endurance and has made her capable of monstrous cruelty and selfishness. Besides, time has devoured what beauty she once had, leaving her with an unnatural ugliness. But it is precisely when she is an image of helplessness and ugliness—"clutching one of his fingers like a child"[60] or appearing like "a joint under a meat cover" (*HOM*, p. 17)—that is, when Scobie sees her most clearly as a victim of a life which he imagines he has been essentially responsible for, that he comes closest to loving her:

> He watched her through the muslin net. Her face had the yellow-ivory tinge of atabrine: her hair, which had once been the colour of bottled honey, was dark and stringy with sweat. These were the

> times of ugliness when he loved her, when pity and responsibility reached the intensity of a passion. It was pity that told him to go: he wouldn't have woken his worst enemy from sleep—leave alone Louise (*HOM*, p. 16).

Scobie values sleep because it represents the time of peace, a form of escape from the terror of life, the little death. He thinks constantly of peace, yearning for it like a mystic for a vision. Ironically, even in sleep he is tormented by its promise. Once he dreamed that it had appeared to him as the great glowing shoulder of the moon heaving across his window like an iceberg, arctic and destructive in the moment before the world was struck; by day he tried to win a few moments of its company, crouched under the rusting handcuffs in the locked office, reading the reports from the sub-stations. Peace seemed to him the most beautiful word in the language; My peace I give you, my peace I leave with you: O Lamb of God, who takest away the sins of the world, grant us thy peace. In the Mass he pressed his fingers against his eyes to keep the tears of longing in (*HOM*, p. 61).

So when Louise begs him to find a way to send her to South Africa for a long rest, and later suggests that he will find peace once she is gone, he is tempted into making a rash promise of consent even though he has no idea how to get enough money together for such a trip.

This decision is his first step toward his fateful end. But even if Scobie could have known the consequences of this promise, he would have acted in the same way, for he was always ready to lift the burden of responsibility, especially when he came upon the suffering of children or child-like adults. Having been absent during the death of his own child, he has ever since felt irrationally guilty and has tried to atone for what he sees as his profound failure. Thus when he is confronted by the pleading of a

Portuguese ship captain not to report his sentimental letter to his daughter that he has tried to get past the wartime censors, Scobie cannot resist giving in to such "an unattractive child, the fat boy of the school" (*HOM*, p. 49). The name of the ship is the *Esperanca*; ironically, it turns out to be the scene of an act that will lead to hoplessness. Here Scobie betrays the integrity of his profession for the first time, not for money but for sentiment, a very treacherous sort of corruption "because you couldn't name its price" (*HOM*, p. 55).

Scobie continues on the road to corruption when, because he can find no other quick means, he goes to Yusef, a shady Syrian merchant, to borrow the money for Louise's trip. Professional discretion demands that he not be under any kind of obligation to a man of Yusef's dubious reputation; however, he is prepared to go this far because he now feels the full weight of his wife's unhappiness. Besides, he is instinctively drawn to Yusef because here seems to be someone else to be pitied. He is one of the unattractive, lonely rejects of life who, it has been Scobie's experience, are fated to be abused. Scobie is deceived, though, when he imagines Yusef to be just another innocent victim of life. Instead, it's Yusef who victimizes others by feeding on and living for business profit, as symbolized by his gold teeth that "flashed instantaneously like a torch" (*HOM*, p. 29). The setting of the loan transaction with Scobie tells us more about Yusef's true nature: "The bungalow was divided into a succession of small rooms identically furnished with sofas and cushions and low tables for drinks like the rooms in a brothel" (*HOM*, p. 158). Its decoration is even more significant, for it reveals that Greene's purpose is to imply that Yusef is a satanic character. The "hideous mauve silk cushions, the threads showing where the damp was rotting the covers: the tangerine curtains . . . the blue siphon of soda" add up to a suggestion of "an eternal air like the furnishings of hell" (*HOM*, p. 159). What seduced Scobie into this unnatural union was the promise of peace. But although he gets the money, the price he pays in return amounts to very nearly the loss of his soul, or at least its temporary defilement.

One should note, by the way, that the affair between Scobie and Yusef is described in highly sexual terms. This is not intended to imply that Yusef's attraction to Scobie is mainly physical but is rather meant to symbolize the corrupt form of Yusef's emotion. His "love" for Scobie is the opposite extreme of pity-adoration. As the story tells us, this kind of blind worship of a man is just as sinister and dangerous as pity. Evidently because Yusef's antithetical kind of affection promises rest from responsibility, Scobie cannot resist it. And because he is seduced by its force, he will thereafter be tormented by feelings of selfdisgust and self-betrayal. Yusef, who comes to represent evil genius, will continue to try to entice him until the time arrives when the power of God's spirit proves to be more potent and Scobie decides he must destroy his own corruption.

After finally seeing Louise off, Scobie looks forward to coming back to an empty house. However, Yusef materializes that night to offer him his debased friendship and to trick him into framing a competing Syrian merchant. Not long thereafter Helen will come into his life. Again he will be drawn to her because of the sentiment of pity. As she is brought ashore on a stretcher, having endured dreadful suffering after her ship was torpedoed by a submarine, his heart goes out to her for he cannot resist such a picture of human wreckage:

> The face was ugly with exhaustion: the skin looked as though it were about to crack over the cheekbones: only the absence of lines showed that it was a young face . . . Her arms as thin as a child's lay outside the blanket, and her fingers

> clasped a book firmly, Scobie could see the wedding-ring loose on her dried-up finger (*HOM*, p. 125).

We realize, of course, that the loose ring is an indication adultery was being carried into Scobie's life. He will later be eager to merely befriend her, since they seem to have important qualities in common—she informs him that she, too, is a loner, hates complexity and complicity, and can talk about death without reservation. But it is the image of her child-like weakness and ugliness that lures and then traps Scobie into a fateful kiss that shatters his illusion of safety from involvement. The fact is that he has only shed one responsibility to assume another. Helen is naturally much younger than Louise; but since she is not essentially different from her in other respects, this new relationship will take the same road to unhappiness, with Scobie increasingly controlled by the feeling that it is his responsibility to save Helen from the various disappointments of life.

Consequently, when Louise unexpectedly decides to return upon learning that there are rumors flying about her husband and a young woman, Scobie finds it impossible to suddenly desert his mistress. And since he cannot give up his wife either, he is caught in an intolerable dilemma. He tries to maintain his dual role of husband and lover, but the results are predictably disastrous. He has a terrible scene with Helen in which she accuses him of hypocrisy when he tells her that he could never marry her because his religion forbids divorce. In her hysteria she screams at him to go to hell, and indeed his path seems to him to lead there. Ironically, a priest comes to see him soon thereafter because of a feeling Scobie can be of comfort at a time when the fear of impotency in saving souls is overwhelming. Then a series of other events accumulate during one day to suggest a quickly closing trap. Wilson, who has been spying on Scobie's activities partly because it is his war-time job to check on security but mainly because he imagines that he loves Louise, leaves a cryptic note in Scobie's office which, characteristic of his ineptitude, fails to hide the fact that he has gone so far as to start checking his rival's files. Scobie finds out that, in a cruel turnabout, the scene of his first crime (the *Esperanca*) is about to return to him. He discovers that the letter he had written to Helen in which he wrecklessly expressed his attachment to her has disappeared without her having seen it, and that someone as a result now has some evidence which could be used in blackmailing him. When he gets home after the already shattering day, he is dismayed by the telegram from Louise informing him that she is on her way back. As if to complete a cosmic conspiracy against him, a typhoon all at once blows up. Pursued so relentlessly by his fate (and Greene sets up this process so that it almost seems foreordained), Scobie begins to think seriously about suicide.

That he hesitates at all is natural enough, for he believes in the church's teaching that it is the worst sin, even though he tries very hard to convince himself that Christ's crucifixion is a kind of precedent:

> The priests told you that it was the unforgivable sin, the final expression of an unrepentant despair, and of course one accepted the Church's teaching. But they taught also that God had sometimes broken his own laws, and was it more impossible for him to put out a hand of forgiveness into the suicidal darkness and chaos than to have woken himself in the tomb, behind the stone? Christ had killed himself (*HOM*, pp. 206-207).

Scobie is indeed pushing moral interpretations to sophistical extremes; but because he has a strong element of logic, he cannot ultimately deceive himself.[61]

These thoughts indicate not so much his theological convictions as his psychological yearning for self-destruction. A dream he has is particularly revealing of his growing awareness of his decadence:

> That night he dreamed that he was in a boat drifting down just such an underground river as his boyhood hero Allan Quatermain had taken towards the lost city of Milosis. But Quatermain had companions, while he was alone, for you couldn't count the dead body on the stretcher as a companion. He felt a sense of urgency, for he told himself that bodies in this climate kept for a very short time, and the smell of decay was already in his nostrils. Then, sitting there guiding the boat down the mid-stream, he realized that it was not the dead body that smelt but his own living one (*HOM*, p. 246).

Scobie imagines with horror that he has reached the point where he is not only the cause of immense pain for Louise and Helen but also for God. As he forsees the possibility of a future of sacrilegious masses, he has a "picture before his eyes of a bleeding face, of eyes closed by the continuous shower of blows: the punch-drunk head of God reeling sideways" (*HOM*, p. 264). The final blow to God is, he imagines, the murder of Ali, his servant of fifteen years, through his complicity with Yusef because of Scobie's unjust suspicion that Ali was capable of betrayal. When he sees the body of Ali, he imagines that of God because he has betrayed both even though he has also loved them. And due to this shock of recognition, which barely averts a damning sort of pride, he recovers the distinction between pity and love.

It is in this final context of love that we must look at Scobie's suicide.[62] It becomes an act of atonement, not of escape or self-crucifixion. His last words—"Dear God, I love . . ." —may seem at first ambiguous.[63] Yet they are ambiguous only if one fails to see that he has undergone an afferent movement from an abstract vision of cosmic pity in which "the heart of the matter" is that one must "feel pity even for the planets" to a faith in the potency of divine love.

Greene has said that a suicide which is successful "is often only a cry for help which hasn't been heard in time."[64] In Scobie's case God, at any rate, has heard. That God's love is present and receptive is suggested in several ways after Scobie has reached the suicidal point. Scobie imagines that a mysterious "someone outside the room" was actually "seeking him" as he approaches his final minutes; the mysterious fingers and voice which try to hold him are those of grace. As he falls to his death, the medal that was given to him by the grateful Portuguese captain strikes the floor and spins "like a coin under the ice-box—the saint whose name nobody could remember" (*HOM*, p. 299). We know, of course, that Scobie will not be canonized; still, in his fall to grace he has experienced the agony of man's impotency and the power of God's love with the terrible intensity of a saint. Significantly, it is God's vicar, Father Rank, who most cleary indicates the inscrutable nature of grace. His answer to Louise's conviction that Scobie was surely damned is "don't imagine you—or I—know a thing about God's mercy (*HOM*, p. 306).

When Greene started on *The Heart of the Matter*, it had been several years since he had actually written a novel due to his service in the Second World War. Thus, as he would admit himself, he was a little rusty in his craft.[65] This hardly ever becomes obvious mainly because, by this time, he had perfected the use of an ironic tone which could act consistently as a form of commentary while it also pulled the story together. Still, there are times when some of the descriptive and religiously weighted passages are clearly overloaded. Moreover, by the end of the novel, there exists a feeling that the facets of the plot and the design of the theme have been controlled too carefully. These problems, in turn, lead back to the fundamental one Greene had with this novel. Significantly enough, this had to do with the question of point-of-view, something that Greene had apparently learned to master long ago.

When Greene settled on using the third person point-ofview for *The Heart of the Matter*, he was following the practice of all of his previous novels. In all those books there is no reason to question Greene's choice. But investing *The Heart of the Matter* with a point-of-view which, in his hands, gives almost total authority to Scobie's view of things led to an unforseen difficulty. Greene had actually set out to write a book whose central character would be a negative expression of the dangers of inordinate pride.[66] However, because we are made to see things from Scobie's perspective so completely, and because the line of the story is laid out in a somewhat rigid way, we eventually learn not only to trust him but to sympathize fully with him. This is why by the time we get to the words of Father Rank about God's grace we are obliged to feel that Scobie was surely not meant for damnation. Beyond that, we might feel that *The Heart of the Matter* is so schematic that perhaps Scobie was never really in danger because he wasn't free enough for us to have ever doubted his fate.

Taken as a whole, *The Heart of the Matter* is by no means a failure. In several ways it even represents some of Greene's best work. Green is, for example, often nothing less than brilliant in the way he manages to capture the African landscape as an authentic reflection of what he experienced while he was stationed there during the war and as a vivid metaphor for what was happening to the war-ravaged world. Moreover, this novel contains several of his most fully developed and striking characters. Yet because of his technical failure to create the kind of essential ambiguity he desired for this novel, Greene realized that he might have to change the strategy in the next novel he was planning in order to more effectively bring out the eschatological issues which would arise from it. Thus in *The End of the Affair*, the last of his Catholic tetralogy, he would finally try out an active first person narrator.[67] Of course, this approach would not lead to a flawless work. The main problem which Greene was aware of but which he could only partially resolve was the inherent nature of this approach to resist a narrative tone which had both variety and ambiguity. Yet largely because he challenged this paradoxical problem by going ahead with a change in his method, Greene would ultimately come up with a book which is at least more sympathetically involving than his previous Catholic novels.

The End of the Affair

If we consider the evidence presented in *Brighton Rock*, *The Power and the Glory*, and *The Heart of the Matter*, we are bound to agree with Mauriac that, up to this point in Greene's career, his primary subject had been "the hidden presence of God in an atheistic world."[68] In these books we are made to be aware that God is ever present, watching, apparently eager to answer if called upon, whispering the way to the lost. In *The End of the Affair* (1951), however, God takes a more explicit and active role. The result is the creation of an unusual drama in which an adulteress finds her way to sainthood and a skeptical and hate-ridden novelist gropes his way toward faith and a deeper comprehension of love.

There are elements in the story of Sarah Miles which make it resemble a conventional hagiography. Notably, her soul travels the path described by St. John as a necessarily nocturnal one in which "the point of departure is privation of all desire, and complete detachment from the world: the road is by faith, which is like night to the intellect; the goal, which is God, is incomprehensible while we are in this life."[69] Then, after her mystical union with God is complete, she is blessed with the gift of miracles. But such a reading would, of course, be far too simple. To begin with, Sarah's story also has some surprising and unorthodox twists and turns, starting with a highly provocative factor—the betrayal of her husband. Moreover, the story is told in such a way that the real focus finally turns on the firstperson narrator, the hate-ridden novelist who eventually reveals his complex nature to himself and to us, but only after the involutions and ambiguities of his drama are put in order through careful analysis and judgment.

The catalyst of the story is the fact that between Sarah and Henry, her husband, exists a relationship which is devoid of passion. Because the most either can expect of the other is kindness, Sarah looks elsewhere to satisfy her intense longings for a more complete union. She appears to find the love she has been searching for in Bendrix, the novelist, and their affair does last for five years. Then Sarah suddenly ends it, and several months later she just as suddenly dies.

Soon thereafter—for cathartic, therapeutic, and professional reasons—Bendrix starts to write a novel about these events. He begins by describing an encounter with Henry which took place a number of months after the end of the affair. Henry is very disturbed by the growing suspicion that his wife is unfaithful to him because of her increasingly strange behavior. He wonders out loud whether he might not engage a private detective to investigate the possibility of adultery, but then he gives it up as an obscene thought. Bendrix, however, follows up the idea on his own initiative because he is consumed by jealousy. To his surprise, he comes to the realization that he has been replaced by God.

The process of Sarah's exchange of profane love for sacred love began the very day that marked the death of the illicit affair. That day Bendrix is surprised by the blast of one of the first V-1 rockets raining on war-time London. Sarah, finding him to all appearances dead, prays wildly: "Dear God . . . make me believe. I can't believe. Make me . . . I'm a bitch and a fake and I hate myself. I can't do anything of myself. *Make* me believe . . . Let him be alive, and I *will* believe. Give him a chance. Let him have his happiness. Do this, and I'll believe. But that wasn't enough. It doesn't hurt to believe. So I said, I love him and I'll do anything if You'll make him alive. I said very slowly, I'll give him up forever, only let him be alive with a chance . . ."[70] And then Bendrix walked in. He believes that he has only been momentarily stunned by the explosion; she is convinced that her prayer has been answered. As a result she attempts to keep her desperate vow.

The ordeal to keep her part of the bargain with God (described, like all of Sarah's subjective facts, in her diary) is naturally painful. She finds that she is terribly lonely, particularly for Bendrix. Besides, there is the persisting temptation to rationalize away the existence of God. To be convinced of this wild hope, she goes to Smythe, a rationalist, for private discussions. Ironically, his arguments that God is only a chimera assure her to the contrary. Then, with belief comes the light of faith followed by a vision of divine love.

When Bendrix discovers that he has been jealous of a spiritual rival, he assumes that he can win Sarah back since he can offer her a love which is not abstract. He calls her on the telephone to insist that he is coming over immediately to take her with him once and for all; but he only succeeds in driving her out into the rain in a wild attempt to escape him. As a result, she catches pneumonia, and within a matter of days she dies. He is naturally embittered and stunned by the events. But it is the discovery that Sarah appears to be the source of a series of miracles that sends him into a terrible struggle with God. First there is what he would have preferred to see as the coincidence that his mock prayer to Sarah at her funeral to save him from becoming involved with a certain available young woman is answered. Then the touch of a relic of Sarah's hair seems to cure Smythe of a facial birthmark that was perhaps the source of his rebellion against God. And the son of Parkis, the detective who spied on Sarah for Bendrix, is cured of intense abdominal pains by what the boy says was a visitation by her in the night. What haunts Bendrix most, though, is Sarah's diary, which Parkis lifted during the course of his investigation and which now possesses Bendrix. Its presence in the hands of Bendrix seems to be assurance that the miracle of his cure from self-indulgent hatred will follow.

All this is told in a slightly disjointed way to reflect not only Bendrix's mental and emotional condition but also the fact that this story has professional consequences for him. Bendrix has been the author of several modestly successful novels in the past. There are some critics and loyal followers who admire his sense of style and his polished technique in particular. Greater success, though, has constantly eluded him because, as he comes to suspect, he has in fact been too finished and slick. He has had methodical control over his works, apparently to the extent that they had no life of their own. Now, however, he starts a story which from the very beginning threatens to progress on its own. His first sentence expresses his belief that he, as a novelist, arbitrarily selects where to begin and end a story; but his second sentence is already a statement of doubt. A few sentences later he declares that this will be a record of hatred; we soon realize, however, that the story will be transformed into a record of love. As he begins, he thinks that if he is writing against the grain of his prejudices he has nothing to fear since his professional pride will encourage him to tell the truth, or at least the near truth. Nevertheless, what becomes most fearful to him is actually his realization that he does not even know the truth about himself and that his story is known in its entirety and can only be told by God. After he comes to the realization that God has replaced him not only as the lover of Sarah but also as the writer of his novel, he tries to resist by expressing his hatred. However, since grace has an active interest in Bendrix, his determination to be an outrage to God is futile. In fact, by trying to deny divine prerogative Bendrix assures his fate, since in Greene's religious world grace seeks out the rebels because by their actions they probe the mystery of God.[71] Besides, as Greene has pointed out about his various sinners, Bendrix might try to sin against God but he does not manage to do so very successfully.[72] His rebellious words actually indicate that he is going through a stage of mental suffering and terror, and in Greene's fiction this is a necessary prelude to spiritual transformation. When the mortal terror becomes unbearable, so does the temptation to surrender to divine power. In a sense, one might say that the book finally develops into a testament of the irresistible nature of grace. Greene has described that faith originally came to him formless but with overwhelming certainty. The apocalypse Bendrix finally experiences is even more disembodied but just as absolute.

If Bendrix's spiritual journey is more prolonged than Sarah's, it is mainly because he is possessed by pride. Sarah's sins are all of the flesh, and hence there is no serious obstacle to her reaching the stage of heroic virtue. Bendrix's sins, however, are of the mind and consequently are much more insidious. His intellectual pride as a novelist allows him to delve into the lives of others with detachment, yet ultimately not with impunity. Since pride is self-devouring, the final consquence is emotional sterility. Fortunately for Bendrix, he is allowed soon after he starts his book to realize that he has really become deficient both in hatred and love. When he finally does recognize his insufficiency, he is taking the characteristically Christian first step toward the possibility of redemption. With humility comes the acceptance of guilt, and with guilt the yearning to confess. That his proposed novel actually becomes a spiritual diary and confession is by now clear, and what is also clear to the reader though not to Bendrix is that it becomes an exemplum of Christian love. We can recognize that Sarah's love imitates the passion of Christ. But we also come to the understanding before Bendrix does that he is entering the territory of Christian love in his growing affection for Parkis, Henry, and Sarah. Since selfless love is strange to Bendrix, he is naturally apprehensive. More frightening to him, though, is the realization of what must surely follow if he gives up his hatred for God. After reading once again the final page of Sarah's diary in which she prays to God to give him peace, Bendrix reveals the depth of his dread of submitting to the divine mystery:

> What I chiefly felt was less hate than fear. For if this God exists, I thought, and if even you—with your lusts and your adulteries and the timid lies you used to tell—can change like this, we could all be saints by leaping as you leapt, by shutting the eyes and leaping once and for all; if *you* are a saint, it's not so difficult to be a saint. It's something He can demand of any of us—leap! But I won't leap (*EOA*, p. 209).

These words of panic, part of the highly charged final scene of the book, are, of course, chiefly ironic. Bendrix is not about to become a saint, but he is on the verge of taking the fearful leap. Exhausted by the relentless pursuit of grace, he glances at the distance he has already traveled and expresses his surrender in quietly ironic terms in the final paragraph:

> I wrote at the start that this was a record of hate, and, walking there beside Henry . . . I found the one prayer that seemed to serve the winter mood: O God, You've done enough, You've robbed me of enough. I'm too tired and old to learn to love. Leave me alone forever (*EOA*, p. 211).

In tracing Bendrix's path to this point of reluctant salvation, Greene exhibits a notable extension of his art. Having combined the subjective narrative method with a kind of novelwithin-a-novel approach, he succeeds in creating a story which contains more structural complexity, emotional resonance, and purposeful ambiguity than any of his previous books. At the same time, it must be said that this book has less of that urgent passion which gives so much power to his previous religious novels. This, paradoxically, seems connected with the fact that there are some things about *The End of the Affair* which ultimately suggest Greene had now perhaps gone further as a writer than he might have meant to in the area of religious abstractions, and that it was therefore inevitable this would be his last pointedly Catholic book.

The End of the Catholic Cycle

In taking Greene's Catholic novels together, it becomes clear that they can be read as a remarkable tetralogy on the subject of grace. One might go so far as to call these books comedies of salvation, since in each of them the protagonist travels through ever widening spheres of infernal terror until he finally emerges into the territory of grace. The progress of each of these characters has unique factors, but a general examination of their spiritual journeys shows us their forms are essentially the same. That Greene begins in *medias res* serves to dramatize the fact the protagonists are all initially suspended between the saving power of grace and the fatal attraction of evil, between heaven and hell. While in this state of suspension, their suffering is dreadful as the supernatural struggle for their souls rages. Their having the imagination to recognize what is at stake while experiencing the relentless tension of the opposing forces is actually the first indication they are not doomed. With the conviction of the reality of heaven and hell, Greene indicates, one is saved from amoral sterility; and with the experience of deep suffering, particularly after one becomes involved with others who also suffer, one is led to the conviction that pain and evil are the way of life. Greene follows the view of St. Augustine in suggesting that this recognition of the ineluctable reality of evil is the first clear concession to the force of grace.[73] What constantly pulls in the opposite direction, though, is pride, since it is the source of that deceptive feeling of self-sufficiency. This is why a shattering experience of failure precedes the ultimate leap to faith. Failure makes one aware of his insignificance when placed against the backdrop of the supernatural dimension, and it also allows one to identify himself with the myth of fallen man. When one has reached the point where he can feel such a sense of rare humility, he is near to attaining that understanding of himself and his spiritual destiny Greene calls the "religious sense."[74] If he then gives himself up to divine judgment, he will discover that the more dreadful his failures, the greater the appalling mercy of God.

If it's obvious that these novels are thoroughly informed with the spirit of Catholic doctrine, in the end they actually offer a personal mythology. Perhaps it is true to say that Greene, feeling deprived of an inherited or unbroken tradition of Christianity, had finally to invent a system of his own in the manner of such other modern writers as Lawrence, Pound, and Yeats.[75] This is not to suggest that there is anything dishonest about his declared religion; yet there is no doubt that Greene's Catholicism is unorthodox. Above all, Greene's view of the mercy of God is distinctive. As we have seen, he assumes that the mystery of God's grace is so great there are no formal religious rules which can comprehend it, and that instead the patterns and means of theological salvation are as strange as sacred love. Greene's quest is not to try to uncover that mystery of God. Instead, as one critic puts it, he moves "stealthily deeper into the darkness, moves through the annihilation of our confidence in human knowledge to an awareness of impenetrable mystery, moves from the deceptive light to the queerly nourishing obscurity. All the truth of things, for Greene, lies hidden in the darkness . . ."[76] That one can never reach the heart of this darkness may be a terrifying fact in Greene's religious novels; paradoxically, though, it's also presented as the source of animating faith.

There are very few novelists who have so compellingly employed the techniques of realism and melodrama to investigate religious themes. Thus it was a surprise to many of Greene's admirers when he declared after writing *The End of the Affair* that his next novel would not be concerned with explicitly Catholic themes.[77] Why Greene made such a decision is naturally intriguing. Had he perhaps become a burnt-out Catholic? There were those critics who guessed this was the case, and that Bendrix's final prayer moreover implied that religion as a creative spring had now simply run dry for Greene.[78] At this point in Greene's career, however, such a conclusion was at least premature and exaggerated. The actual fact seems to be that Greene stopped writing Catholic novels after his fourth one not because he was then losing his religion but because he had been led so far by his religious considerations in general and the theme of grace in particular that he felt his art threatened.

Greene has made the standard disclaimer that his characters should not be mistaken for their author. Neverthless, after reading *The End of the Affair* one comes away with the strong impression that the alarming situation of Bendrix is at least to some extent symptomatic of the state of Greene's mind. There appears no doubt that Bendrix's soul will be saved; but what about his art? As Bendrix prepares for the religious leap, he reveals that he is ready to reject the validity not only of reason and consciousness but also of the aesthetic approach to life.[79] The implications of his climactic frame of mind are extensive, going so far in fact as to suggest that Bendrix could not indeed be saved without giving up his intellectual vocation. At this point one might begin to wonder if Greene does not appear to show that art, which is the product of ego, is not mutually exclusive from faith, with follows the surrender of ego. In making the reluctant Bendrix a captive of the irresistible force of grace, Greene leaves the impression that spiritual determinism is the explanation for both what happens and what is written. Bendrix's story ends up differently from his original intention not because he has become indecisive in his work but because God is the master artist who conditions his vicar novelist.[80] Greene has agreed with the view that in *The End of the Affair* he has written "a novel about plot making . . . not only about a novelist making a plot, but about God making a plot."[81] Significantly, he has also made the statement in referring to the introduction of the miracles without natural explanations that he had "made an appalling mistake . . ."[82] Consequently, we have an implicit paradox here that is disturbing. Who is responsible for those "mistakes," as the book was written, Bendrix, Greene, or God? One wonders where Greene meant to draw the line between God's province and the province of his own artistic imagination. In describing his state of mind as he approached his conversion to Catholicism, Greene has indicated that he had earlier feared the possibility there was no such dividing line at all.[83] Eventually this issue would cease to bother Greene. At that point in his career, however, he was still devout enough in his religion to be troubled deeply by this dilemma.

The fact that Greene's Catholic novels didn't clearly resolve the issue of spiritual determinism is what was behind a minor critical war. Because these novels are so dominated by the theme of God's mercy, various critics became occupied with trying to interpret Greene's precise understanding of evil and grace. Thus John Atkins, for example, is convinced that what Greene had written about the presence of evil in the works of Dickens is really true of his own novels: "the eternal and alluring taint of the Manichee, with its simple and terrible explanation of our plight, how the world was made by Satan and not by God, lulling us with the music of despair . . ."[84] Sean O'Faolin concludes that Greene is clearly writing in the tradition of Pascal and Jansenism.[85] Francis Kunkel is not so sure, for he is bothered by an occasional theological paradox: "To believe, as Greene obviously does, that some characters are forever outside the pale of grace and so incapable of religious belief and experience is to cast a gratuitous slur on God's mercy and to flirt with Jansenism. Greene's position here is inconsistent because ordinarily he follows Pascal in setting no limits to God's mercy."[86] Refining his interpretation, he concludes that Greene is not Pelagian nor completely Manichaean, but half Manichaean.[87] It is no wonder that the drift toward theological esoterica by his critics eventually prompted a complaint from Greene:

> People who think they are getting at Jansenism in my novels usually do not know what Jansenism really means. They probably mean Manichaenism. This is because in the Catholic novels I seem to believe in a supernatural evil. One gets so tired of people saying that my novels are about the opposition of Good and Evil. They are not about Good and Evil, but about human beings.[88]

Despite Greene's objection, however, one is prone to come away from these religious novels with the feeling he has been a witness to dramas less human than divine. This is due primarily to their conclusions. These novels slide rather conspicuously from realism to abstract didacticism as they approach the end. As a consequence, one is bound to agree with a view of David PryceJones that because "finally nothing in the novels seems to derive from human vagary, there is a discrepancy between the involved world which Greene sets out to portray in all its complications and the rigid solutions he imposes at the end."[89] And as Morton Dauwen Zabel in particular has pointed out, the drift in these novels toward explicitly theological conclusions has unfortunate artistic consequences. He suggests that the fiction that embodies such arguments soon runs into the difficulty which all tendentious or didactic fiction sooner or later encounters. It no longer "argues" the problems and complexities or character in terms of psychological and moral forces; it states, decides, and solves them in terms of pre-established and dictated premises. Grace is always held in reserve as a principle of salvation . . . Greene . . . shirks nothing in presenting his men and women as psychically complex and morally confounded. But as he advances out of parable into realism, out of the tale of violence into the drama of credible human personalities, he still keeps an ace up his sleeve, and grace is called upon to do the work that normally would be assigned to moral logic and nemesis.[90]

Needless to say, it is debatable just how much Greene might have been influenced by such criticism into deciding to write novels with different forms and perspectives. There seems no doubt, however, that because of his venturesome temperament he experienced increasing impatience and frustration with what had become something of a formula. Beyond that, it's easy to imagine this peripatetic writer simply deciding to compose novels which did not explicitly focus on the subject of religious salvation because of a restless ambition to explore new regions. He had surveyed the territory of grace; the map was as complete as the imagination would allow. What lay beyond was also absorbing. In explaining how he came to choose his subjects, Greene once said: "What it really adds up to is that I write novels about what interests me and I can't write about anything else. And one of the things which interests me most is discovering the humanity in the apparently inhuman character."[91] We have seen that the protagonists of the Catholic cycle reveal their humanity primarily in their struggles with supernatural forces, most obviously with grace. In the novels which follow *The End of the Affair*, however, one can recognize a shift in emphasis and direction, with the dramatized conflicts of the protagonists now clearly presented in less abstract, more secular terms.

Beginning with the publication of *The Quiet American* in 1955, Greene is seen to explore the problem of what man himself can do to salvage something meaningful and worthwhile from the here and now.[92] This shift is not an extreme one, it should be stressed. Greene's techniques and obsessions remain essentially the same. Even the protagonists are reminiscent in many ways of their predecessors. Bendrix in particular seems to be their model, but with important differences. He is saved from withering hatred and cynicism by the intervention of a divine energy. The protagonists who follow Bendrix, however, are increasingly less confounded by the divine challenge and are progressively more involved with the insistent demands of the social, political, and human spheres.[93] They might be faced with a variety of difficult moral problems, too; but their decisive acts finally depend not on theological dogma but on secular considerations. If faith is still the operative term, it is now used in a more personal and existential sense. In this regard, the critic Stanford Sternlicht is quite correct in his claim that Greene's hope now begins to reside "not only nor primarily in after life, but in the distinctly encouraging possibility of living in dignity during this worldly existence."[94] Yet he is not wholly accurate when he goes on to say that what saves these later protagonists from corrosive despair is a belief in some system.[95] Their actual means of liberation turns out to be less abstract and surprisingly conspicuous. In the Catholic novels the apparently doomed characters can find their way to God through a radical experience of spiritual immolation. In the subsequent novels, though, the protagonists must, as a rule, venture through the treacherous maze of egoism to the point where they come upon the discovery that what can save them is the resolution to become engaged in the hazards of human affection.

SUMMARY

Although Greene has long ago reached an age when one would expect him to consider retirement, he has indicated that his urge to write continues unabated.[96] Therefore, it's possible *Monsignor Quixote* may not turn out to be his last book of fiction. But even if Greene manages to keep on publishing, it now seems possible to outline his achievement as a novelist without the danger of the sorts of premature summations which so many of his earlier critics have run up against. With the appearance of *Monsignor Quixote* it seems that his greatest thematic subject has now been fully imparted, or has at least reached a resolute, inescapably abstract conclusion which in future novels could only be repeated, whatever different stylistic forms might be tried.

In summarizing Greene's accomplishments, it's useful to begin with the question of his contemporary reputation. Among most critics, not to mention the general reading public, it's indeed very high. Yet Greene also has his share of detractors, especially in some academic circles. This is all to the good when these critics point out the flaws which can be found in Greene's various efforts. Certain of these same critics, however, go much further, concluding that Greene shouldn't even be considered as a major novelist. What is the basis for such a conclusion? Almost without exception, these critics feel that Greene, even if he possesses great natural talents, falls through in two important ways. One, he isn't consistent enough in his moral vision and, two, he isn't an entirely original writer. Obviously, if true, these would be legitimate reasons for attacking Greene's reputation. However, the first of these objections can be dismissed immediately by recalling how the theme of salvation ties all of his novels together. As for the second objection, it seems to have basis in fact only if one is arguing from a modernist bias.

If one is to judge Greene's achievement properly, it should be recognized that he *consciously* has tried to write a new kind of novel which at the same time is traditional. To see this, one has to first imagine Greene as a beginning novelist standing at a crossroad, pulled in two different directions. On the one hand, there was the traditional side. Here would lie the typical British novel in which character, story, and moral theme were the primary virtues. Here would be found the socially realistic fiction which, it may be argued, began with Chaucer and has continued through such writers as Fielding, Thackeray, Dickens, and Hardy. On the other hand, there was the modernist possibility. This possibility—with its emphasis on experimental technique as a means of primarily expressing not social issues but the resonant contingencies of an isolated artistic sensibility and medium—actually held most of Greene's interest during the first part of his career. Feeling the great influence of James Joyce and other experimentalists writing at that time, Greene injected his earliest novels with a highly poetic, purposely devised language. These novels were failures, and Greene, recognizing that the modernist way was actually alien to him, turned for guidance toward such writers as Henry James and Joseph Conrad. In other words, he opted for an older, pre-modernist heritage. To a number of his critics, this apparently seemed simply a retreat to a safer, more popular way. Greene's writings, once he took this step, did become increasingly popular. This happened, however, not because Greene played it safe, but because he then began to risk injecting an old tradition with thoroughly contemporary ideas and patterns. Subsequently, he became so adept at this process that, in effect, he would up re-creating the realist novel for our times.

In producing such a novel, Greene has combined four essential facets. To begin with, he has re-emphasized narrative, functional style, and other artistic virtues closely associated with the realist tradition. He has also cultivated the possibilities of various popular genres and themes and employed them for dramatic effect. Then, through the main force of a moral vision, he has raised his novels to psychological and symbolic levels which are characteristic of the most serious kind of art. Finally, by focusing directly on contemporary issues with a vivid religious and political imagination, Greene has shown how pertinent and alive the realist novel can still be.

At this juncture a question concerning Greene's influence might be raised. If one claims that he has rejuvenated the traditional novel, does this mean he actually has followers? The answer is, only indirectly. This was bound to be so since Greene is such a highly obsessive and privately romantic writer. With regard to his artistic vision, it seems that he is wholly unique. Yet, in looking especially at the literary scene in England, it's possible to see a definite measure of his influence. For a long time after the modernist revolution, it was difficult to find a serious realist writer in England. Without getting into a debate as to the comparative merits of these opposing literary fashions, it's clear that for historical and ideological reasons, the realist rather than the modernist novel seems more natural to the British writer as a whole. But it's only after Greene came into his own and provided (along to an important extent with Evelyn Waugh) an influential example that the realist novel made a sort of comeback in England. Today, the modernist tradition seems still to be the most influential one in France and America, for example. In England, however, only a handful of writers still appears to subscribe to its tenets. There it's essential traditionalists who are now in the forefront of critical acclaim.[97] The likely indications are that all these writers were touched by the long shadow of Greene, and, not to make exaggerated claims, were at least encouraged to try his direction.

In summarizing Greene's achievement, though, what should be stressed above everything else is something which he has in common with all major writers of whatever tradition. That is that Greene has managed to create an imagined world which is immediately recognizable as his alone. What's under consideration here isn't mainly the characters and placement of his stories, although they are strikingly unique. More important is Greene's moral system. This is where Greene is finally most creative. Feeling the powerful need for a moral system, but ultimately finding none which he could unquestionably adopt, he has done what other great novelists before him were compelled to do.[98] In effect, he has invented a personal moral system which gives integrity and completeness to his whole fictional world. At the heart of this system lies the conviction that we must all be driven by inner pursuits of our salvation.

NOTES

1. As well as on the art of film, one might add. See his book, *The Pleasure Dome* (London: Secker & Warburg, 1972).
2. See his essays on Henry James in *Collected Essays* (New York: The Viking Press, 1969), pp. 23-53.
3. The most important sources for this kind of commentary are his autobiographical works *A Sort of Life* (New York: Simon and Schuster, 1971) and *Ways of Escape* (New York: Simon and Schuster, 1980). In addition, there is his very revealing essay "The Revolver in the Corner

Cupboard" in *The Lost Childhood* (New York: The Viking Press, 1951).

4. *A Sort of Life*, pp. 117-118.
5. *Journey Without Maps* (New York: The Viking Press, 1965), pp. 220-221.
6. *Another Mexico* (New York: The Viking Press, 1967), p. 2. Known primarily as *The Lawless Roads* in England.
7. *Ibid.*, pp. 2-3.
8. *Collected Essays*, p. 17.
9. *Ibid.*, pp. 18-19.
10. *Ibid.*, p. 18.
11. This was not Greene's first time to flirt with suicide. Some five or six years earlier he had, on various occasions, tried hypo, hayfever lotion, nightshade, and twenty aspirins before taking a swim as means of suicide. Then he was driven primarily by a romantic sense of rebellion.
12. Greene took this trip during the winter of 1934-35. One year later he published his observations in his *Journey Without Maps*, quite a unique travel book which reveals much more about the traveler than about the land.
13. *Journey Without Maps*, pp. 262, 279.
14. Kenneth Allott and Miriam Farris, *The Art of Graham Greene* (New York: Russell & Russell, Inc., 1963), p. 15.
15. *A Sort of Life*, p. 196.
16. It was, for example, praised for its "brisk" and "exceptionally fresh and readable story" of "vitally delineated" characters (Thomas Gilbert, "First Novels," *Spectator*, June 22, 1929, p. 982); for its "honesty and subtlety" (Bartlet Brebner, *The Saturday Review of Literature*, October 19, 1929, p. 287); and for the "skill and complexity with which the psychological tissue is woven" (Anonymous, *The Times Literary Supplement*, June 20, 1929, p. 492).
17. Also known as *Orient Express* in the United States.

18. The most noteworthy of which is Quin Savory, the popular writer. On one hand, he is satirized for writing trash. On the other, he is a kind of sly parody of Greene himself. Greene, as fond of self-deprecating humor as anyone, attributes certain qualities to him which he recognizes in himself. For example, he makes Savory out to be a kind of "spy" who has learned some of his craft from films and who feels that the world is an "adventurous place."
19. *A Sort of Life*, p. 203.
20. This is apparently one reason why Greene decided to make up the label of "entertainment" for it.
21. Interestingly enough, part of the original inspiration for this book was a famous film, Grand Hotel. But in its make-up, it resembles much more the work in the *film noir* genre of Fritz Lang, a director whose films Greene admired.
22. Greene believes that this practice was due to "the influence of my early passion for playwrighting," a passion "which has never died" and which eventually led to several plays. *Ways of Escape*, p. 32.
23. *Stamboul Train* (London: William Heinemann & Bodley Head, 1974), p. 203.
24. In certain ways, Czinner is a type of figure which continued to fascinate Greene and which he eventually split into two characters, the whiskey priest and the lieutenant in *The Power and the Glory*.
25. Another modern novelist who used authorial comments was Francois Mauriac, a writer whom Greene admired and who apparently influenced him.
26. David Lodge, "Graham Greene," *Six Contemporary British Novelists*, George Stade, ed. (New York: Columbia University Press, 1976), p. 24.
27. Greene's recollection that the novel's subject "was suggested by a dream, the fruit of anxiety-ridden weeks, in which I had been condemned to death for murder" and that as he wrote it he felt he was going through "an

act of self-destruction" may help to explain the book's unrelieved gloom. *Ways of Escape*, pp. 34-35.

28. Also known as *The Shipwrecked* in the United States.
29. Greene says that the rise of Hitler was one of the factors that "cast a shadow on this book." *Ways of Escape*, p. 37.
30. *England Made Me* (London: William Heinemann & Bodley Head, 1970), p. 256.
31. Even though, as he recalls, this is "the only occasion when I have deliberately chosen an unknown country as a background and then visited it, like a camera team, to take the necessary stills." *Ways of Escape*, p. 37.
32. He managed this in part by the use of suggestive cataloguing, a practice which he may have learned from Auden and his followers.
33. This is true despite Greene's belief that the brother and sister are two of his very best portraits. *Ways of Escape*, pp. 39-40.
34. Also known as *This Gun for Hire* in the United States.
35. In *Ways of Escape* Greene says that in looking back to the two books "Raven the killer seems to me now a first sketch for Pinkie in *Brighton Rock*," p. 75.
36. This initial inconclusiveness was reflected by the fact that when the book first appeared it was listed as a novel, then an entertainment, then back to a novel in Greene's bibliography.
37. *Ways of Escape*, pp. 78-79.
38. In *Ways of Escape*, Greene admits that this is so and wishes that he had the "strength of mind" to "start the story again," p. 80.
39. Interview with Gene D. Phillips, "Graham Greene: On the Screen," Graham Greene, Samuel Hynes, ed. (Englewood Cliffs, Prentice-Hall, Inc., 1973), p. 173.
40. Evelyn Waugh, "Felix Culpa?" Graham Greene, Samuel Hynes, ed. (Englewood Cliffs: Prentice-Hall, Inc., 1973), p. 96.

41. R.W.B. Lewis, "The 'Trilogy'," *The Power and the Glory*, R.W.B. Lewis and Peter J. Conn, eds. (New York: The Viking Press, 1970), p. 377.

42. Frederick R. Karl, *The Contemporary English Novel* (New York: Farrar, Straus and Giroux, 1965), p. 93. Even Charles A. Muller, who has written convincingly about Greene's recent novels, holds this view: "Graham Greene and the Justification of God's Ways," *UES 10*, i (1972), pp. 2335.

43. Robert O. Evans, "The Satanist Fallacy of Brighton Rock," Graham Greene, Robert O. Evans, ed. (University of Kentucky Press, 1963), p. 154.

44. Graham Greene, *Brighton Rock* (London: William Heinemann & Bodley Head, 1975), p. 120. All further references to this book will be incorporated into the body of the text, with abbreviations for the title BR followed by page numbers both within parentheses, a system which will be used with subsequent novels by Greene.

45. This is at least partly explained by an admission Greene made in his second autobiographical work: "I fell back for the first and last time in my life on Benzedrine. For six weeks I started each day with a tablet, and renewed the dose at midday. Each day I sat down to work with no idea of what turn the plot might take and each morning I wrote, with the automatism of a planchette, two thousand words instead of my usual stint of five hundred words." *Ways of Escape*, p. 92.

46. *The Confidential Agent* (London: William Heinemann & Bodley Head, 1971), p. 167.

47. Also known as *Another Mexico*, in the United States primarily.

48. *Ways of Escape*, p. 86.

49. Kunkel has pointed out a number of parallels between the two: the priest is betrayed by a Judas figure, spends a night in a cell that is remindful of Gethsemane, is tempted by worldliness in the desert-like land across the border, gives solace to a "good thief" in the person of

the Yank, is more the target of the state than the Barabas-like criminal, is denied by a fallen disciple of the church as his death approaches, and finally dies a martyr for the corrupt and abandoned. Francis L. Kunkel, *The Labyrinthine Ways of Graham Greene* (New York: Sheed and Ward, 1959), p. 118.

50. Lynette Kohn, *Graham Greene: The Major Novels* (Palo Alto: Stanford Honors Essays in Humanities, no. IV, 1961), pp. 41-43. Or, if one wishes, circles of another kind. Patten thinks that there is a "radiant" pattern, with the priest "at the center, and all of the others characters . . . symbolically related to him, as the spokes of a wheel relate to the hub." Karl Patten, "The Structure of The Power and the Glory," *The Power and the Glory*, R.W.B. Lewis and Peter Conn, eds. (New York: The Viking Press, 1970), p. 311.

51. Karl goes too far, though, when he says that " Greene's mission in his major novels . . . is to write Greek tragedy without forsaking a Christian God." Karl, p. 88. More credible is Patten's suggestion that in the figure of the priest we have both "the type of Everyman, that primitive product of the late medieval imagination" and someone who resembles Bunyan's Christian. Patten, p. 321.

52. Graham Greene, *The Power and the Glory* (New York: The Viking Press, 1948), p. 45.

53. Atkins' argument that the priest was able to go on because he was sustained less by faith than by force of habit and "nihilism of the opposition" is a rather cynical one based less on textual evidence than, one must assume, on personal bias. John Atkins, *Graham Greene* (London: J. Calder, 1957), p. 124.

54. The fact that Greene chose to call it an "entertainment" signals, though it doesn't explain, this fact.

55. *Nineteen Stories* (London: Heinemann, 1947).

56. Graham Greene, *The Ministry of Fear* (London: William Heinemann, 1956), p. 71.

57. Several critics have discovered a Greek element in this book. Two of the more noteworthy arguments are by De

Vitis and Lewis. De Vitis sees Scobie as a Greek tragic figure. A.A. De Vitis, *Graham Greene* (New York: Twayne Publishers, 1964), pp. 102-103. Lewis analyzes the novel in Artistotelian terms. Lewis, pp. 388-393.

58. King has a noteworthy Danteian interpretation. Bruce King, "Graham Greene's Inferno," *Etudes Anglaises*, XXI (1968), 35-51.

59. W.H. Auden, "The Heresy of Our Time," Graham Greene, Samuel Hynes, ed. (Englewood Cliffs, Prentice-Hall, Inc., 1973), p. 94.

60. Graham Greene, *The Heart of the Matter* (New York: The Viking Press, 1948), p. 41.

61. Kenneth Allott and Miriam Farris, *The Art of Graham Greene* (New York: Russell & Russell, Inc., 1963), p. 224.

62. Even if, for example, all this seems to be beyond Waugh's comprehension. See Waugh, p. 101.

63. There exists an important letter by Greene in which he says that his "own intention was to make it completely vague as to whether he was expressing his love for the two women or his love for God." Marie-Beatrice Mesnet, *Graham Greene and The Heart of the Matter* (London: Cresset Press, 1954), pp. 103-104.

64. Graham Greene, *A Sort of Life* (New York: Simon and Schuster, 1971), p. 85.

65. *Ways of Escape*, p. 123.

66. *Ibid.*, p. 125.

67. Prior to the publication of *The End of the Affair* in 1951, Greene had actually tried out the first person narrative approach before, but only in a very limited and rather tentative way—in some short stories and in *The Third Man* (1950), a book which was meant to be read as a screenplay and was not meant to be published as a finished work of fiction.

68. Charles J. Rolo, "Graham Greene: The Man and the Message," *Atlantic Monthly*, CCVII (May 1961), 65.

69. Nathan A. Scott, Jr., "Graham Greene: Christian Tragedian," Graham Greene, Robert O. Evans, ed. (University of Kentucky Press, 1963), p. 45.

70. Graham Greene, *The End of the Affair* (London: William Heinemann & Bodley Head, 1974), pp. 99-100.

71. Karl, p. 90.

72. Martin Shuttleworth and Simon Raven, "The Art of Fiction: Graham Greene," Graham Greene, Samuel Hynes, ed. (Englewood Cliffs: Prentice-Hall, Inc., 1973), p. 161.

73. Kohn, p. 2.

74. Shuttleworth and Raven, p. 159.

75. Paul West, *The Wine of Absurdity* (University Park: The Pennsylvania State University Press, 1966), p. 176.

76. Lewis, p. 394.

77. Shuttleworth and Raven, p. 159.

78. David Pryce-Jones, *Graham Greene* (Edinburgh: Oliver and Boyd, 1970), p. 114.

79. Herbert R. Haber, "The End of the Catholic Cycle: The Writer Versus the Saint," Graham Greene, Robert O. Evans, ed. (University of Kentucky Press, 1963), p. 134.

80. Pryce-Jones, p. 86.

81. Frank Kermode, "The House of Fiction: Interviews with Seven English Novelists," *Partisan Review*, XXX (Spring 1963), 67.

82. *Ibid.*

83. *A Sort of Life*, p. 167.

84. Atkins, p. 179.

85. Sean O'Faolain, "Graham Greene: 'I Suffer, Therefore I Am'," *The Power and the Glory*, R.W.B. Lewis and Peter J. Conn, eds. (New York: The Viking Press, 1970), p. 436.

86. Francis L. Kunkel, "The Theme of Sin and Grace," Graham Greene , Robert O. Evans, ed. (University of Kentucky Press, 1963), p. 51.

87. Kunkel, *The Labyrinthine Ways of Graham Greene*, p. 20.
88. Phillips, p. 175.
89. Pryce-Jones, p. 109.
90. Morton Dauwen Zabel, "Graham Greene: The Best and the Worst," *The Power and the Glory*, R.W.B. Lewis and Peter J. Conn, eds. (New York: The Viking Press, 1970), p. 368.
91. Philip Toynbee, "Graham Greene on the Job of the Writer: An Interview," *The Power and the Glory*, R.W.B. Lewis and Peter J. Conn, eds. (New York: The Viking Press, 1970), p. 502.
92. Between 1951 and 1955, the publication dates of *The End of the Affair* and *The Quiet American*, Greene composed such a wide variety of things that, in retrospect at least, it seems clear he was actually signaling a restless desire for a shift away from the kind of writing which had established his reputation. During those years he published volumes of essays in 1951 and 1953; his first play, entitled *The Living Room*, in 1953; an expanded edition of his previously published short story collection in 1954; and *Loser Takes All*, a comic novelette which he rightly considered to be a frivolity, in 1955. In subsequent years, Greene would return to these modes during periods of creative restlessness. Of these, drama became the favorite because, to him, its social nature provided the greatest means of escape from the sometimes painful experience of writing a novel. It might be noted that although some of his plays did well enough on the stage, none represents a truly major achievements. As for short fiction, during the course of his career Greene has written several stories ("The Basement Room," for example, or "The Destructors") which are of the highest quality. However, there is no denying that his gift for the novel far exceeds that for any other form of creative writing.
93. David Lodge, "Graham Greene's Comedians," *Commonweal*, LXXXIII (1966), 604-605.
94. Stanford Sternlicht, "The Sad Comedians: Graham Greene's Later Novels," *Florida Quarterly*, I (1968), 77.

95. *Ibid.*, p. 65.

96. As late as in the fall of 1982, for instance, Greene indicated a plan to write a full-length memoir of the late Torrijos Herrera, Panama's political leader for many years. See: J.D. Reed, "The Surprise of Spiritual Slapstick," *Time* (September 20, 1982), p. 75.

97. The reference is to such writers as Angus Wilson, Anthony Powell, Alan Sillitoe, Margaret Drabble, John Fowles, and V.S. Naipaul.

98. Greene is especially remindful of Hardy, Lawrence, and Conrad in this regard.

2

From Granite to Grass: Graham Greene, Travel and the Primitive

—Adam Schwartz

In 1962, Evelyn Waugh reflected that "one of the many sharp differences" between his generation of British authors and writers of other eras was that "we got about the world, noting that the likes of himself, Robert Byron, Peter Fleming and "Mr. Graham Greene" "spent much of their youth in enterprising and arduous journeys . . . For some—Mr. Greene in particular—the habit has proved ineradicable" (Essays, Articles and Reviews 592). Waugh's remarks suggest two important truths about some of the British intellectuals who came of age between the two world wars: first, they traveled outside of the United Kingdom more extensively than their predecessors had and brought a distinct vision to the places they observed; second, Graham Greene was especially and enduringly affected by the experience of travel abroad.

Greene was bitten by the travel bug that swarmed among the British literati in the 1930s, and he remained restless for the remainder of his days, as he eventually traversed distant lands as diverse as the Congo, Kenya,

Vietnam, Malaysia, Israel, Haiti, Cuba, Argentina, Panama, and Nicaragua. Greene frequently filed newspaper and magazine dispatches on the political situation in such countries and often set his fiction in these locales; indeed, eighteen of his twenty-six novels have a non-English setting. But Greene's most sustained and extensive reflections on remote places were inspired by two sojourns of the 1930s: a three-month excursion through Sierra Leone, French Guinea and Liberia in 1935, chronicled chiefly in Journey Without Maps (1936); and a two-month trip to Mexico in 1938 to observe the effects of the revolutionary regime's religious persecution of Catholics there that had commenced in 1925, which he reported on primarily in The Lawless Roads (1939). Greene's reactions to what he saw on these voyages, especially the contrasts he drew between the "primitive" abroad and "civilized" Britain and Europe, became crucial components of the religious and cultural framework with which he critiqued both foreign nations and his homeland thenceforth.

Greene recognized the pivotal nature of these two trips (Cassis 222), a judgment that several scholars have seconded (Lewis 235, Boardman 51-2, Harmer 170, Gunn 191, Walker 164-5). Yet critics have not adequately realized that Greene's travel writings are a microcosm of his distinctly Roman Catholic protest against modern Western secularism and materialism. Greene echoed many of his peers in asserting that the primitive had a superior cultural ethos to that of European industrial civilization. But his version of this general judgment was highly individualized, being shaped crucially by formative personal experiences and by Catholicism, to which he had converted in 1926. To Greene, the primitive was more aware of and respectful of the sempiternal significance of human life, evil's persistence, the supernatural, tradition, and elemental faith, while also being more able to integrate life's various activities and stages. He also found it a repository of virtues like a sense of community and social justice that he associated with Europe's pre-industrial places and past. Greene concluded that all these beliefs, institutions and values that he thought the primitive upheld were threatened by modern civilizing forces and were best conserved by Roman Catholicism. But the tragic view of life that he derived from early personal suffering and found confirmed by Catholicism kept him from idealizing primitive people and places. Analyzing the motives for Greene's trips, the components of the differences between the primitive and civilization that he adduced from them, and the role of Catholicism in shaping this outlook will thus reveal both Greene's participation in the travel literature of protest that his generation pioneered, and the particular stamp of his religious faith on his rebellion against modernity. It will hence complement discussions of his travel writings that are less detailed (Fussell), less comprehensive (Davis, Gunn, Walker) or more focused on the aesthetic implications of these journeys (Boardman, Davis, Harmer); and it will help correct unnuanced treatments that dismiss the centrality and gravity of Greene's religious concerns (Meyers).

Paul Fussell has defined well the sort of travel and travel writing that Greene's generation undertook. Fussell notes that the travel book is a distinct genre, one characterized by an "active, organic, and, if you will, `creative' mediation between fact and fiction" (214), as "the autobiographical narrative arises from the speaker's encounter with distant or unfamiliar data, and in which the narrative—unlike that in a novel or a romance—claims literal validity by constant reference to actuality" (203). Although this form was not invented by Greene's generation of thinkers, Fussell explains that it was given a special shape by them. In broad terms, growing disillusionment with liberal values and industrial capitalism occasioned by the Great War and the Hungry Thirties made discontent with all things English both a dominant motive for travel during this period and a rhetorical feature of books about these excursions; an almost obligatory "I Hate It Here" section became a unique feature of interwar travel writing: "literary travel between the wars constitutes an implicit rejection of industrialism and everything implied by the concept `modern northern Europe'" (16, 210). In addition, the increased sensitivity to international issues stimulated by the war and Fascism's rise allowed epistles from abroad to perform a function exercised by sages and men of letters in less cosmopolitan days, becoming "a subtle instrument of ethics, replacing such former vehicles as sermons and essays" (204). A further moral feature of these accounts is their use of spatial voyages as vehicles for internal examinations of consciousness and conscience, making them both "a record of an inquiry and a report of the effect of the inquiry on the mind and imagination of the traveler" (39). In short, travel books act out "the basic trope of the generation ... journey itself, the most insistent of `thirties metaphors'" (Hynes 229).

Although Greene's travels continued long after the thirties ended, the kinds of places he visited and the concerns he expressed in his writings about them varied little. In a sense, then, all his travel books are thirties travel books, for his travelogues and fiction based on trips, both in the thirties and later, fulfill this model's general terms, as well as other more specific elements of it, while also being molded distinctively by his religious considerations and convictions.[1] Greene often attributed his wanderlust to boredom (Sort 133; Cassis 196, 247-8, 449), but he also admitted to being influenced by adventure stories he read as a youngster (Sort 55; Collected Essays 15), and to having been fascinated by some of the places he visited, such as Africa and Panama, from boyhood (Journey 20; General 19); and even before he went abroad, he made experience of foreign lands crucial to a character in It's a Battlefield (127).[2] Other aspects of his childhood and his reactions to it also shaped his reasons for traveling, and these impinged on his religious and cultural interests directly.

Initially, Greene sought in travel A.E.'s "ancient shadows and twilights/Where childhood had strayed" that he invoked in discussing his own lost childhood. The seminal event of Greene's life was an adolescent breakdown that occurred in 1919-1920. Greene at this time was a boarding student at Berkhamsted public school, where his father was headmaster, a situation that permanently divided Graham's loyalties between his schoolmates and his family. Other pupils preyed on the isolated boy, tormenting him physically (with dividers) and manipulating his craving for affection emotionally. When one of his few friends conspired with his worst foe to betray his friendship, Greene became desperate and even attempted suicide. His alarmed family soon sent him to London for psychoanalysis. Greene derived from this episode a vivid sense of evil's reality, a corresponding deep skepticism of innocence, and a scorn for his parents' liberal Christianity and humanitarian progressivism, which now seemed fatally insensitive to human malevolence. These incidents and attitudes helped spur his eventual conversion to Catholicism and became a permanent subtext of his adult writing (Schwartz 3-7).[3] In his travel works, Greene frequently juxtaposed memories of his youth and school years with his accounts of occurrences abroad; but he was particularly straightforward about this personal motive for travel in his rendering of his journey without maps to Liberia. In 1935, he associated Africa with "death and forest and maps and school and dust and darkness, unhappiness . . . the face of an unpleasant boy and evensong and a pair of dividers" ("Analysis" 459-60). He further compared his trek directly to the kind of psychoanalysis he had undergone as a teen:

> The method of psychoanalysis is to bring the patient back to the idea which he is repressing: a long

> journey backwards without maps, catching a clue here and a clue there, as I caught the names of villages from this man and that, until one has the face, the general idea, the pain or memory. This is what you have feared, Africa may be imagined as saying, you can't avoid it, there it is creeping round the wall, flying in at the door, rustling the grass. (Journey 97)

Greene makes the twin meaning of his book's title obvious here, but a similar dynamic is at work in all his travel writings, which is unsurprising given his fixation on his painful memory of his school experiences of evil: "As the vision of evil becomes crusted over with characteristically deadening maturity, the need becomes urgent to seek it out again by returning to the youthful terror" (Lewis 236). Although governed by such particular concerns, then, Greene's travel books are like his fellow travel authors' in being reports of both external and internal inquiry, something Greene acknowledged in fact and fiction (Search 19, Burnt 131, Short Stories 212, Allain 98).[4] Yet Greene's chosen destinations reveal that he was pursuing not only his own lost childhood, but his race's as well. He sought out what he deemed primitive locations because—as Auden's words used as an epigraph for Journey Without Maps indicate—when Greene's footsteps felt from granite to grass, he was diligently looking to discover what was lacking in modern industrial society. Greene tried to uncover the stage of social development at which Britain and cultures like it began to decline, as though he could isolate original sin anthropologically: "when one sees to what unhappiness, to what peril of extinction centuries of cerebration have brought us, one sometimes has a curiosity to discover if one can from what we have come, to recall at which point we went astray" (Journey 21). In attempting to suggest a sense of what Britain's past may have been like through descriptions of other nations' presents, with this purpose of moral instruction, Greene is acting as both sage and prophet; and his accounts often read like extended sermons and essays, making them again typical of the travel genre.

They also demonstrate Greene's tendency to think in polarities, for "the primitive" and "civilization" are clear antitheses in his reports. In this respect, his work belonged to a Western literary tradition dating from at least the late eighteenth century that posits the particular virtue of primitive people and places (Fussell 38); but his use of this paradigm was shaped by his more personal perception of industrial modernity's religious and cultural effects. Greene distinguished between two attitudes to reality, belief in Good and Evil and belief in Right and Wrong: the former, epitomized by Catholicism, is teleologically-oriented, stressing ends, theology and metaphysics, and the transcendent; while the latter, reaching its quintessence in modern secularism, is deontologically inclined, accenting means, ethics, and the solely natural and human. Greene thought that only believers in the absolutes of Good and Evil are fully human, for their moral imaginations alone are attuned to the eternal dimension of existence; believers in the mediated reality of Right and Wrong have had their sensibilities attenuated by exclusive focus on ephemerals, making them a kind of sub-humanity. He began to formulate this distinction between "the ethical mind and the religious" (Greene to Nancy Pearn, 9 April 1937; quoted in Sherry 1: 639) in the mid-1930s, arguing that modern secularists have a "much thinner reality, they are not concerned with eternal damnation" or salvation, and thus cannot comprehend those, like Catholics, who assert the importance of "eternal issues, of the struggle between good and evil, between vice that really demands to be called satanic and virtue of a kind which can only be called heavenly" (Collected Essays 131-132). He elaborated this dichotomy and its implications most fully in Brighton Rock (1938) through the clash of the Roman Catholics, Pinkie and Rose, and archetypal secularist Ida Arnold: "the idea is that Pinkie and Rose belong to the real world in which good & evil exist, but that the interfering Ida belongs to a kind of artificial surface world in which there is no such thing as good & evil but only right & wrong" (Greene to Laurence Pollinger, 4 March 1943; quoted in Sherry 2: 163). Ida's ethic of adherence to social conventions and pursuit of material success and pleasure is hence painted as radically incompatible with, and deficient in comparison with, the two "Romans'" belief in eternal verities and in the supernatural dimension and destiny of human life. Ida's mantra that "I know the difference between Right and Wrong" can thus not persuade Rose to leave the murderous, manipulative Pinkie:

> Rose didn't answer; the woman was quite right; the two words meant nothing to her. Their taste was extinguished by stronger foods—Good and Evil . . . she knew by tests as clear as mathematics that Pinkie was evil—what did it matter in that case whether he was right or wrong? . . . "Right and wrong. That's what she talks about . . . As if she knew ... Oh she wouldn't burn. She couldn't burn if she tried." (Brighton 199-200, 112)

Greene applied this taxonomy to societies that he observed, asserting, in general terms, that primitive societies uphold Good and Evil but civilized ones profess Right and Wrong. He claimed that "there is no peace anywhere where there is human life . . . the horror may be the same, it is an intrinsic part of human life in every place: it attacks you in the Strand or the tropics" (Lawless 33-4). Yet he argued further that places like the tropics or Mexico are more sensitive to that aboriginal horror than are the Strand or the United States because they have been less narcotized by consumerist civilization:

> So many years have passed in England since the war began between faith and anarchy: we live in ugly indifference. Over here lay the grave of Pro, Tabasco with every Church destroyed, and Chiapas, where the Mass was forbidden. The advertisements for aerated waters and patent medicines line the modern highway which leads to the front line and the tourists go back and forth, their cars laden with serapes and big hats, and their minds sprightly with the legend of a happy and picturesque Mexico . . . life among the dark groves of leaning crosses [in Chiapas] was at any rate concerned with eternal values. (Lawless 33-4, 207)[5]

Greene put this contention in explicitly theological terms in 1939, appropriate to his views at that time, when reflecting on his stay in "civilized" San Antonio: "Original sin under the spell of elegance had lost its meaning . . . The horror and beauty of human life were both absent" (Lawless 27).[6] Greene believed that he had discovered human life and nature stripped of their elegant veneer in primitive areas, and hence exposed in their more genuine horror and beauty. Even before he first went abroad, Greene asserted that the British cloaked disreputable occupations with an elaborate air of respectability (Battlefield 112-113). Such euphemism was part of why he hated it here and wanted to "get out of this bloody country" (Greene to Hugh Greene, 16 Jan. 1938; quoted in Sherry 1: 659). He claimed that abroad, people—British and otherwise—were more transparent, as Scobie's ruminations on Sierra Leone (where Greene was also stationed for part of World War II) reveal:

> Why, he wondered . . . do I love this place so much? Is it because here human nature hasn't had time to disguise itself?. [Here] flourished the injustices, the cruelties, the meanness that elsewhere people so cleverly hushed up. Here you could love human

> beings nearly as God loved them, knowing the worst: you didn't love a pose, a pretty dress, a sentiment artfully assumed. (Heart 35-6)[7]

It was because Greene, like his character Arthur Rowe, "prefer[red] human nature plain" that he sought out areas as unlike civilization-encrusted Britain as he could envision (Ministry 102). NOT surprisingly, given his tragic view of life, Greene focused more on the horror, the injustices, cruelties, and meannesses, of the areas he visited. He maintained that Liberia attracted him because "there seemed to be a seediness about the place you couldn't get to the same extent elsewhere;" and seediness satisfied a core need that drove his excursions, "the sense of nostalgia for something lost; it seems to represent a stage further back." Because it is closer to human origins, Greene argued, primitive seediness is "not, after all, so far from the central darkness," making it "deeper and purer" than its civilized counterparts: "it hasn't reached so far away as the smart, the new, the chic, the cerebral." He argued that civilization teaches people to forget this primitive "finer terror," and thus replaces a sense of "supernatural evil" with Right and Wrong's "small human viciousness": "There was cruelty enough in the interior, but had we done wisely exchanging the supernatural cruelty for our own?" He thus concluded that his African sojourn had only "reinforced a sense of disappointment with what man had made of the primitive, what he had made out of his childhood," and hence had strengthened his distaste for Progressive ideologies, "a distrust of any future based on what we are" (Journey 19, 249, 225, 226, 224, 20).[8] The primitive, then, substantiated Greene's tragic view of life by providing an entire culture as an objective correlative for the intuitions about evil's presence and power, and about civilized modernity's ignorance of its force and perdurance, that he had possessed since Berkhamsted. Although Greene was in many ways seeing what he wanted to see abroad, possible factual inaccuracies should not obscure this tactical importance of primitive areas to his rebellion against modernity.

Greene was not blind to what he considered the beauty of life in its primitive forms, though. Just as he felt that the primitive had a sharper sense of evil, so he deemed its discoveries and displays of goodness sweeter than civilization's corruptions. He held that among African natives he met "gentleness, kindness, an honesty which one would not have found, or at least dared to assume, was there in Europe" because "Love . . . existed here without the trappings of civilization" (Journey 80). Greene extolled specific virtues of primitive societies, such as a more authentic art; a greater acceptance of the unknown; increased sensitivity to natural rhythms; more just treatment of racial minorities; and enhanced recognition of public charity's value, all of which made them superior in his mind to modern civilization (Journey 108, 154, 183, 237; Lawless 181). To him, the primitive social order as a whole was rooted in "a greater simplicity, an older, more natural culture, and traditions of honesty and hospitality" (Journey 244). Because the primitive's apprehension of Evil is more acute, Greene implied, its comprehension of Good is equally astute. Only with civilization's corroding effects, he thought, are these perceptions diluted into the confused perversions of Right and Wrong. Despite his paeans to primitive culture's charms, though, Greene was finally more fascinated by its abominations, regarding these as life's more vivid portion in a fallen world: to him, "failure, ugliness, the primitive are in some sense truer than success, beauty and civilization with their deceptive gloss" (Allott and Farris 16).

In addition to his broad use of trips as an opportunity for Eliot's backward half-look over the shoulder towards the primitive terror, Greene also isolated more specific differences between primitive and civilized societies. Initially, he judged the primitive to be more religious. In

1939, Greene claimed that Africa's fascination for him was "a religious fascination: the country offers the European an opportunity of living continuously in the presence of the supernatural," something he no longer deemed possible in post-Christian Europe ("Three Travelers"); and he repeated this conviction over forty years later (Ways 208). This disparity between primitive native and secular European attitudes to religion was a persistent theme of Greene's factual and fictional presentations of remote places. For instance, he felt that civilized, modern ideas, even religious ones, were so saturated with Right and Wrong that they failed to comprehend the horror and beauty of primitive religions based on Good and Evil. Evaluating the liberal Christian missionaries of his youth retrospectively, Greene commented that they were "not only innocent beside our own masters, they were innocent among the blacks they taught." He contended that they were more concerned with raising money to support "the hideous tin church" than with the "sense of sin," and he thus doubted that they could have had much influence among men "whose secret ritual it is to sacrifice a child once a year to the great python" (Journey 169). Greene reiterated this perceived incompatibility between civilized and primitive approaches to religion often, as in confidential agent D's contrast between "the civilized" ethic of "no religious faith, but a lot of Gregorian chants and picturesque ceremonies" and his preference for "the distrust, the barbarity, the betrayals . . . even the chaos" that accompanied eras of authentic faith, like the Dark Ages (Confidential 30). Even in the mid-1960s, Greene portrayed an exemplar of modern civilization as incredulous that a Sorbonne-educated poet could be attracted to Haitian voodoo ceremonies (Comedians 180).

As well as asserting this general contrast, Greene posited further that primitive religion was closer to the essentials of faith, enriched other aspects of culture, and was better equipped to deal with matters shunned by civilized moderns. His Mexican whiskey priest reflects that "life without books, without contact with educated men, had peeled away from his memory everything but the simplest outline of the mystery" (Power 65); and Dr. Colin judges the Congolese leper colony's less intellectualized Catholicism to be closer to the Apostles' than Europe's civilized scholasticism is (Burnt 58). It was this focus on the elementary, suprarational elements of Catholicism that led Greene to state expressly, "I like the so-called `primitive' manifestations of the faith" (Allain 146). Not only is Christianity reduced to its basic components in primitive settings, Greene thought, but native religions share this uncomplicated character: "One felt that the two religions here were appealing on the simplest terms" (Journey 87). He held that this emphasis on fundamentals keeps such religions closer to actual religious experiences, and hence avoids the ratiocinated "abstractions of the Methodists and Anglicans" and Catholic scholastics (Allain 146), which he found less convincing and lasting than the "magical heart of the faith" (Power 154) that he took note of among Mexican Indians and chided civilized Europeans for neglecting: "we are too apt to minimize the magic elements in Christianity—the man raised from the dead, the devils cast out, the water turned into wine" (Lawless 171). Put another way, primitive religion (Christian or indigenous) corresponds to fulfilling, enduring, mystical "faith" in Greene's schema and civilization's to arid, ephemeral, rationalistic "belief" (Schwartz passim).

Beyond exemplifying Greene's dictum that "religion is simple, dogma is simple" primitive religion also illustrated for him the correct relationship between religion and the rest of life (Collected Essays 106). In the case of art, for example, whereas D's civilized nemeses find religion of only cultural interest, Greene argued that primitive societies consider artistic expression valuable only because of its religious significance. His description of the Liberian bush devil's dance exemplifies this perceived contrast: "it was a carnival, but it wasn't a carnival in the vulgar sense of Nice and the Battle of Flowers: it wasn't secular and skittish; like the dancing in the Spanish cathedral at Easter, it had its religious value." More generally, Greene praised one African tribe for making "a work of conscious art in the service of a belief," while criticizing another for their "lack of religious enthusiasm," which "diminishes their artistic talent" (Journey 92, 113), a view anticipating his 1945 assessment of literary modernism as a failure due to its lack of a religious sense (Collected Essays 91-96). Besides providing proper focus for life's creativity, Greene also postulated, the primitive deals better with its conclusion. South African expatriate Sarah Castle tells her English husband, Maurice, that "we used to have better funerals in Africa" than civilization's cremations; and she chides the English boast of being a venerable civilization, to which Maurice responds, "old civilizations are not always famous for feeling deeply about death" (Human 191), especially when their modern avatars have embraced Ida Arnold's fear of it:

> Death shocked her, life was so important. She wasn't religious. She didn't believe in heaven or hell, only in ghosts, ouija boards, tables that rapped and little inept voices speaking plaintively of flowers. Let Papists treat death with flippancy: life wasn't so important perhaps to them as what came after; but to her death was the end of everything. (Brighton 32)[9]

Such juxtapositions between the primitive and civilization and between Catholicism and secular modernity function throughout Greene's travelogues and fiction both as a "no" to modernity and a simultaneous "yes" to an alternate path for Britain and the civilized world to follow. As Carolyn Scott explains, "Greene sees in primitive ritual and myth making something which can potentially revitalize our own civilized institutions, most of which have their origins in ancient rites . . . [the] hope that a supernatural power can permeate all things. In this realization Greene hopes for a coherent ritual not incompatible with modern institutions" (243-4). Greene sought to fill this modern form with the traditional content of his own faith, for he felt that "in the civilized world Catholicism held something of the mystery the primitive offered . . . religious experience offered unspoken understanding. It was, in its literal, root meaning, a bond (religare), something by which people might be linked together" (Adamson 35-6). In addition to replicating the primitive's mystical coherence in civilization, Greene contended further, "the Catholic attitude gave a unity and a purpose, and thus a permanence" to those primitive societies that had accepted it. It hence created a "solid block of culture" that he considered superior to the "polo, Sunday school teachers and ministers" that typified modern British Protestantism and its cultural concomitants to him, and that he thought was its evanescent legacy abroad and at home (Cassis 164).[10] Because Greene believed that Catholicism and the primitive share a teleological bent; a tragic view of life; an emphasis on mystery, simplicity, and experience (at least when "faith" is prioritized over "belief"); and a sacramental perspective on life's activities and its termination, he considered Roman Catholicism the best vehicle for subverting "civilized" norms, and for protecting these "primitive" values and inculcating them into Western cultures too long starved of their finer taste and terror."[11] Primitive beliefs and practices not only resonated with Greene's specifically religious concerns about culture, but also with his respect for tradition. He asserted that traditions are both more enduring and more venerated in primitive areas than in industrial civilization. The Human Factor's John Hargreaves rebukes the idea advanced by a representative of modern civilization that the "old Africa" is gone forever by drawing on his (and his creator's) experiences in that continent: "if we destroy the world, the roads will become overgrown and all the new luxury hotels will crumble, the forests will come back, the chiefs, the witch doctors—there's still a rain queen in the northeast Transvaal" (135). The Quiet American's Fowler had expressed the same idea in discussing Vietnam's ancient peasant culture (95), and Greene had even asserted the persistence of Mexican traditions of which he disapproved (Lawless 44, 123). In the main, though, he considered this primitive sense of continuity beneficial, especially given the alternative he saw of accepting civilization's rootlessness. Thus he described favorably a leper who shuns a modern clinic's amenities when death approaches because "he was prepared to die only where his ancestors had died, in the darkness surrounded by the smell of dry mud and leaves" (Burnt 19), rather than in the antiseptic anonymity in which It's a Battlefield's Conrad Drover had breathed his last in a London hospital (197).

As admirable as Greene judged these sorts of religious and cultural attitudes, he was also convinced of the constant peril posed to them by industrial civilization. He opined in 1936 that in Africa (and primitive areas everywhere), "Civilization here remained exploitation; we had hardly, it seemed to me, improved the natives' lot at all" either physically or spiritually, for to "have been touched by civilization" was to "have learnt to steal and lie and kill" (Journey 61, 224). Subsequent history only strengthened these sentiments, as twenty-five years later he challenged the notion that natives who fear the consequences of introducing modern technology are simple-minded Luddites: "in our century you could hardly call them fools. Hola Camp, Sharpeville, and Algiers had justified all possible belief in European cruelty" (Burnt 43). Nor did Greene consider this cruelty confined to Europeans. He perceived in Mexico the extent to which an indigenous government could exercise it against citizens' religion when corrupted by "dusty rationalist" ideologies like naturalism and Marxism imported from civilized lands. Yet he also asserted the existence of a more insidious attack on traditional religion by modern civilized values. For instance, Greene contrasted a Mexican cathedral, where "the mortification goes on. This is the atmosphere of the stigmata," with a "squalid" tourist market and its firewalker who practices "mortification for money, the stigmata of the pleasure fair." It is in places like Mexico City or Puebla, which Greene found most dominated by commercial values, that he thought religion becomes superstition, esteemed for the price its quaintness can fetch among visitors from post-Christian lands. He contended that this sort of environment contaminates even those attempting to adhere to authentic faiths. Among his co-religionists in Puebla, for example, he detected degeneration into "a kind of social Catholicism" that seemed worlds away from the "wild region of great crooked crosses, of the cave dweller faces bowed before the crucified Christ, of the talking saint," that was more rustic Chiapas, where life was palpably concerned with eternal values (Lawless 21, 44, 201, 194).[12] In short, Greene worried that primitive societies, perhaps without realizing it, were in danger of succumbing to the secularizing and fetishizing pressures he associated with civilization, ones that he considered it essential to rebel against both at home and abroad.

Modern civilization must also be resisted, in Greene's mind, to prevent the primitive from losing the traditional way of life already smashed in metropolitan areas. In particular, he feared that the machine that had blighted the shire now threatened to blemish the savanna and pampa, warning in 1940 that "heartless industrialization" imperiled "the wide rapid river, the dense tangled forest and the volcanic mountains" of primitive lands (Film 270). Greene was encouraged by Liberian areas in which "the forest stayed forest, it was hardly pitted at all by the little holes white prospectors had dug . . . the minerals remained where they were in the soil of the country, and the images had certainly not been pulled down out of the temples." Yet he saw ominous signs elsewhere in Africa, such as the advent of cars in Sierra Leone, which frightened natives "as civilization went terrifyingly by them in a fume of evil smoke" (Journey 134, 57). In many ways, he deemed Mexico even more degraded, often complaining that there was little difference between it and the "bloody country" he had left behind, but finding the growing hegemony of an ethic rooted in "the petty social fulfillment, the tiny pension and the machine-made furniture" to be "peculiarly unnatural" where it had taken root in Mexico (Lawless 49, 122).

Greene felt that a more genuine way of life was available in pastoralism, especially the kind mythologized in his own green and pleasant land. Although he reproved the Romantics' view of nature as sentimental throughout his travel books (see, e.g., Journey 158; Lawless 61-2), he was at one with them in using rural England as a standard for judging social orders. Greene was charmed by a Liberian village because there was something "peculiarly English" about it (Journey 182); and this cross-cultural comparison was even more overt in Mexico, as he admitted evaluating the country according to the works of Trollope and Cobbett he had brought with him. Mexico's inability to provide tangible equivalents to the society described in those "English book[s]" made Greene homesick, for "there was nothing in this country so beautiful as an English village" (Lawless, 128, 157). His use of this template indicates, as Mafia Cuoto explains, that his concerns about the course of African and Mexican development were prompted by "an agonizing recall of the loss of the innocent beauty of undespoiled, rural England," and the contrast between that arcadia and the "soulless brashness of [the] urban bourgeoisie" in modern Britain, one that led him to warn against and lament industrial civilization's expansion (13). In doing so, Greene's travel writing not only fits within a tradition of British religious and romantic anti-industrialist protest writing dating to the eighteenth century (Williams;

Wiener; and Veldman); but it also meets a convention of its own genre, as "[the] pastoral is a powerful element in most travel books" of this period, serving as a salutary counterpoint for their authors to the industrial world they hated there (Fussell 210).

One pre-industrial value Greene deemed especially besieged was the sense of community. Again revealing his debt to the myth of meerie England, Greene described his brief residence in a Chipping Camden thatched cottage as living out "that pastoral Georgian dream of the industrial twenties" and maintained that "the life of a village is intimate and dramatic. There is a sense of community. People talk. In a city there may be a suicide in the next street and you will never hear of it" (Sort 204-5). Even before he went abroad, Greene considered civilization afflicted with "Metroland loneliness" (Lawless 18), for the sense that "loneliness was only too easily attained" in urban modernity pervades It's a Battlefield (150). Greene argued consistently that societies under industrial civilization's sway discover community only in such ersatz venues as partnership in crime, madness, prison, refuge from political oppression, and television (See, e.g., Gun 212, 214, 222; Lawless 74; Power 128; Honorary 209; Ministry 85; Short Stories 178). He blamed public schools in part for weakening what he deemed a student's natural loyalties to the society of his birthplace and producing class-conscious prigs instead (Old School 7, 255-56); but he regarded schools as only agents of the urban, industrial, consumerist culture underlying this erosion of solidarity. As Cuoto concludes,

> the sense of a rich and close community life replaced by an urban desert is very strong in all Greene's fiction and an important element of the dream England that died with "growing up" . . . the fiction is underpinned by disgust with the endless

> gratification of consumer tastes, of a civilization that panders to human acquisitiveness. (108)

Greene held that less acquisitive societies existed in primitive areas. For example, he described his Liberian trip as a deliberate exodus from "the depraved individualists to the old, the unfamiliar, the communal life" of Africa (Journey 74). Additionally, he maintained that Europeans who live in primitive areas soon unlearn their snobbery and develop a sense of social solidarity because "a common danger, purpose or way of life can very nearly destroy differences of intellect and class" (Journey 23-4). Yet Greene also feared that these victories might be hollow. He regarded the Europeans' new-found communitarian sensibility as based more on the circumstances of their relative isolation than on commitment to a less individualistic culture; in fact, he considered Europeans incapable of comprehending fully the African taste for the other: "they seemed to like to touch each other, as if it made them feel good to know the other man was there. It wasn't love; it didn't mean anything we could understand" (Journey 33).[13] This ignorance made Greene anxious that the primitive sense of community could not survive industrial capitalist civilization's steady encroachment. In the areas of Africa that had accepted its influence by 1935, for instance, he discerned a change even in the rationale for forced labor from one that "at least pretends to be for the good of the community" to one that stresses "the good of shareholders" (Journey 233). Given his sense of communitarian values' existential frailty, Greene sought some institution to ground them in. As with other virtues he associated with the primitive, he seems to have concluded that Catholicism was their best repository. Maurice Castle is driven into a Roman Catholic church by an "emotion of loneliness," and this search for fellowship also appears to have motivated his creator (Human 205). Even after excommunicating himself in the 1950s due to an inability to repent his sexual sins (Schwartz 13-14),

Greene claimed that he still went to Mass for, amongst other things, exactly what he had found in village life, "a sense of community" (Donaghy 56). Because it rebels against modernity and its atomizing tendencies, Greene believed, Catholicism's centripetal bond of common convictions and practices gives its adherents the sense of place and purpose that It's a Battlefield's Jules Briton found salvific: "He wanted to be saved from the counter and the tea urn, the 'Weights,' and the heartless flippancy of the café . . . Always in the badly lit church, surrounded by the hideous statues of an uncompromising faith, listening to the certainty of that pronouncement—peche, peche, peche he was given confidence, an immense pride, a purpose. However lost in the cafe ... here he was at home" (41, 140). The Church is hence a positive and distinct alternative to both acquisitive anomie and the impersonal, degraded substitutes that Greene thought civilization offers for pre-industrial fellowship, even as its sense of purpose gives primitive areas a permanent source of cultural unity (Cassis 164). To Greene, then, Catholicism was the best contemporary upholder—for himself, civilization, and the primitive alike—of the ideal of social fraternity that he had derived from a myth of rural "Englishness," and that primitive locales had exemplified to him.

If the English village and its contemporary primitive counterparts were Greene's spatial referents for anti-modern values, his temporal one was often the Middle Ages. Greene had a youthful interest in things medieval, as "the first stories I tried to write were of the Middle Ages" (Sort 30). Yet even in these early tales, Greene depicted medieval ideals as precarious, having a knight declare, "I and my kind are dead" (The Berkhamstedian, March, 1921; quoted in Sherry 1: 81). In his adult trips abroad, medievalism was one of Greene's standards for assessing primitive places and practices. In Africa, he dubbed villages that gave him the sense of being "a small courageous community" as "like medieval towns" (Journey

79). He deemed a mined Mexican palace and chapel "as beautiful as anything out of the Middle Ages" (Lawless 40); and one of his initial impressions of the Indo-China that he would grow to love was of its being "a very strange medieval place" (Greene to Marion Greene, c. 12 Feb. 1951; quoted in Sherry 2: 376). Additionally, Greene affirmed medieval mores and beliefs. He defended a corporatist economic model that he uncovered in Mexico, differentiating the moral economy he thought practiced by General Saturnino Cedillo and the peasants who worked for him from the wage-labor system adopted by other Mexicans:

> The General gave them no pay, but food and clothes and shelter and half of everything the farm produced, and ready cash too if they asked for it and he had it . . . And they gave him labor and love. It was not a progressive relationship; it was feudal; you may say it was one-sided and he had everything . . . but they possessed at any rate more than did their fellow-peasants in other states, living at best on the minimum wage of thirty five cents a day, with no one caring if they lived or died. (Lawless 56)

Greene did not consider this paternalism a form of despotism, but rather an example of a governor who did not abdicate his responsibilities. Yet, as laudable as he judged medieval principles and social orders based on them to be, he also continued to think them tenuous. In 1935, for instance, he labeled pre-invasion Abyssinia "the last medieval State" and warned that it is "more worth preserving than the bright slick streamlined civilization which threatens it" (Film 6), one that had already reduced Britain from a place where people "lived here once and died with their feet crossed to show they had been on a crusade" to a "Metroland" dominated by "the estate agents, the cafes and the two super-cinemas" (Nineteen Stories 219; Lawless 16). As this passage implies, Greene ascribed such cultural decline to a fundamentally religious cause, feeling that modern secularism could not sustain the cultural integrity that the primitive derived from faith in the supernatural's pervasive presence, a spiritual coherence he thought medieval Christendom had shared and that the industrial, individualistic West had lost. As D puts it, extending his comparison of the primitive, pious Dark Ages and the civilized, disenchanted Modern Age, "Roland had companions at Roncesvalles—Oliver and Turpin: the whole chivalry of Europe was riding up to help him. Men were united by a common belief . . . Now there were so many varieties of economic materialism, so many initial letters" (Confidential 56). It was thus in that common belief uniting the actual medievals that Greene thought their norms were best preserved in modern times. A Mexican bishop symbolized to him how Catholic, medieval Good and Evil survives in the midst of secular, modern Right and Wrong: "In the modern city—among the American tea shops, the advertisements for safety razors, the dapper night clubs—there existed, besides medieval violence, this medieval sanctity" (Lawless 211). Greene also praised the Papal social encyclicals for their condemnation of both capitalist and communist economic materialism in his Mexican travelogue, suggesting further that he regarded Catholicism as a philosophical ally of the medievalist, anti-modern economic system he found more just in practice (Lawless 28-9). Unlike fellow Catholics like G.K. Chesterton or Christopher Dawson, Greene did not detail how Catholicism should give such medieval notions currency in contemporary cultures; but he did share their sense of an essential link between the two outlooks, making medievalism yet another ideal associated with the primitive that Greene thought his church guarded best, and could embody most credibly in the post-Christian world. As these mores are ultimately rooted in the timeless truths of Catholicism, they are equally timely for all cultures and ages: "if one believes in Christianity at all, one must believe in its universal validity. A Christian cannot believe in one God for Europe and another God for Africa," nor in one for the medieval era and another for the modern epoch (Journey 84). To Greene, then, Catholicism was both a source of internal cultural unity and a transcendent tie across cultures and generations.

Although Greene clearly preferred his perception of the primitive to his conception of civilization, his view was not uncritical. His travelogues and letters from abroad contain a frequent tension between approval of more primitive conditions and yearning for modern amenities (See, e.g., Lawless 132; Journey 211). Greene admitted that some of his more outrageous outbursts were largely a result of trying to do too much in an unfamiliar climate, but other criticisms of primitive life were more substantive (See, e.g., Journey 223; Lawless 145-6; Greene to Lawrence Pollinger, 19 June 1942, quoted in Sherry 2: 141; Search 58). For example, he charged that there was "a virtual enslavement of women" in Africa (Search 60). Moreover, Greene satirized the kind of primitivist who refuses to recognize native people's vices in The Comedians's Mr. and Mrs. Smith. These absurdly well-intentioned American vegetarians try to excuse the corruption and persecution practiced by Papa Doc Duvalier's Haitian regime by asserting, amongst other things, that "we must not judge a colored dictatorship as we judge a white one" (116-117). If the primitive's cruelty is supernatural, Greene thought, it is still cruel; and he distanced himself explicitly from a Rousseauean rendering of remote peoples: "The `noble savage' no longer exists; perhaps he never existed" (Journey 61).[14]

The reason for that possibility, in Greene's mind, is the most salient motive for his only partial embrace of the primitive, his tragic view of life. He concluded that, whatever its considerable virtues, the primitive can only approximate prelapsarian perfection: although people "can never quite forget" such a paradise, it is "a way of life we have hopelessly lost" (Lawless 170). He held that, despite its many advantages, the primitive is essentially similar to civilization ontologically: "what had astonished me about Africa was that it had never really been strange . . . The `heart of darkness' was common" to both Africans and Europeans (Journey 248); and he reiterated this sentiment about Mexico: "Did I really expect to find there what I hadn't found here? ... The world is all of a piece, of course; it is engaged everywhere in the same subterranean struggle" (Lawless 17, 33). At the conclusion of both his Thirties travelogues, Greene juxtaposes the civilization he has returned to with the primitive just departed to stress this likeness (Journey 250; Lawless 223-24). This rhetorical strategy reinforces his belief that all people are implicated in the aboriginal calamity; and it also subverts a norm of the travel genre by having an "I Hate It Here" section conclude as well as originate the book, leaving the inference that in coming home "one is not fleeing to something nicer, one is returning to something which travel has exposed as equally loathsome" (Fussell 223).[15]

This perception of his own culture's loathsomeness was widely echoed by Greene's generation of travel writers, but its cause and cure took a distinctive shape in his mind. Greene shared his fellow authors' motive in going abroad, as he wished to discover social orders less touched by industrialism; and, like many of them, he used his accounts as jeremiads about the condition of England and of modern civilization generally. Greene also followed the common pattern of using these journeys as internal explorations, particularly of outlooks stemming from his school sufferings. Yet his travelogues were also molded by his distinct, Roman Catholic rebellion against modernity. Whether it was in choice of location (as in Mexico), topics discussed, or criteria used to evaluate what he witnessed, Greene's religion was an indispensable lens through which he viewed remote places. His conviction that Catholicism could best preserve for the primitive and transmit to the civilized West traditional beliefs and virtues that he found more vivid and vital in primitive areas exemplifies how much this element of his cultural criticism depended at times on his religion. In positing that industrial, post-Christian Britain also was one of the dark places of the earth, Greene discerned that its enlightenment would arise from renewal of its pre-industrial patrimony and the ever-ancient, ever-new faith that had infused it: the modern "Dark Age of . . . civilization" (Film 73) would be redeemed by recovery of the permanently pertinent principles of the creed and culture that dawned in the original Dark Ages. He descried hints of this explanation in various primitive places; but he felt that these diverse avenues of cultural deliverance must converge along a wider concourse, one that the crooked timber of (both civilized and primitive) humanity could never make straight by itself. Like J.R.R. Tolkien, Greene believed that the road goes ever on and on, until it joins some larger Way where many paths and errands meet.

NOTES

1. Denis Donoghue opines more generally: "how much a writer of the thirties Greene is . . . if not his best work, it is his most typical, producing his major themes, situations and images. Greene's mind, like Auden's during the same decade, was appeased mainly by lurid occasions . . . frontiers, maps, passports . . ." (324-6).

2. Greene later recognized the "curious foreshadowing" concerning travel in this novel (Ways 36).

3. Newman's assertion in the Apologia Pro Vita Sua that humanity is implicated in an aboriginal calamity became Greene's mantra in his early Catholic years, summarizing for him the Roman Catholic attitude toward life (Greene notes, Redway Papers, Box 3, Folder 3). Tellingly, Greene used that passage as an epigraph for The Lawless Roads and referred to it several times in that volume.

4. Jeffrey Meyers has pointed out that, like Greene's novels, these travel books help reveal important sides of Greene's

life about which he is relatively reticent in more direct settings (67).

5. The prominence of this idea in Greene's mind at this time is further substantiated by its presence in a novel he wrote in 1939. Confidential agent D muses, "If this was civilization—the crowded prosperous streets, the women trooping in for coffee at Buzzard's, the lady-in-waiting at King Edward's court and the sinking drowning child—he preferred barbarity" (Confidential 51).

6. This view persisted even after Greene claimed that he had stopped believing in the doctrine of original sin, beginning in the 1950s, as did his general sense of the ubiquity and permanence of evil in temporal life. See General 11-12; Cassis 385; Cuoto 217; and Schwartz 14-18.

7. At least on this topic, Greene claimed Scobie's view as his own (Donaghy 17). He anticipated this statement in a 1940 film review (Film 270).

8. He reprised many of these themes four decades later in Burnt 76; and Comedians 196.

9. See also Greene's description of African tribal funeral rites (Journey 86-8); and his contrast between memories of genuine primitive burial ceremonies and ones staged for civilization and tainted by it (Search 31-2).

10. Catholicism's superior suitability to primitive peoples than Protestantism was a frequent and consistent theme of Greene's reflections on non-European cultures (Search 21-22, 33; Burnt 86; Ways 208; Allain 146). For modern Protestantism's insubstantiality in British contexts, see, e.g., Battlefield 81-4; Brighton 31-2; Confidential 178-9; Lawless 14-15.

11. Although Greene was often sharply critical of Pope John Paul II, the pontiff shares many of Greene's ideas about the affinities between Catholicism and primitive religions, especially in Africa, and also seems to imply that the Church can be a bridge between their more elemental religiosity and the West's materialism. See Cowell 11, 28.

12. In 1961, Greene reiterated this criticism of Catholicism abroad corrupted by civilization, condemning Mass of "a most unreligious kind" that he attended in Africa with "most unattractive colonial types" (Search 70-1).

13. His perception of European ignorance of African affection made a strong impression on Greene, as he repeated this passage almost verbatim in a contemporaneous short story (Short Stories 98); and he noted a similar tactile bent among Latin Americans over thirty years later (Honorary 8-9, 162).

14. Greene also highlighted Chesterton's condemnations of romantic primitivism in his copy of The Everlasting Man (Greene Personal Library). Moreover, he became a keen observer, and staunch critic, of the corruption and tyranny prevalent in many post-colonial native governments, concluding by 1988 that "ordinary Africans were better off under most colonial regimes" (Cassis 449). Recognizing such remarks should temper the criticism of those who overemphasize Greene's elegiac evocations of primitive life, such as Meyers 56; and the work of S.E. Ogunde discussed in Cuoto 11-12.

15. Fussell applies this idea only to The Lawless Roads, and thinks that Greene changes the placement of the "I Hate It Here" section rather than adding a second one to bookend his analysis and bring it full-circle.

REFERENCES

Adamson, Judith. *Graham Greene: The Dangerous Edge.* New York: Macmillan, 1990.

Alan Redway Papers. Georgetown University, Washington, D.C.

Allain, Marie-Francoise. *The Other Man: Conversations With Graham Greene.* New York: Simon & Schuster, 1983.

Allott, Kenneth and Miriam Farris. *The Art of Graham Greene.* New York: Russell & Russell, 1951.

Boardman, Gwenn. *Graham Greene: Aesthetics of Exploration.* Gainesville: U of Florida P, 1971.

Cassis, A.F., ed. *Graham Greene: Man of Paradox*. Chicago: Loyola UP, 1994.

Cowell, Alan. "Challenge to the Faithful." *The New York Times Magazine*. 27 Dec. 1992: 10-11, 28, 31-4.

Cuoto, Maria. *Graham Greene: On the Frontier: Politics and Religion in the Novels*. New York: St. Martin's Press, 1988.

Davis, R.M. "The Rhetoric of Mexican Travel: Greene and Waugh." *Renascence* 38 (1986): 160-169.

Donaghy, Henry J., ed. *Conversations With Graham Greene*. Jackson: UP of Mississippi, 1992.

Donoghue, Denis. *England, Their England: Commentaries on English Language and Literature*. Berkeley: U of California P, 1989.

Fussell, Paul. *Abroad: British Literary Traveling Between the Wars*. Oxford: Oxford UP, 1980.

Greene, Graham. "Analysis of a Journey." *Spectator* 27 Sept. 1935: 459-60.

——. Brighton Rock. 1938. Reprint. New York: Bantam, 1968.

——. A Burnt-Out Case. 1960. Reprint. New York: Penguin, 1977.

——. *Collected Essays*. New York: Penguin, 1969.

——. *Collected Short Stories*. New York: Penguin, 1986.

——. *The Comedians*. 1965, 1966. Reprint. New York: Penguin, 1968.

——. *The Confidential Agent*. 1939. Reprint. New York: Penguin, 1971.

——. *Getting to Know the General*. Toronto: Lester & Orpen Dennys, 1984.

——. *Graham Greene on Film: Collected Film Criticism, 1935-40*. Ed. John Russell Taylor. New York: Simon & Schuster, 1972.

——. *This Gun for Hire*. 1936. Reprint. New York: Viking, 1982.

——. *The Heart of the Matter*. 1948, 1971. Reprint. New York: Penguin, 1978.

——. *The Honorary Counsel*. 1973. Reprint. New York: Pocket Books, 1974.

——. *The Human Factor*. 1978. Reprint. New York: Avon Books, 1979.

——. *In Search of a Character*. New York: Viking, 1961.

——. *It's a Battlefield*. 1934. Reprint. New York: Penguin, 1977.

——. *Journey Without Maps*. 1936, 1946. Reprint. New York: Penguin, 1980.

——. *The Lawless Roads*. 1939. Reprint. New York: Penguin, 1976.

——. *The Ministry of Fear*. 1943. Reprint. New York: Viking, 1982.

——. *Nineteen Stories*. New York: Viking, 1949.

——, ed. *The Old School: Essays By Divers Hands*. London: Jonathan Cape, 1934.

——. *The Power and the Glory*. 1940. Reprint. New York: Penguin, 1971.

——. *The Quiet American*. 1955, 1973. Reprint. New York: Penguin, 1977.

——. *Reflections*. Ed. Judith Adamson. New York: Penguin, 1990.

——. *A Sort of Life*. New York: Simon & Schuster, 1971.

——. "Three Travelers." *Spectator* 8 Dec. 1939: 838.

——. *Ways of Escape*. New York: Simon & Schuster, 1980.

——. Graham Greene Personal Library. John J. Bums Library. Boston College. Boston, MA.

Gunn, Drewey Wayne. *American and British Writers in Mexico, 1556-1973*. Austin: U of Texas P, 1974.

Harmer, Ruth Mulvey. "Greene World of Mexico: The Birth of a Novelist." *Renascence* 15 (Summer 1963): 171-182.

Hynes, Samuel. *The Auden Generation*. London: Bodley Head, 1976.

Lewis, R.W.B. *The Picaresque Saint: Representative Figures in Contemporary Fiction*. Philadelphia: J.B. Lippincott, 1956, 1958.

Meyers, Jeffrey. "Greene's Travel Books." *Graham Greene: A Revaluation*. Ed. Jeffrey Meyers. New York: Macmillan, 1990. 47-67.

Schwartz, Adam. "Christianity's Dangerous Edge: `Belief,' `Faith,' and Doubt in Graham Greene's Writing." *Thematica: Historical Research and Review* 3 (May 1996): 2-29.

Scott, Carolyn. "The Witch at the Corner: Notes on Graham Greene's Mythology." *Graham Greene: Some Critical Considerations*. Ed. Robert O. Evans. Lexington: U of Kentucky P, 1963.

Sherry, Norman. *The Life of Graham Greene*, Vol. I: 1904-1939. New York: Viking, 1989.

——. *The Life of Graham Greene*, Vol. 2: 1939-1955. London: Jonathan Cape, 1994.

Veldman, Meredith. *Fantasy, the Bomb, and the Greening of Britain: Romantic Protest, 1945-1980*. Cambridge: Cambridge UP, 1994.

Walker, Ronald. *Infernal Paradise: Mexico and the Modern English Novel*. Berkeley: U of California P, 1978.

Waugh, Evelyn. *The Essays, Articles and Reviews of Evelyn Waugh*. Ed. Donat Gallagher. Boston: Little, Brown & Co., 1984.

Wiener, Martin. *English Culture and the Decline of the Industrial Spirit: 1850-1980*. Cambridge: Cambridge UP, 1981.

Williams, Raymond. *Culture and Society: 1780-1950*. 1958. Reprint. New York: Columbia UP, 1983.

3

Modernism's Shell-Shocked History: Amnesia, Repetition and the War in Graham Greene's The Ministry of Fear

—Damon Marcel Decoste

> [T]he 1930s quickly became associated with the rejection of high modernism as it had developed after the war and with a renewed dedication to realism and political commitment.
>
> —Brian Diemert (23)

> [T]o fight against forgetting means to fight to remember that one forgets as soon as one believes, draws conclusions, and holds for certain.
>
> —Jean-Francois Lyotard (10)

In his timely study of Greene's early "entertainments" and their use of the thriller format,[1] Diemert argues convincingly for the seriousness of these works and of The Ministry of Fear, "one of [Greene's] most skillful and complex novels" (151), in particular. Further, as my first epigraph testifies, Diemert sees much of the complexity of this novel as stemming from Greene's attempt, through his adoption of such a popular narrative form, to repudiate the aesthetic elitism and dubious politics of that generation of high modernist writers that preceded his own (28, 35). Indeed, in so situating Greene's early works, Diemert concurs with the standard critical wisdom on British writers of the 1930s and their relationship to the modernists who went before them.2 Yet it is my contention that Greene's work, and The Ministry of Fear especially, cannot be so neatly disentangled from the project of Anglo-American modernism. Indeed, Greene's sole novel written during the war years[3] remains an essentially moderni st one, in that the Second World War is made comprehensible here by taking its place in that history of repetition that was the touchstone of those modernists whom Orwell saw as "temperamentally hostile to the notion of 'progress'" (507). That is to say, the war, as Greene figures it, is both understandable and inevitable precisely as it is mandated by a Western history conceived, in modernist terms, as the ceaseless rehearsal of past atrocity. Greene, in The Ministry of Fear's "attempt to find a discourse to make a sense of the world of the blitz" (R. Smith 115), thus extends the modernists' own repudiation of the meliorist historiography of liberal thought, presenting instead a history that inexorably reenacts past rituals of violence.

This bloody repetition, moreover, perpetuates itself, for Greene, through a process of forgetting akin to that which Lyotard decries in my second epigraph. Central to the story of Arthur Rowe is not only the shellshock amnesia that disrupts the narrative but also his persistent forgetting, not, significantly, of the past but of the present real condition of self and others. Greene's novel, in its treatment of Rowe's steady adherence to the adventure-tale ethics learned in childhood and of his resulting susceptibility to pity as a destructive emotion, shows both Rowe and his war-torn world more generally to be repeating their respective pasts in the form of deadly force. While the engine of such dire repetition is thus revealed as a kind of remembering, this memory acts also as a forgetting in Lyotard's sense, a holding for certain of an inherited ethos that is oblivious both to the actual character of the self and to the very selfhood of others. In this way, Greene's text, in its presentation of the war as r ehearsal, repeats, in its turn, the modernists' antiliberal sense of history, but does so by diagnosing Western history as the necessary, if slaughterous, result of a refusal to grant the other particularity and autonomy, to grant her, in other words, selfhood in liberal terms.

Yet before proceeding to examine Greene's explication of the war as an instance of modernist thinking on history, I want first to proffer some defense for my claim that Anglo-American modernism centers on this sense of history as tragic repetition. To be sure, current formulations of modernism tend to paint a rather different picture, with many critics, indeed, reading modernism as nothing other than a retreat from questions of history.[4] Thus Marianne DeKoven sees modernist fiction as deliberately suppressing the historical referent, seeking instead "to save the world through an art purified of history" (138),[5] though, on her account, this suppression is doomed to the happiest of failures, such strategies only serving "to render those [historical] facts with greater power than direct representation would give" (151). When, moreover, critics do acknowledge how "the problematic of time occupies a central place" in modernist thought (Nicholls 165), they tend to cast this problematic in terms of rupture rather than repetition. Thus, for Paul Fussell, modernist literature adheres to "[t]he image of strict division [which] dominates the Great War conception of Time Before and Time After" (80). As this claim would suggest, the notion of history thus ascribed to modernism is one not only of discontinuity but of decline as well, and perhaps the most prevalent understanding of modernism in recent scholarship is one that sees it as essentially nostalgic or elegiac, driven, in

Frank Lentricchia's words, by a "need to turn back the clock" (8). Thus many critics agree with Surette that modernism is an articulation of "the antique view of history as a decline from some pure origin" (253). Art Berman, for example, proclaims this elegiac sense of history's course the very sine qua non of Anglo-American modernism: "this decline is modernism's subject: there would be no modernism without it" (212). Likewise, Meisel argues that what he deems the Eliotic assumption of "a lost golden age in the Renaissance" constitutes a "crucial myth of the modern" (77, 78). Even Levenson, while he insists that Anglo-American modernism was "anti-traditional before it was traditional" (79), nonetheless claims that the very seeds of modernism in Conrad are already moving "toward the undermining of the sovereign individual and toward nostalgia for more traditional, precapitalist values" (34).

Modernism, as depicted in recent scholarship at any rate, is thus a project that, when it deigns to consider history at all, does so in the mode of nostalgic lament, calling for the resuscitation "of values which [are] explicitly anti-modern" (Nicholls 167). Yet I contend that such an account largely mistranslates what modernism has to say about the nature and value of Western history. If, as Nicholls noted above, the problematic of time is central here, it is so because history, for the modernists, represents not a process of decline but rather a persistent repetition of the past, figured not as some forfeit Golden Age but as the site of senseless violence. The masterworks of high modernism, in other words, convey a dread of the historical present, not as it fails to sustain past grandeur but as it tiresomely reenacts past enormity. Indeed, if we examine two signal texts from 1922, British modernism's annus mirabilis, what we find is not, in Eysteinsson's phrase, "the music played to the imminent decline of Western culture" (30), but rather an anatomy of the history of that culture which identifies it as horribly consistent in its rehearsal of past bloodshed.

Thus despite Batchelor's claim, consonant with so much modernist criticism, that all of Woolf's major novels are written in the elegiac mode (22), Woolf's modernism, as reflected in the watershed of Jacob's Room at any rate, is obsessed with history, not as a counterpoint to, but as the prime determinant of, a martial present. This sense that the world of the doomed Jacob Flanders is a legacy bequeathed by a still vital cultural past is captured early on, in Woolf's portrait of Cambridge before the Great War:

> The stroke of the clock even was muffled; . . . as if generations of learned men heard the last hour go rolling through their ranks and issued it, already smooth and timeworn, with their blessing, for the use of the living. (42)

While the undergraduate Jacob basks in the favor of this gift, pleased to think "himself the inheritor" and fulfillment of this seamless history (42), it soon becomes clear that this inheritance is not quite the boon he thinks it is. To be sure, this sense of himself as beneficiary of the treasures of a glorious occidental past ironically engenders in him a sense of a ruptured history and a nostalgia for a classical Golden Age: "Ages lapped at their feet like waves for sailing. And surveying all this, looming through the fog, the shades of London, the two young men decided in favour of Greece" (72). Yet Woolf's narrator refuses to let us endorse this lapsarian view of history, or that sense of history as cultural treasure trove from which it springs. If, musing on the press's treatment of Europe's march to war, this narrator must note, "[w]hen a child begins to read history one marvels, sorrowfully, to hear him spell out in his new voice the ancient words" (93), it is because present history is figured here a s repetition, and this is itself worthy of lament, not Jacob's celebration. Indeed, the war that finally claims his life must, for Woolf, be seen not as a break in, but as a bloody extension of, Western history as a martial continuum. Thus the war's onset is cast here in terms binding it to those very "glories" of Greece that Jacob saw as incommensurate with a peculiarly modern squalor:

> But the red light was on the columns of the Parthenon, and the Greek women who were knitting their stockings and sometimes crying to a child . . . were as jolly as sand-martins in the heat, quarreling, scolding, suckling babies, until the ships in the Piraeus fired their guns. (167)

Thus the Woolf who, in 1938, would lament that "[i]t seems as if there were no progress in the human race, but only repetition" (Three Guineas 76) mounts this same case 16 years earlier, and it is, I suggest, this argument that is central to her literary modernism, as indeed it is integral to that even more formidable literary monument of 1922, Joyce's Ulysses. If Stephen's history lesson in "Nestor" centers, significantly, on the exemplary story of Pyrrhus, of "progress" revealed as bloodiest failure (20), it is clear that this history, "a tale like any other too often heard" (21), is still very much an operative and oppressive presence: "As it was in the beginning, is now" (24). Indeed, in the "old wisdom" kept alive and transmitted by Mr. Deasy (28), this persistence of the past is the persistence, too, of violence, as Stephen sees in Deasy's "[g]lorious, pious and immortal memory" visions of "[t]he lodge of Diamond in Armagh the splendid behung with corpses of papishes" (26). Further, the lesson, according to this custodian of the living past, to be gleaned from its bloody course is one that, in its anti-Semitic fervor (28), can serve only to reproduce historical violence—thus Stephen's conclusion that "[h]istory . . . is a nightmare" (28) from which he must strive to awake. While Stephen is hardly reliable as the conscience of Ulysses, he seems, in his sense of history both as continuous and as cruel, to be borne out by the text, for we shall indeed see Mr. Deasy's lesson taken to heart and acted upon by the Citizen in

"Cyclops" (280-81), an attempt at unholy repetition—"By Jesus, I'll crucify him [Bloom] so I will" (280)—which, by means of this chapter's mock-epic recourse to past idioms of heroism, is placed firmly in a still vital occidental tradition. Likewise, that this history persists in the present specifically as nightmare is amply demonstrated by the passion play of "Circe," where history, both personal and cultural, explodes as a sinister phantasmal force still scourging the living.

For these seminal works of British modernism, then, history is indeed a depressing, and murderous, form of repetition, and not some squandered estate we must work to reclaim. Yet Quinones, noting the early modernist sense of history as "a kind of repetitive sameness" (38), nonetheless sees modernism as moving, by the 1930s, toward a new embrace of the cultural past, now "humanized and regarded as necessary to the comforts and continuities of civilized life" (232). I contend, however, that that sense of history traced above is reiterated by certain writers of this period, and that modernism, so understood, persists as the primary schema for understanding the Second World War in Greene's Ministry of Fear. To be sure, as Diemert, Sharrock, and others have stressed, Greene does at times take issue with the modernist project as he sees it, and particularly with its Bloomsbury variant.[6] Thus, in his literary criticism, we see him attacking the fiction of Woolf and Forster for a lack of religious dimension that renders their characters mere "cardboard symbols [wandering] through a world which [is] paper-thin" (Essays 115). Likewise, in a 1938 essay on Dorothy Richardson, Greene suggests that the hyper-subjectivism of Richardson's stream-of-consciousness technique can only make us pine for "the old dictatorship" of plot (Essays 152). Yet, such barbs notwithstanding,[7] Greene consistently traces for his own work a decidedly modernist pedigree. In a 1949 interview, for example, Greene, when asked to name his own literary staples, mentions not only Conrad, James, and Ford but also such "high" modernists as Eliot and Pound (Donaghy 23). Such a modernist personal canon is proffered in Ways of Escape, as well, with Greene there declaring Eliot and Herbert Read "the two great figures of my young manhood" (28), and still noting with fondness "a kind phrase from Ezra Pound, and some words of praise from Ford Madox Ford" for It's a Battlefield, published in 1934 (23). This high estimation of modernist writers persists, indeed, even in the posthumously published dream diary, A World of My Own, in which Greene's dream meetings with writers are almost wholly devoted to such figures as Ford, James, and Eliot (8-10).[8]

This affinity for much of the modernist movement in English is, further, matched in Greene by that modernist sense of history as tragic rehearsal outlined above. If the modernists do hold a certain allure for him, it is because they share with him a common conception of, and moral judgment on, Western history. Certainly, Greene himself proclaims his own fascination with history; as he tells us in Ways of Escape, what the 1930s gave him above all was a passion, not for politics or religion but for history, "a desire to be a spectator of history, history in which I found I was concerned myself' (59). Yet as such a witness to history, Greene, like the modernists generally, has been commonly read as chronicling a history of rupture and decline. Grahame Smith's claim that "Greene's melody is elegiac" (217) is representative of much critical consideration of Greene's treatment of history,[9] and such scholarship thus figures him as fundamentally nostalgic in his outlook. But if Greene is, as Evans notes, in revolt against "that liberal, optimistic view of the world nurtured by the Enlightenment and brought to fruition in the nineteenth century" (xiv), his revolt consists, I argue, not in reversing the trajectory of this linear history, so that progress becomes degeneration, but by, in modernist fashion, replacing this line altogether with a sense of history as something both cyclical and terrible. Thus when pressed, in a 1949 interview, to comment on the apparently unprecedented horrors of the present century, Greene dismisses the notion that such violence can be seen as any great departure from past history. Rather, the crises and bloodshed of the first half of the century are, for him, "humanity's normal state. Certain epochs create the illusion of being calmer, but they are rare" (Donaghy 22). The horrors of the present, then, are, in Greene's view, continuous with a past figured in rather grisly terms, a point made again in Ways of Escape, in Greene's reflections on postwar conflicts. Here, present violence is understood explicitly as a rehearsal of more ancient barbarity, such that war in Vietnam constitutes "the return of the watchtower and the border castle in Saigon" (161; my emphasis), and the Kenya of the Mau-Mau uprisings has "gone back to the bamboo tower, the wall of pointed thorns, the stakes slanting in the ditch" (161).

Thus for Greene, as Friedman notes, life is cast "as accretion, endless repetition, rather than as expansion or repletion" (132).[10] In other words, history for him wears the same wearisome face it presented to the modernists who went before him. And this specifically modernist understanding of history is precisely the medium through which the Second World War becomes comprehensible in his work. If, as McEwen argues, Greene understands war generally as continuous with putative "peace," as only "bring[ing] into the open conditions which peacetime disguises" (118), it is also clear that modern war is, in his mind, congruous not only with the prewar condition but also with more ancient history, with indeed the whole cultural heritage of the West. Thus D. of The Confidential Agent is, in his own participation in a war narrative, presented as existing thereby as a kind of cultural avatar and fulfillment: "Five hundred years of inbreeding had produced him, set him against an exact background, made him at home, and at the same time haunted—by the vices of ancestors and the tastes of the past" (33). D., then, has been made for war, precisely insofar as he has been fashioned in the image of a remote cultural past, and that the war he has been so readied to participate in is itself likewise a repetition is underscored by the novel's use of The Song of Roland, its tale of medieval warfare stressing both the present's status as repetition and history's bloody nature. This sense of history, here applied to the Spanish Civil War, is also deployed as the means for coming to terms with that more global conflict that followed. Writing during the London blitz, Greene, in a 1940 essay, marvels at the ease with which the British have accommodated themselves to the war, yet deems this, given his understanding of European history, as perhaps not so marvelous after all: "Violence comes to us more easily because it was so long expected—not only by the political sense but by the moral sense. The world we lived in could not have ended any other way" (Essays 447). Again, the war here is predictable, indeed inescapable, because it is the very culmination of our cultural traditions, the latest conflagration for which Western history, in its insatiable restaging of old conflicts, has served to prepare us, just as D. has been prepared.

This view of European history as of a piece with, rather than distinct from or superior to, the present's destructive course is central, too, to Greene's fictional exploration of World War II in The Ministry of Fear. Here, both the carnage of the blitz and the fascism of Greene's fifth columnists are presented, not as in opposition to, but rather as rehearsals of, the more or less remote prewar past. Both the nihilistic Willi Hilfe and the more apparently compassionate Dr. Forester, for example, share more than just their Nazi sympathies, in that these sentiments themselves are revealed, in both, as being tied to the past. Thus Willi and sister Anna seem, to Rowe, to form "a Victorian family group" (43), and Willi speaks always in "antiquated slang," more at home in the last century (44; see also 45-46). Likewise Forester presents to Rowe a face "hawk-like and noble and a little histrionic, like the portrait of a Victorian" (113). Those characters, then, who by their struggles for the Nazi enemy, may be seen as engines of the present war are conspicuous in their being palpably of another, earlier time. So, too, is the destruction they and their allies visit upon England. London bombarded, here, represents not novelty but repetition of an age-old suffering, such that Rowe remarks "the strange, torn landscape where London shops were reduced to a stone ground-plan like those of Pompeii" (40). If such an echo of past violence would thus liken the war to natural disasters, it is clear elsewhere that the present war must be seen, even more, as a rehearsal of a human perversity of some long historical standing. Thus Rowe, in a book auction, comes upon an antique Roman Catholic missal that serves to underscore the present's implication in a history of violence seemingly as old as history itself: "oddly enough, it was the only thing that spoke of war in the old quiet room. Open it where you would, you came on prayers for deliverance, the angry nations, the unjust, the wicked" (74). In this passage, Greene situates the present war in a very human past, one which, in its most ancient occidental documents, already chronicles repeated war, oppression, and lament.

Yet this is not, to be sure, the way Rowe himself views the war and its place in history. Rather, his understanding of history is one that accords instead with those critics who take both Greene, and modernism more generally, to write a literature of nostalgia; indeed, many have taken Rowe's elegiac yearning for the pastas proof of Greene's own nostalgic outlook.[11] As we first meet Arthur Rowe, mercy killer and self-styled pariah, we see him drawn to the fete that will embroil him in the novel's thriller plot precisely as it seems to offer access to a personal and national past he deems both edenic and irrevocably lost: "The fete called him like innocence: it was entangled in childhood, with vicarage gardens and girls in white summer frocks" (11). The past for which Rowe, from the very outset, is desperately searching is both the ostensibly innocent age of his own childhood and the utopia of a pastoral British prewar existence. What is conveyed on this very opening page, then, is that Rowe experiences hist ory, both biographical and cultural, in terms not only of rupture but also of decline. Despite the fact that Greene, even here, undermines such sentiments—the fete band, after all, plays "a faded song of the last war" (12), thus signaling the present conflict as very much in line with the past—Rowe remains, like the Little Duke of the novel's many epigraphs, a quester, and what he seeks is the retrieval of a past he sees as lamentably divorced from the present. Thus he experiences the fete as instructional, as demonstrating for him just this rupture and the consequently dire necessity of his quest: "it was as if Providence had led him to exactly this point to indicate the difference between then and now. These people might have been playing a part in an expensive morality play for his sole benefit" (15).

Rowe certainly takes the moral of this perceived performance very much to heart, clinging throughout the novel to a belief in the past's superiority and thus to an acute longing for its resuscitation. Indeed, as outlined in Book One, his character is that almost of an acolyte before the altar of past history, striving through a private liturgy to keep it alive; thus he ritually reads his two Dickens novels "as people used to read the Bible, over and over again till he could have quoted chapter and verse, not so much because he liked them as because he had read them as a child" (20). In other respects, too, his wartime home remains a kind of temple to the cult of childhood, with his radio dial producing "a homely effect like a nightlight in a child's nursery" (23), and his "last remaining treasure—a big schoolboy's knife" holding talismanic significance for him (24). This brand of piety, which we will see again in Rowe's devotion to the heroic virtues of his childhood adventure-tale reading, draws its rigor from Rowe's firm belief that history is a process of decline and fall, a downward-tending line catastrophically broken by war, on the one hand, and his killing of his wife, on the other. Thus as he dreams of his mother who "had died before the first great war" (64), Rowe insists that the enormity of his present could only have been as inaccessible to her understanding as the past world she represents for him is to his grasp: "She could no more have imagined this than that her small son in his brown corduroy knickers...should grow up to be a murderer" (65). If, then, the prewar past of which Rowe dreams here "isn't real life any more" (65), this is tragic because Rowe remains convinced that it was once real and undeniably more human than the present world he suffers.

Yet holding certain, as he does, the chasm that exists between then and now, Rowe, all his devotions notwithstanding, cannot reconstruct Eden; his private theology admits no New Jerusalem. As he is told by the policeman in the above dream, this war-tom world "is home. There isn't anywhere else at all" (67-68). This being the case, Rowe's quest for the past becomes a longing not so much for memory as for oblivion. That is, if the past he defines in polar opposition to a degraded present is truly inaccessible to all but memory, then what is required, in lieu of its recapture, is forgetting, a forgetting specifically of this postlapsarian present.[12] This wish will find its fulfillment in the amnesia of Book Two, whose title, "The Happy Man," underscores that equation between ignorance and bliss Rowe has made throughout the novel's first 100 pages. From the very outset, Rowe's desire for the past has been tied to a concomitant longing for the obliteration of present historical reality, the fete serving to heighten his need "to mislay the events of twenty years" (13). And in ways Rowe himself never seems to become aware of, the text highlights how this nostalgic longing for the erasure of the present dovetails with the wholesale destruction of modern war itself. Thus Rowe, eager to forget, welcomes the violence of the blitz, as it quite forcibly eradicates that present life he, burdened with dreams of an idyllic past, cannot abide: "After a raid he used to sally out and note with a kind of hope that this restaurant or that shop existed no longer—it was like loosening the bars of a prison cell one by one" (22). In a paradoxical way, then, the war he seeks to escape through forgetting garners his blessing precisely because in violence, in death—and, of course suicide, too, remains a persistent temptation for him (92-95)—his beloved oblivion beckons.

If Rowe's nostalgia, through its transformation into an ethics of forgetting, is thus presented as implicated in, rather than at odds with, the war from which it ostensibly recoils, this same forgetting is cast by Greene as indeed definitive of the war. The project of forgetting thus not only sanctions massacre but also generates a history at odds with its own nostalgic underpinnings, that is, one not of rupture but of repetition. The war symbolizes—but also, through the bomb that induces Rowe's amnesia, enables—forgetting, and does so by making his life history mirror the war's own status as historical rehearsal. For through his amnesia, Rowe wins not only that oblivion for which he has ached but also something more, namely, a return to that childhood he has idealized. In Forester's "shell-shock clinic," Rowe still retains some memories, but only those that will make of his present condition a reenactment of his own past: "You see, I remember things quite clearly until, say, eighteen" (110). What Rowe, through the agency of the war, has forgotten, then, is his adult identity, and this forgetting permits a joyous repetition of his own age of innocence. Thus his regular visits with Dr. Forester are, now, "like visiting a benign headmaster out of school hours" (111), and his stirring affection for Anna Hilfe is experienced as an "adolescent love" (130). Even in his ultimate rebellion against Forester's strictures, his clandestine foray into the clinic's "sick bay," Rowe, as

Greene's narrator underlines for us, is repeating the antics of youth: "He was back in his own childhood, breaking out of dormitory, daring more than he really wanted to dare, proving himself" (137). In Rowe's forgetting, then, personal history, at least, is shown to follow patterns, not of decline and fall but of continuity and recurrence.

And as the last citation demonstrates, what recurs here is a particular kind of childhood past, one suffused with the conventions of romantic adventure as delineated by boyhood reading. As Diemert has noted, in The Ministry of Fear "the war . . . is fought not only with bombs and guns but with texts as well" (177). Indeed, Greene is famous for believing in the great power over us of those texts, in particular, which we read as children. For him, only this reading has any lasting influence on the adults we become: "In later life we admire, we are entertained, we may modify some views we already hold, but we are more likely to find in books a confirmation of what is in our minds already" (Essays 13). For Rowe, at least, this is certainly true, and he returns to his past in large part by returning to a system of belief nurtured by childhood reading of such adventure tales as Yonge's The Little Duke. As longingly recalled in Book One, such reading involved for Rowe an education in a stable and optimistic worldview, one in which "[o]ur heroes are simple: they are brave, they tell the truth, they are good swordsmen and they are never in the long run really defeated" (89). Indeed, it was as just such a hero that the young Rowe understood himself, a dashing figure "capable of extraordinary heroisms and endurances which would make the girl he loved forget the awkward hands and the spotty chin of adolescence" (73). If this passage indicates how such aggrandizing self-definition is at odds with, is a kind of forgetting of, the self's actuality, such adventuretale dreams nonetheless became, in his youth, as much an article of faith as his nostalgia would become in later life: "It was like the religious discipline: words however emptily repeated can in time form a habit . . . until one day to your own surprise you find yourself acting on the belief you thought you didn't believe in" (73).

That such an ethos of romantic heroism has indeed persisted in him is underscored by Rowe's actions as the amnesiac Digby. In speculating on the true nature of his forgotten adult identity, Rowe wonders, for instance, whether he became an explorer, a la Burton and Stanley, as he had dreamed of being in childhood (111). Indeed, his sole complaint about his apparently idyllic existence at the clinic is that it does not afford him the properly heroic narrative he believes should be his. As the fortune-telling Mrs. Bellairs astutely observed at the fete, Rowe "sometimes feel[s] [he has] not been allowed a proper scope for [his] gifts. [He wants] to do great deeds, not dream them all day long" (16). This same self-estimation and frustration surface even in Rowe's return to the Eden of childhood, as he laments, "[t]here was no satisfaction in shining before [assistant] Johns....He dreamed wildly between the box hedges" (123). When, finally, he embarks upon his great adventure, his search for the dreaded "sick bay, " it is at least in part because this will satisfy his thirst for adventure, his desire to be the romantic hero of childhood storybooks: "He was afraid of undefined punishments and for that reason he felt his action was heroic and worthy of someone in love" (136). Such attempts at casting himself in the role of the extraordinary, heroic protagonist of adventure tales continue, even after his expulsion from Forester's garden. In his reimmersion in the novel's thriller plot of wartime espionage, Rowe stays true to this same heroic ethos, so "happily drunk with danger and action" that even "[t]he ruins from which [he and investigator Prentice] emerged were only a heroic back-cloth to his personal adventure" (176).

This last point is significant, for what it highlights is that the rehearsal of childhood Rowe's amnesia permits does not, as O'Prey argues, leave him "detached from the chaos and violence" of the war (49). In returning, through forgetting, to the past and its notions of heroism, Rowe is repeating not only his own personal history but also the characteristic actions of the war to which he sees his past as opposed. For despite Diemert's claim that the novel "discredits the ethos of the romantic adventure tale by contrasting it with the thriller world of war-ravaged London" (158; my emphasis), The Ministry of Fear effects its debunking of this ethos precisely as it identifies it with the horrors of war. Rowe's persistent desire to be the hero of children's literature does not, as he thinks, distinguish him from that "History of Contemporary Society" he deems rightly written in the thriller mode (66). Rather, his need to be the extraordinary man, living out a life of derring-do, allies him with those very fifth columnists who drive the novel's thriller plot. It finds an echo, for instance, in Poole's solicitous talk of "the sheep" to whom both he and Rowe are, naturally, superior (25), and this spy's use of the first-person plural here (28) is both telling and astute. Likewise the spy-ring's chief, Willi Hilfe, admits that he, too, is "a romantic" (44), and that "a story [of intrigue] like [Rowe's] excites [him]. It seems to give an opportunity, well, to take a more violent line" (48). No wonder, then, that Rowe himself is convinced, on first meeting the Hilfes, that "these were the allies he needed" (44). And such an alliance, or affinity, continues throughout the novel, as the amnesiac Rowe's lust for romantic adventure keeps him at the center of this very contemporary tale of war and espionage. Not only is the clinic in which his wholesale return to this ostensibly dated worldview takes place run by the very spies and traitors who populate the modern thriller world, but also it is his childish need to be the her o in the spotlight that prompts him to withhold from police the telephone number that will lead to the spies and the stolen film (187). Thus does the hero of his boyish imaginings find himself at home in the war-torn present that itself endorses such a heroic ethos.

Rowe's forgetting does not, then, release him from the present but rather highlights the continuities between his idealized childhood world and the treacherous world of the war. Thus the "Arcady" in which his amnesia lands him in Book Two (109) is revealed to be a myth, the past being, in its vision of valor and heroism, at one with the carnage of the present. Indeed, it is this shared ethos, and the sense of self and others on which it rests, that Greene proffers as the very principle of a forgetting that constitutes Western history as modernism's nightmarish process of repetition. For in dreaming oneself the noble hero, one does not only, in Greene's view, elide one's own "spotty" imperfections but further justifies actions that deny, and even destroy, the selfhood of other human beings. The deadly force of this heroic self-conception Rowe shares with his Nazi foes, and the present shares with the past, is made clearest in the novel's dissection of Rowe's defining quality, namely, pity. For despite Watts's claim that the morality of Greene's fiction centers on "the value of the charitable action—the altruistic deed motivated by pity" (107),[13] Greene's treatment of this "virtue" puts it at the heart of the psychology of the war and of his explanation of history's repetitive and murderous course. It is, after all, this trait that is the source of Rowe's own status as wife murderer, and thus of his ties to such wartime villains as Willi and Poole. Like these characters, Rowe too is a killer, and what has driven him to emulate their war ethos is nothing other than the quality of mercy—" [m]ercy to [his wife] or mercy to me," remaining, as Rowe himself notes, unclear (37). Pity for his ill wife, his inability to stand her pain, has made him a killer, and the text underscores how this, too, figures as a repetition of, rather than fall from, the past by relating a cognate, if lesser, "murder" from his childhood: "Suddenly he couldn't bear the sight of the [wounded] rat's pain any more; he picked up a cricket-bat and struck the rat on the head over and over again" (66). Thus, for Greene, this mercy is and was indeed "dangerous pity" (26), for what it sanctions are actions akin even to those of murderer Willi Hilfe, whose suggestive last name (German for help) signals such kinship between Rowe's "virtue" and the workings of war. Indeed, Greene makes this connection even more explicit in his narrator's gloss on the meaning of the Catholic missal: "It wasn't only evil men who did these things. Courage smashes a cathedral, endurance lets a city starve, pity kills" (74).

But in order to clarify how pity, for Greene, can exemplify the ostensibly pitiless violence of war and the West's war-tom history, we must follow the hints this passage gives us and trace the links between pity and that adventure-tale ethic already seen to be definitive of the prewar past, as much as the World War II present. For despite Rowe's own belief that pity stands in opposition to this ethos as maturity to immaturity (187), pity counts, as the passage from page 74 quoted above indicates, as one of the cardinal virtues of the hero of the adventure tale. If the heroic faith of the past that Rowe has learned so well centers on such concepts as "sacrifice, courage, virtue" (73), so does their restatement as sources of destruction on the very next page situate Rowe's pity as part of the hero's constitution, and part of the danger he represents for others. Pity may be so embraced by the romantic values of past and present, of war and prewar, because at its heart, for Greene, lies the conviction he deems definitive of heroic self-conception, namely, that one is extraordinary and uniquely equipped to serve more, presumably, ordinary others. If Rowe's dreams of himself as hero, both in adolescence and amnesiac adulthood, focus, as we have seen, on service to, trials endured for, a beloved other, so, too, is pity revealed as validating action in the best interests of others, even to the point of their annihilation. Thus the amnesiac Rowe, caught up in adventure-filled plans for his illicit trip to the "sick bay," is appalled by the pacifism he reads in Forester's copy of Tolstoy's What I Believe. Such a worldview jars with Rowe's heroic persona and its need for Willi's "more violent line," but the way he articulates this to himself stresses the connections between the proper virtues of the hero and pity's own capacity to sanction any action: "why does he write as if the worst thing we can do to our fellow-man is to kill him? Everybody has to die and everybody fears death, but when we kill a man we save him from h is fear" (132). This line of reasoning thus defends the murder of others as, indeed, for their own good, and thus consonant with heroism. So long as we act heroically, so long that is, as we act in the interests of another, any act, for Rowe, may be justified: "there was the point—not to kill for one's own sake. But for the sake of people you loved, . . . it was right to risk damnation" (132). Such thinking, that of the "immature," romantic Rowe, seems, then, very much in accord with that of the "mature," pitying Rowe who would serve his wife the poisoned milk, for her own good, to end her pain, even though "he could never know whether [her] fear [of his act] had been worse than the pain" (89). Though he cannot, as he himself admits, ever know whether she might well have preferred "any sort of life to death" (89-90), he has been able, with pity and romantic heroism both to guide him, to decide what her preference should be, and act on her behalf, to the point even of her own destruction.

As the threads of historical continuity, then, both heroism and pity serve to make of history a continuum of violence, through a shared paternalism that underwrites any action at all that can be argued to serve or to spare another. Such paternalism is also, for Greene, the very pith of the forgetting that is the very essence of the war and of the history of which it constitutes an emblematic part. As the above passages make clear, what it entails is the forgetting or repression of the other, of her actual preferences, of her capacity to decide and act upon her own "best interests." Likewise are the actual interests and weaknesses of the heroic/pitying self elided and in their place erected a form of heroic infallibility, a certain knowledge of what is best for the other that can cloud both what the other might desire and what the heroic agent might truly be seeking through such "other-centered" action—hence Rowe's post facto fears that he might well have acted to end his own pain, not his wife's (89). This is, then, forgetting in Lyotard's mode, a forgetting of the other as agent that substitutes instead a certain belief in the rightness of one's own actions, as well as of one's right to undertake them. And it is such forgetting that, in its erasure of the other as a self capable of self-determination and its dictation of certain goods for all, Greene sees at the root of the twentieth-century's own genocidal reenactment of the historical nightmare. Thus, as McEwen notes, for Greene "it is dreadful to be sure of oneself" (20), for what such certainty, in its heroic or pitying justifications, permits is an imposition of will, a quashing of the other, very much at home with the violence of war:

> Do you know what happens . . . when you wish the world to be neat and orderly and precise, a closed, untroubled place? You try to make it that way. And when people don't respond (and they don't), you end up with Belsen. (Donaghy 33)

Certainly, The Ministry of Fear attempts to provide plenty of evidence that this is so. Not only does Rowe's pity drive him to murder, just as his desire for adventure implicates him in the murderous plot of Hilfe and his confederates, but also such certainty as to one's right to decide for others is the common foundation for what will become the novel's "massacre on an Elizabethan scale" (180). Like Rowe, the Nazi spy Poole also believes that "even murder can sometimes be excused," a truth he relates, tellingly, with "an intolerable confidence," as he appeals to Rowe as another man of intelligence, a cut above the sheep who may or may not have to be excusably murdered (25). So, too, the idealist Dr. Forester, a man of sufficient pity that he does "not approve . . . of taking animal life" (119), is nonetheless in league with Poole, Hilfe, and the others, and is "quite unmoved by the story of the Nazi elimination of old people and incurables" (182). Indeed, he will be party to the murder of muddled Major Stone, a crime he defends in advance as "the greatest mercy we can ask for him" (183). Forester's own death is, in apt and illuminating fashion, brought about for his own good, with "respectable, hero-worshipping Johns" (181) killing his idol, the fulfillment of his own romantic dreams of heroism, to protect him:

> he was saving him from the interminable proceedings of the law courts, from the crudities of prosecuting counsel, the unfathomable ignorances of the judge, and the indignity of depending on the shallow opinion of twelve men picked at random. (182)

Even Anna Hilfe, with whom a loving Rowe ends up in the novel's conclusion, is, as herself part of her brother's ring, presented as a character of suspect, even oppressive, pity. Thus, visiting an amnesiac Rowe freed from the memory of his wife's murder, Anna refuses to tell him the truth and admits she prefers him so protected from the truth, even if it consigns him to Forester's clinic-cum-prison: "This is how you should be. This is how I like you" (129).

If in all these characters the alchemy of pity and self-certainty yields a precipitate of murder and confinement, Willi Hilfe reveals the violence of such an imposition of will shorn even of pity's respectability. While the above instances serve to demonstrate, in Webster's words, how suffering in Greene's fiction "is made by idealists who fancy themselves God" (15), Willi, who makes no pretense to ideals of any sort, still starkly illustrates the essence of their idealism and the ends to which it tends. For as Silverstein argues, Willi's nihilism, like Nazism itself, "only carr[ies] Rowe's sense of pity to its logical and terrifying extreme" (41). While Anna posits her brother's service to the Nazis as the antithesis of Rowe's pity—"they can bear pain—other people's pain—endlessly" (100; Greene's emphasis)—the narrative rather reveals Willi's mercilessness to be the obverse, not the inverse, of Rowe's quality of mercy. We have, for example, already seen how Willi's own brand of romanticism, and his surname, work to establish a tie between the pitying Rowe and the amoral spy. Such connections are made here because Willi's amorality involves, albeit in a more nihilistic mode, the same kind of erasure of others as does the apparent compassion shared by Rowe, Anna, and Johns. If Willi, for Greene, embodies "the grace and attraction of nihilism—of not caring for anything" (203), what this involves is the use of other people as pawns to further his own ends, a manipulation that can easily lead, as in his attempted murder of Rowe and Anna at the end of Book One, to their destruction. This is, indeed, a matter of course for Willi, simply how the game is played, such that he is offended and amused by Rowe's throwing the attempted murder in his face: "He seemed to accuse them of a lack of humour; it was not the kind of thing they ought to have taken to heart" (204). What is important, however, is that Willi's own brand of indifferent disregard for the lives of others sheds light on that ethics of care shared by the novel's other characters. They, too, as we have seen, are ready to judge for, manipulate, and kill other people to serve what they take to be the right, and thus the novel argues that their "caring" tends, by its forgetfulness of others, to the same deadly presumption that is the essence of Nazism and the war; in this sense, they are indeed Nazi sympathizers.

What, then, all the novel's characters share, just as the present shares it with the past, is a lethal forgetting of the other and a sure sense of their own entitlement to use her as they see fit. The engine that drives the war and the past that it emulates is, finally, an egotism that denies other human beings dignity, agency, and respect. What, in other words, is forgotten here, as Rowe seems momentarily at least to see, is the value and rights of particularized others, human beings with their own desires and preferences:

> Over there among the unknown tubes a woman was giving birth, rats were nosing among sacks of meal, an old man was dying, two people were seeing each other for the first time by the light of a lamp; everything in that darkness was of such deep importance that their errand lithe pursuit of the stolen film] could not equal it—this violent, superficial chase, this cardboard adventure. (178)

In the words of Greene's narrator, then, the novel works to demonstrate that "[o]ne can't love humanity. One can only love people" (184), and that to do so entails a respect for the way they conduct their own lives. What this means is that Greene's modernist rejection of liberal Enlightenment's progressive history is itself one rooted in a very liberal sensibility. That is, if history is, as both the war and the past illustrate, a repeated nightmare, it is so because what it ceaselessly repeats is the forgetting of the worth and rights of others. The essence of Greene's hellish history in The Ministry of Fear is the persistent betrayal of the Millian principle that "[o]ver himself over his own body and mind, the individual is sovereign" (Mill 69; his emphasis). And indeed Greene's dissection of pity accords with Mill's own insistence that this individual "cannot rightfully be compelled to do or forbear because it will be better for him to do so, because it will make him happier" (68).[14] Greene, then, accepts the modernists' bloody view of history and sees as its source our continued failure to engage liberally with other human beings. Thus liberal history, in The Ministry of Fear, is revealed to be a myth because of a failure of liberalism: our inability to respect the liberty of other selves.

With such a diagnosis of the maladies of history, the question then arises: can the murderous cycles of history identified by Greene and the modernists actually be broken? On this point, Greene, in The Ministry of Fear at least, remains ambivalent. For while Rowe does come to the insight, cited above, that true value must lie in the integrity of other people's lives, and not in their status as stage props for the self's heroic drama, this truth seems once again forgotten by the novel's conclusion. If the narrator insists that we attend to people, rather than solely to our power over them, Rowe returns to the pitying mode in which he began, driven by "the need to protect [Anna] at any cost" to spare her the fact that he now knows the truth about his past, that he has killed his wife (221). Likewise does she, with "the air of someone perpetually on guard to shield him" (221), withhold this truth from him. Thus the two of them remain part of the "permanent staff" of the "Ministry of Fear" (220), the phrase tellingly used by Johns to describe the novel's fifth columnists (121). In the end, despite the lessons their story might have provided, these characters only repeat that form of paternalism which the novel has been at such pains to condemn. Thus the question of whether this failing, and the modernist history it generates, affords a remedy remains an open one, yet perhaps aptly so. For if this nightmarish history feeds on forgetting qua self-certainty, it is fitting indeed that the novel proffer no certain answer, conveying finally the only message its author would later avow, namely, "fallibility. Doubts" (Donaghy 171).

NOTES

1. While I will, in what follows, take issue with his formulation of Greene's attitudes toward, and indebtedness to, Anglo-American modernism, his book remains a nuanced and compelling case for the importance of these often-neglected works to our understanding of Greene's project as a writer, and as such, is a book long overdue. Indeed, the only other book-length study of Greene's many "entertainments" remains Wolfe's 1972 monograph, Graham Greene, The Entertainer, and Wolfe's text, stressing the Catholicism that may be traced in these novels, their status as tales of "the potential saviour[,] not only a man with a mission [but] also a man on the run" (9), largely elides the generic specificity of these texts, their status as the thrillers they advertise themselves to be. Apart from Wolfe's analysis, these early works have been all too often ignored or treated as of interest solely as they presage the more "serious," Catholic novels to follow. Thus, for example, The Ministry of Fear itself often rates mention as anticipating that exploration of pity more ably undertaken in *The Heart of the Matter* (see, as examples of such cursory treatments, DeVitis 61—64, Atkins 134—38, and Sharrock 151). Such a dismissal of the early "entertainments" as inferior works continues even in most recent Greene scholarship. Thus Mudford, in his 1996 introduction, Graham Greene, ignores the thrillers altogether, and Watts's 1997 Preface to Greene disdains them as "blithely preposterous" and "strained and implausible" (45, 50). In such a critical context, Diemert's cogent argument for the thrillers' role "as part of a widespread response to the literature and criticism of high modernism . . . and to the political, socio-economic, and military crises" of their day (5) is indeed welcome.

2. Diemert's portrait of this "rejection" of high modernism largely accords with the assessment of Stevenson, who argues that the rejection of modernist experiment, in favor of a return to more traditional literary realism, is "one of the clearest trends of the age" (65). Likewise is Gorra "startled by how little [writers of the 30s] owe to

their modernist predecessors" (8). Though less concerned with the question of modernism per se, Johnstone makes a similar claim, when he identifies as the common characteristic of 30s literature "the mixture, often uneasy, of realism and romance" (15). Nor have such judgments been alien to Greene scholarship. Sharrock asserts that Greene has remarkably little connection to the modernist canon, though he does concede "a kind of indirect, diffused modernism" in his work (45), and Miller contends, much like Diemert, that Greene is attracted to the thriller form precisely because it puts him "somewhat at odds with the modernist tradition" (9). As I hope to establish in what follows, such readings ultimately misconstrue the troubled relationship between Greene, at any rate, and what Orwell dubbed "the Joyce-Eliot generation" (511), and do so precisely insofar as they insist on treating modernism as strictly a matter of form rather than as a meditation on the moral significance of Western history.

3. It is worth noting, however, that, as Diemert points out, virtually all of Greene's novels of the 30s can be fruitfully read as "war novels," stressing "the violence and savagery lurking beneath a seeming peace" (117). Adamson concurs, noting how, from the 1932 Stamboul Train "to the end of the decade, war became a constant and complex metaphor in his books" (20). This is, in any event, true of the "entertainments" of the 1930s, as can be seen in A Gun for Sale (1936), a story of a second European war narrowly averted yet still impending, with Greene's England only "safe for a few more years" (242). Here, as O'Prey observes, is a text that would not function without the "atmosphere of expectation" of another war (45). Likewise, *The Confidential Agent* (1939), in its thinly veiled reliance on the history of the Spanish Civil War, also projects war as not only a future but indeed a present, pan-European condition: "You couldn't escape a war by changing your country: you only changed the technique" (44). It is worth noting, as well, that this obsession with the war far outlived, for Greene, its actual duration, such that A World of My Own records his dreams of a Second World War still playing itself out in the 1960s (40-42), and Jones, protagonist of *Doctor Fischer of Geneva*

(1980), is a character still haunted and physically scarred by the London Blitz (11).

4. This is especially true of scholarship on British writers of the 30s. In arguing for these writers' rejection of modernism, such critics commonly define the latter in terms of an elision, not only of historical realities but also of the external world itself. Thus for Stevenson, modernism represents an "exclusiveness of concentration within the envelope of individual consciousness" (16), which writers of the 1930s correct with a renewed focus on political realities and material conditions of life. Likewise, Gorra sees British modernism as subordinating the social world "to the free play of the individual mind" (5), as an entity somehow abstracted from its cultural and historical context. Diemert concurs with this "subjectivist" reading. For him, too, modernism "made individual perception and subjectivity the governing means of representing the world" (33), and thus the move away from modernism in the 1930s sprang, on Diemert's account, from the sense that modernism tended "to negate history and attenuate reality" (31). As I hope to show, however, whatever their concerns for a more acute rendering of inner life, the modernists were above all concerned with this life as it participates in, or indeed is trapped by, historical processes.

5. This claim captures nicely another reading of Anglo-American modernism that still enjoys considerable critical currency, namely that which sees modernism as, above all, concerned with formal concerns and with the aesthetic autonomy of the literary text vis-a-vis the social and political world. This conception of modernism, first put forth in such New Critical assertions as Frank's claim that, in modernist literature, "[w]e are asked only to accept the work of art as an autonomous structure" (59), still resounds through modernist criticism. Thus if Maurice Beebe would, in 1974, follow Frank by defining modernism in terms of "a preoccupation with form" (1072), critics, even after the deconstructionist deluge, have continued, in modernist studies at least, to travel these same New Critical paths. For Levenson, for example, modernism "sought to purge the human, the organic,

the mental, the vital, and insisted instead on the independence and objectivity of form, value and meaning" (102). This formulation dovetails with Schwartz's delineation of "the Modernist creed," with its "emphases on the impersonality of the artist, the 'swift perception of relations,' [and] the autonomy of the text" (51). Similarly, Surette takes as axiomatic "the modernist principle of the autonomy of art" (3), and Berman contends that "[f]ormalism ultimately comes to be the most essential feature of the movement called modernism" (24). As I hope will become clear, this reading is, in my view, an incomplete one, occluding what I deem a definitive modernist concern with history and human affairs.

6. Indeed, it is by focusing on Greene's quarrel with Bloomsbury that these critics, and Cuoto as well, can so cast him in the role of antimodernist. Thus for Diemert, the modernism toward which Greene enacts an "oedipal" rejection (43) seems to entail only the writers of Bloomsbury, especially Woolf and Forster on the one hand, and the elitist literary criticism of the Leavisites on the other (30, 35). So construing modernism, Diemert can then acknowledge Greene's debts to Eliot (19, 38, 41) and to an earlier generation of modernists, including Conrad and Ford Madox Ford (43), while still situating him as part of a generational repudiation of high modernism. A similar pattern is found in Sharrock, who, as noted earlier, sees Greene as antipathetic to the modernists, yet then proceeds, by way of delineating Greene's most important influences, to enumerate what amounts to a modernist canon, including Eliot, Conrad, Joyce, and even Woolf herself (58-72). Cuoto sees this distaste for Bloomsbury as frankly definitive of Greene's work of the 30s, arguing that his putatively nonmodernist use of the thriller form was intended as an open renunciation of the literary practice of Woolf and her circle (216).

7. Indeed, The Ministry of Fear, in its sinister Dr. Forester and its fifth columnist coterie—complete with a philosopher, a critic, a proletarian poet, and an abstract painter (53)—convening for séances on Campden Hill,

may be articulating Greene's animus toward Bloomsbury in an even more caustic fashion.

8. While Greene critics have been reluctant to thrust upon him the mantle of modernism, such connections to earlier modernist writers have not gone unremarked. Thus, for example, Wolfe sees in the character of Stamboul Train's Myatt a figure inspired by Joyce's Bloom, just as his dream sequences are reminiscent of the "Circe" episode of Ulysses (48). In a similar vein, Miller proffers a refreshingly sympathetic reading of Brighton Rock's Ida, suggesting that she is modeled after Joyce's Molly (42). Both DeVitis and Watts concur with Diemert (see note 6) regarding the centrality of Eliot, and of The Waste Land in particular, to the thrillers' rendering of modern urban life (DeVitis 54, Watts 127). Watts also argues for Conrad as perhaps the overriding influence on Greene's work, judging the latter, somewhat uncharitably, "less powerful but enviously and industriously emulous" of the former (124). For an exhaustive and enlightening treatment of this last instance of literary influence, see Pendleton's study of Graham Greene's Conradian Masterplot, which, while insisting that both Conrad and Greene are more firmly rooted "in Victorian realism than other 'high' modernist novelists such as James Joyce and Virginia Woolf' (5), nonetheless sees Greene's entire corpus as tied to Conrad's work, in an attempt to achieve what Pendleton reads as Conrad's fusion of "political, interior and adventure narratives" (25).

9. Joining Smith in this assessment are Cuoto, who sees Greene's depiction of modern, urban England as one "tinged with nostalgia for a lost world which is composed of the ordered certainties of prewar England" (93); Watts, who argues that Greene's work "mourns a fallen world and a defiled beauty" (171); and Silverstein, who sees such nostalgia at the root of Greene's decision to write thrillers, as this genre affords him the opportunity to paint "a world fallen from unity and order into the abyss and chaos" (33). Such sentiments are echoed by Spurling, who identifies in Greene's grim disclosure of the present a longing for a lost world of Victorian security (55), and implicitly by Adamson, who suggests that the final effect

of Greene's rendering of the political crises of the 1930s "is an overwhelming feeling that the individual is at the mercy of an often incomprehensible and increasingly violent historical reality" (22; my emphasis). Such readings miss what I take to be Greene's critique, in his literary work, of just such nostalgia itself, one also made quite forcefully in a 1941 essay in which Greene explodes pastoral romanticism by stressing such rural realities as "the strange incestuous relationships of the very poor, the wife starved to death according to country gossip, the agricultural laborers who lived on credit all the winter through" (Essays 361), precisely those things that, in his view, such conservative nostalgia seeks, through omission, to conserve. In what follows, I hope, in any event, to establish Greene's kinship with a modernism typified not by pining for some Golden Age but by outrage at both past and present.

10. Hesla concurs, reading in Greene's work a treatment of history as inferno, a place where human beings are doomed to repeated suffering. Thus for Hesla, Greene's world "is a place where man ought not to be, or would be better off in being out of; the world, or historical existence, is hell" (104). A similar sense of history as cyclical is identified by Feldman in his reading of the short story, "The Destructors," but unlike Hesla and Friedman, and indeed unlike myself, he sees this cyclicality as tending, in Hegelian fashion, ultimately toward human betterment (243).

11. Thus for Spurling, the novel, through the character of Rowe, only enacts Greene's own nostalgia for a lost Victorian idyll of peace and innocence (28). O'Prey agrees, reading the novel as exemplifying Greene's own persistent elegizing of lost childhood (50), and Cuoto, too, sees the novel as endorsing Rowe's "longing for the past amid the incoherence and chaos of the present" (105). More acute, to my mind, is Diemert's claim that the novel undertakes a critique of the past precisely "because its values have led to the destruction of the war" (160). In any event, as I hope to show, Greene's novel, far from underwriting the nostalgia of its protagonist, instead

implicates this nostalgia itself in the violence, past and present, which it posits as definitive of Western history.

12. It should be noted that this treatment of repression/amnesia makes Greene's analysis of a pathological history in The Ministry of Fear quite different from that proffered by Freud. Despite Pierloot's claim that the novel presents a virtual case study of a mental disturbance remedied by "a regressive process, similar to a therapeutic psychoanalytic process" (35), the novel actually casts a rather critical light on Freudian psychoanalysis; after all, its sole practitioner in the novel is the treacherous Dr. Forester, and it is made clear that Rowe, whether we take him to be ultimately "cured" or not, is never submitted to psychoanalytic treatment (Ministry 110). In any event, Greene's novel departs from the Freudian thesis that neurotic pathology, both in individuals and in cultures, follows the three-step process of past trauma, repression, and the (symptomatic) return of the repressed (Freud 93-95). While Greene's vision of forgetting does, as we shall see, share with Freud's the production of repetition, such repetition occurs in Greene precisely insofar as the present is repressed and the past fetishized. What is required, then, in Greene's articulation of an amnesia more akin to Lyotard's, is not regression but attentiveness to the present and its realities.

13. Such readings of Rowe, and even more so, The Heart of the Matter's Major Scobie, abound, notwithstanding Greene's own insistence that both these novels were intended to demonstrate how "pity can be the expression of an almost monstrous pride" (Ways 101). Thus DeVitis reads Rowe's pity as positive, creating in him "a sense of responsibility which at once sets him apart from his fellow beings and, paradoxically, causes him to love them more for being apart" (61). Grahame Smith concurs, arguing that Rowe's pity becomes an instrument of pain only because of the fallen world in which he is forced to act (51). Far more extravagant claims are made for Scobie, with many critics echoing ErdinastVulcan's assertion that his pity "leads him back to the truest Christian ideal of altruistic love" (53; see also Sharrock 146, Laitinen 176, Cuoto 78, Spurling 37). While such scholarship tends to

lend credence to Pendleton's view that Scobie's status as villain, rather than saint, "is not clear from the novel itself' (1 07), Greene has consistently held to the position that Scobie is an object of critique, rather than emulation, and has himself judged The Heart of the Matter a failure because readers have so vociferously disagreed (Donaghy 95). One can certainly point to the novel's description of this sentiment—"Pity smouldered like decay at his heart" (Heart 170)—and to the model of human relations it entails—after all, Scobie's servant Ali represents, for him, "all he needed of love or friendship" (80)—to raise questions concerning the prevalent reading of a sanctified Scobie. In The Ministry of Fear, in any event, pity figures, as I hope to show, as destructive, not only, as Pierloot notes, a form of aggression (89) but also an emblem of the pathology of the war, and of the history of which it forms a seamless part.

14. It is this outlook that is at the root of the liberalism, or "humanism," so often identified in Greene's work. See, for example, Cuoto 148, DeVitis 41, McEwen 14, and O'Prey 8. Indeed, Adamson even suggests that Rowe's problem is "the moral dilemma of the liberal," bound to look at all sides of an issue (73). While I would argue that Rowe is, through most of the novel, rather blind to others as anything but extensions of himself and thus fails to attain the liberal perspective for which Greene's novel calls, this observation nonetheless points toward what I take to be the heart of Greene's novel.

REFERENCES

Adamson, Judith. *Graham Greene: The Dangerous Edge Where Art and Politics Meet.* New York: St. Martin's, 1990.

Atkins, John. *Graham Greene.* Rev. ed. London: Calder, 1966.

Batchelor, John. *Virginia Woolf: The Major Novels.* Cambridge: Cambridge UP, 1991.

Beebe, Maurice. "What Modernism Was." *Journal of Modern Literature* 3.5 (1974): 1065-84.

Berman, Art. *Preface to Modernism.* Urbana: U of Illinois P, 1994.

Cuoto, Maria. *Graham Greene on the Frontier: Politics and Religion in the Novels.* London: Macmillan, 1988.

DeKoven, Marianne. "History as Suppressed Referent in Modernist Fiction." *ELH* 51.1 (1984): 137-51.

DeVitis, A.A. *Graham Greene.* New York: Twayne, 1964.

Diemert, Brian. *Graham Greene's Thrillers and the 1930s.* Montreal: McGill-Queen's UP, 1996.

Donaghy, Henry J. *Conversations with Graham Greene.* Literary Conversations Series. Jackson: UP of Mississippi, 1992.

Erdinast-Vulcan, Daphna. *Graham Greene's Childless Fathers.* London: Macmillan, 1988.

Evans, Robert O., ed. *Graham Greene: Some Critical Considerations.* Lexington: U of Kentucky P, 1967.

_____. *Introduction.* Evans v-xv.

Eysteinsson, Astradur. *The Concept of Modernism.* Ithaca: Cornell UP, 1990.

Feldman, Hans. "The Idea of History in Graham Greene's 'The Destructors.'" *Studies in Short Fiction* 19.3 (1982): 241-45.

Frank, Joseph. "Spatial Form in Modern Literature." *The Widening Gyre: Crisis and Mastery in Modern Literature.* Ed. Joseph Frank. New Brunswick: Rutgers UP, 1963. 3-62.

Freud, Sigmund. *Moses and Monotheism.* (1939). Trans. Katherine Jones. New York: Vintage, 1967.

Friedman, Alan Warren. "'The Dangerous Edge': Beginning with Death." *Meyers* 131-55.

Fussell, Paul. *The Great War and Modern Memory.* New York: Oxford UP, 1975.

Gorra, Michael. *The English Novel at Mid-Century: From the Leaning Tower.* London: Macmillan, 1990.

Greene, Graham. *Collected Essays.* London: Bodley Head, 1969.

_____. *The Confidential Agent: An Entertainment.* (1939). London: Heinemann, 1961.

_____. *Doctor Fischer of Geneva, or The Bomb Party*. Harmondsworth: Penguin, 1980.

_____. *A Gun For Sale*. (1936). London: Heinemann, 1961.

_____. *The Heart of the Matter*. (1948). Harmondsworth: Penguin, 1968.

_____. *The Ministry of Fear: An Entertainment*. (1943). Harmondsworth: Penguin, 1985.

_____. *Ways of Escape*. n.p.: Lester & Orpen Dennys, 1980.

_____. *A World of My Own: A Dream Diary*. Toronto: Knopf, 1992.

Hesla, David H. "Theological Ambiguity in the 'Catholic Novels.'" *Evans* 96-111.

Johnstone, Richard. *The Will to Believe: Novelists of the Nineteen-Thirties*. Oxford: Oxford UP, 1982.

Joyce, James. *Ulysses: Student's Edition*. (1922). Ed. Hans Walter Gabler et al. Pref. Richard Ellmann. Harmondsworth: Penguin, 1987.

Laitinen, Kai. "The Heart of the Novel: The Turning Point in The Heart of the Matter." *Evans* 169-80.

Lentricchia, Frank. *Modernist Quartet*. Cambridge: Cambridge UP, 1994.

Levenson, Michael H. *A Genealogy of Modernism: A Study of English Literary Doctrine, 1908-1922*. Cambridge: Cambridge UP, 1984.

Lyotard, Jean-Francois. *Heidegger and "The Jews."* Trans. Andreas Michael and Mark Roberts. Intro. David Carroll. Minneapolis: U of Minnesota P, 1990.

McEwen, Neil. *Graham Greene*. Macmillan Modem Novelists. London: Macmillan, 1988.

Meisel, Perry. *The Myth of the Modern: A Study in British Literature and Criticism after 1850*. New Haven: Yale UP, 1987.

Meyers, Jeffrey, ed. *Graham Greene, A Revaluation: New Essays*. New York: St. Martin's, 1990.

Mill, John Stuart. *On Liberty*. Ed. and Intro. Gertrude Himmelfarb. London: Penguin, 1988.

Miller, R.H. *Understanding Graham Greene*. Columbia: U of South Carolina P, 1990.

Mudford, Peter. *Graham Greene. Writers and their Work Series*. Plymouth: Northcote, 1996.

Nicholls, Peter. *Modernisms: A Literary Guide*. Berkeley: U of California P, 1995.

O'Prey, Paul. *A Reader's Guide to Graham Greene*. Worcester: Thames and Hudson, 1988.

Orwell, George. *The Collected Essays, Journalism and Letters of George Orwell*, Volume One: *An Age Like This, 1920-1940*. Ed. Sonia Orwell and Ian Angus. New York: Harcourt, 1968.

Pendleton, Robert. *Graham Greene's Conradian Masterplot: The Arabesques of Influence*. London: Macmillan, 1996.

Pierloot, Roland A. *Psychoanalytic Patterns in the Work of Graham Greene*. Psychoanalysis and Culture Series. Amsterdam: Rodopi, 1994.

Quinones, Ricardo J. *Mapping Literary Modernism: Time and Development*. Princeton: Princeton UP, 1985.

Schwartz, Sanford. *The Matrix of Modernism: Pound, Eliot and Early Twentieth-Century Thought*. Princeton: Princeton UP, 1985.

Sharrock, Roger. *Saints, Sinners and Comedians: The Novels of Graham Greene*. Notre Dame: U of Notre Dame P, 1984.

Silverstein, Marc. "After the Fall: The World of Graham Greene's Thrillers." *Novel: A Forum on Fiction* 22.1 (1988): 24-44.

Smith, Grahame. *The Achievement of Graham Greene*. Brighton: Harvester, 1986.

Smith, Rowland. "A People's War in Greeneland: Heroic Virtue and Communal Effort in the Wartime Tales." *Meyers* 104-30.

Spurling, John. *Graham Greene. Contemporary Writers Series*. London: Methuen, 1983.

Stevenson, Randall. *The British Novel Since the Thirties: An Introduction*. Athens: U of Georgia P, 1986.

Surette, Leon. *The Birth of Modernism: Ezra Pound*, T.S. Eliot, W.B. Yeats, and the Occult. Montreal: McGill-Queen's UP, 1993.

Watts, Cedric. *A Preface to Greene*. London: Longman, 1997.

Webster, Harvey Curtis. "The World of Graham Greene." *Evans* 1-24.

Wolfe, Peter. *Graham Greene, The Entertainer*. Pref. Harry T. Moore. Carbondale: Southern Illinois UP, 1972.

Woolf, Virginia. *Jacob's Room*. (1922). Harmondsworth: Penguin, 1968.

_____. *Three Guineas*. (1938). Harmondsworth: Penguin, 1982.

4

Greene, Tolkien and the Mysterious Relations of Realism and Fantasy

—Thomas A. Wendorf

If realist Graham Greene could draw criticism that his works were products of his own psychological distortion, a projected "Greeneland" (Ways of Escape 60), it is no wonder that, as Tom Shippey has recently pointed out, J.R.R. Tolkien's fantasy The Lord of the Rings has provoked shrill criticism from the literary academy because, as a work of fantasy, it is "intrinsically less truthful than realistic fiction," and so presumably forfeits serious critical consideration (327). Writing in 1961, C.S. Lewis zeroes in on the problem: "The dominant taste at present demands realism of content" (Experiment 60). Lewis helpfully distinguishes between "Realism of Presentation—the art of bringing something close to us, making it palpable and vivid, by sharply observed or sharply imagined detail" (57)—and "realism of content," which demands that fiction be "probable or `true to life'" (59). As Lewis and Shippey rightly imply, there's something mistaken in upholding strict realism of content as the test for literary worth, particularly since such realism is a relatively recent development in literary history. There is also something mistaken in denying fantasy any claims to truthfulness.

Writing such different kinds of fiction, Greene and Tolkien might seem odd literary bedfellows. However—both English, both Roman Catholic, both writing over long careers during the 20th century—Greene and Tolkien, in their fiction and other writing, suggest that realism and fantasy, often contentiously opposed in critical debate, have more complex relations and can effect similar truths. Because Greene's The Power and the Glory and Tolkien's The Lord of the Rings both effect a vision of the world governed by divine imperatives, the divide they might represent between realism and fantasy becomes less precise, insofar as both works embody mythic dimensions, both suggesting the kind of revelatory power that theologian David Tracy ascribes to religious classics:

> To enter the conversation of religious classics through real interpretation, therefore, is to enter a disclosure of a world of meaning and truth offering no certainty but promising some realized experience of the whole by the power of the whole. That world affords no technically controlled comprehensibility yet it does release the self to the uncontrollable incomprehensibility of an experience of radical mystery. (177)[1]

The Power and the Glory and The Lord of the Rings, the masterpieces of their respective authors, arguably suggest in their different literary approaches the kind of paradoxical disclosing and concealing "of the whole of reality by the power of the whole" and that essential oneness of morality, mystery, and reality that Tracy attributes to religious classics (163). As Greene and Tolkien together suggest, placing realism and fantasy on opposite ends of a continuum of truthfulness (and by direct implication, on a similar continuum of literary merit) is a move that ignores realism's relations with fantasy and downplays fiction's power to reveal mystery through a mythic dimension. The surface similarities between Tolkien's trilogy and Greene's novel are striking, and here for a moment we take that view from a distance that Northrop Frye describes as the vantage point from which we can best see the archetypal organization of a work (140). Both the whisky priest and the ring-bearer are reluctant heroes whose journeys lead them where they had not intended to go but where they find they are compelled to go by their sense of calling, the priest because he is a priest, Frodo because he is the ring-bearer. Frodo often moves forward, particularly in the realms of Mount Doom, without hope, and the whisky priest, even when he has accepted martyrdom over escape, has little hope for his own salvation or much conviction that his death will prove honorable in the eyes of God or others.

Both journeyers also become swallowed in landscapes marked by heat, filth, desolation, and danger (Frodo through the marshes and vast, decimated territory of Mordor, the whisky priest in the harsh land of Tabasco and amid human squalor—a trash heap where he encounters his daughter, the jail where he finds communion with fellow sinners, among the great crosses and in the bitter rain as he approaches the state border). Both are pursued, Frodo by every power allied with Sauron, the whisky priest by the lieutenant and soldiers. Both with some reluctance show mercy to figures who betray them (Frodo to Smeagol/Gollum and the whisky priest to the yellow-fanged mestizo), and this mercy proves crucial in both stories to the success of the journeyers (Smeagol/Gollum completes the destruction of the ring when Frodo wavers; the whisky priest makes his extraordinary decision to give up his life only after receiving the Yankee fugitive's scrawled note from the mestizo). Finally, both of their journeys involve a renunciation of power—Frodo gives up the Ring, and the whisky priest gives up his life. Within the narratives both become a part of stories foretold and told later (Frodo's role is prophesied, and his providential success becomes the stuff of Middle-Earth history and song; the whisky priest's life ironically becomes the story of a Catholic martyr/saint).

These parallels of their journeys, of course, exist amid great conceptual and aesthetic differences. Greene's priest is a figure living very much in what Tolkien calls the "Primary" or actual world, and this is the most crucial difference between the two works; it marks the aesthetic divide between realism of content and fantasy. Even if Greene creates what some critics have, in various ways, called "Greeneland," even if he unavoidably projects his own psychology onto his scene, he is still representing early twentieth-century Mexico. Greene's represented world is also explicitly and historically shaped by Christianity. His whisky priest is, as R.W.B. Lewis puts it, a rogue whose particular sins as a priest (habitual drinking, begetting a child) emerge in all their mundane humanity amid other sins equally human but more theological (pride, despair). As such, he is unlike the Halfling Frodo whose moral character is more exclusively figured in terms of how he deals with the Ring and his role as ring-bearer. The whisky priest journeys mostly alone while Frodo almost always has a companion. The sacraments of the Catholic Church have an explicit place in Greene's novel, as does worship and a more general sense that God works through nature; Tolkien's creatures in The Lord of the Rings, while the most noble among them allude to the presence of a benevolent and omnipotent Providence and sometimes show prayer-like reverence, are not religious in any modern sense of the word and do not engage in explicit worship.

Clearly there is no magic in Greene's novel, nothing fantastic in the sense of overt supernatural action, though the sacraments are certainly fantastic to those who don't believe in them; the lieutenant certainly sees them as bogus. The evil the priest encounters is always ordinary human evil—use of power to dominate others, egotism, lust, gluttony, nihilism, merciless accusation, pride, greed, sensuality—and Greene represents all of these with his characteristic ambiguity. The nihilistic lieutenant is motivated by a desire to help the poor and sometimes shows mercy to match that of the whisky priest; the pious woman in prison judges the sexual intercourse of the inmates, while the whisky priest recognizes a possible goodness in it and the worse sin in her pious judgments. On the other hand, Tolkien's most evil creatures in The Lord of the Rings—Sauron, the Orcs, the Nazgul—seem more purely and irredeemably so, though Elrond, implying the goodness of creation and the larger mythic history out of which the trilogy grows, emphasizes that "nothing is evil in the beginning. Even Sauron was not so" (261).

Graham Greene, in fact, could imagine pure evil in the world, although his fiction has always proved more ambiguous and complex here than his extra-fictional commentary might suggest. By his own account, he first experienced literature's power to reveal the nature of reality and particularly the mystery of evil in a historical romance, Marjorie Bowen's The Viper of Milan (1906). Greene famously claims, "[Bowen] had given me my pattern—religion might later explain it to me in other terms, but the pattern was already there—perfect evil walking the world where perfect good can never walk again, and only the pendulum ensures that after all in the end justice is done" ("The Lost Childhood," Essays 17). Greene found Bowen's historical romance true to life because it mirrored his already acute sense of the human capacity for evil.

In Greene's earliest sense of realism, mystery and the fantastic were already important. Biographer Norman Sherry has well noted Greene's early attraction to fantasy not only in his reading but also in his writing (Volume I 113). In 1922 Greene wrote a story for the school newspaper

The Berkhamstedian tellingly titled "The Tyranny of Realism," an allegorical story that suggests a reconciliation between "Fantasie" and "Realism." In it a boy, bound before the throne of King Realism, sees a sad maiden named "Fantasie" at the King's feet. After bewailing the King for taking away his "unknown country of dark caves and hidden ways, and sun-splashed woods" and for keeping the boy's love, "Fantasie," a slave, the King, with a "little, whimsical smile" instructs the boy to try his bonds. The bonds disappear, the King takes him to the throne, and the walls around them disappear, exposing "great, dark rolling plains, and the star-encrusted sky." In the final moment of the story, the boy sinks to his knees before the King, whose face is "the face of a God," and the boy sees that King Realism looks not at him but at Fantasie, who has taken her place on a throne beside the king. Realism and Fantasie kiss "in a long passion of joy" (2-3). Sherry perceptively suggests that "the allegory is probably a pointer to Graham's hope that because he felt he must in the future write in a more realistic vein it did not mean (as clearly he had feared) that his fantastic imaginings could not also flourish" (Volume I 114). Greene's boyhood story reflects not only a reluctance to sacrifice fantasy to realism but also a desire to unite them.

Greene continued to dabble with fantasy during his long literary career. Characters recalling haunting childhood memories often provided the realistic frame for such forays. In the short story "The Hint of an Explanation" (1948), a provocative childhood encounter with a pitiful, evil-bent, anti-Catholic baker changes the life of the story's central figure. In "Under the Garden" (1963), a childhood "fantasy" narrative, a "memory" of a visit to two strange people living underground becomes a compelling, if ambiguous, reflection of truth and mystery for the terminally ill main character Wilditch. Even in his last novel The Captain and the Enemy (1988), Greene teases us with an ambiguously allegorical father figure dubbed "the Devil," suggesting that Greene's interest in the fantastic never died, even if he would only present these dimensions under the garb of irony and in a realistic frame, leaving the nature and imperatives of mystery ambiguous.

Graham Greene, of course, is not primarily a fantasy writer, but he did have a religious vision that found literary expression after his conversion to Roman Catholicism in 1926, particularly in the string of novels explicitly dealing with Catholic themes of sin and salvation, good and evil—Brighton Rock (1938), The Power and the Glory (1940), The Heart of the Matter (1948), and The End of the Affair (1951). Because Greene's realism here includes that wider reality embraced by Catholic belief, involving both the natural and the supernatural, the seen and the unseen, it already exceeds the limits of naturalism or radical realism. Given its theological dimension, Greene's explicitly religious fiction might seem fantastic, might even seem to fit C.S. Lewis's broad definition of literary fantasy: "any narrative that deals with impossibles and preternaturals" (Experiment 50).

But Greene's commitment to referential narrative placed even his explicitly religious fiction in a more realistic mode with its own challenges. Catholic writer Flannery O'Connor recognized well the difficulty that Christian writers like Greene and herself faced in writing for an increasingly secular audience:

> The problem of the novelist who wishes to write about a man's encounter with . . . God is how he shall make the experience—which is both natural and supernatural—understandable, and credible, to his reader. In any age this would be a problem, but in our own, it is a well-nigh insurmountable one. (Mystery and Manners 161)

In his realism of content, Greene rises to the challenge that O'Connor describes. Though always heterodox and doubtful in a way that O'Connor was not (Greene's fiction and life, even by his own account, attest to this), Greene still reveals in his explicitly Catholic fiction a similar gritty sacramentality, a stubborn sense that nature and human nature are the privileged sites in which and through which any kind of divine grace works. Indeed, he was rarely heavy-handed in his narration, rarely overleapt the human and the natural to get to the divine dimension.[2] His works often suggest, amid great suffering and absurdities, eternal possibilities and consequences for human action, a dramatic effect he praised in Henry James and found lacking in Virginia Woolf and Somerset Maugham. But as it was with Henry James, Greene's treatment of the spiritual dimension is subtle and grounded in the physical and psychological dimensions of character and place. Few would mistake Greene for a fantasy writer even in C.S. Lewis's terms—indeed the "preternatural" is rarely laid bare in his fiction and virtually all that he represents is wonderfully and terribly possible in the actual world. While Greene was writing The Power and the Glory in 1939, Tolkien was beginning painstaking work on his own masterpiece, one set not in twentieth-century Brighton, Mexico, Sierra Leone, or war-ravaged London, but in Middle-Earth. While Greene's aesthetic emphasis involved realism of content, Tolkien's was decidedly different from the start.[3] In his essay "On Fairy-Stories," originally written for a 1938 lecture, Tolkien describes many of his own aesthetic aspirations. Like his Oxford colleague and friend C.S. Lewis, Tolkien defended fantasy against dismissal by prevailing champions of realism of content. Fantasy, he first explains, is etymologically and semantically connected with the "fantastic." Both involve "images of things that are not only `not actually present,' but which are indeed not to be found in our primary world at all, or are generally believed not to be found there" (67). He then describes fantasy as a "form of Art" that represents a "Secondary World" as opposed to our "actual" or "Primary World," a form of Art remarkable for its "arresting strangeness" and inherent challenges for the writer (67-68). Fantasy and realism were not mutually exclusive modes of writing for Tolkien. They were, by necessity, mutually related: fantasy demands an "inner consistency of reality" and that inner consistency "is more difficult to produce, the more unlike are the images and the rearrangements of primary material to the actual arrangements of the Primary World" (68). In other words, the secondary worlds of fantasy demand their own realism of presentation. Tolkien argues, for example, that it is particularly difficult to create a credible Secondary World in which a "green sun" is not only imaginable but also believable. So if fantasy and the fantastic involve "freedom from the domination of observed `fact'" (67), artistically they demand their own internal realism to achieve what Tolkien calls "Secondary Belief" in both the designer and the spectator, the writer and the reader, what Tolkien rightly identifies as a function of all Art.

Yet even in distinguishing the images of Primary and Secondary worlds, Tolkien hints at their aesthetic and analogical relationship. Fantasy, he implies, is inescapably linked to the Primary world, for it is an "art which plays strange tricks with the world and all that is in it" ("On Fairy-Stories" 71). While this art in some sense re-imagines "the world and all that is in it" so that its images are strangely unlike the world, the likeness, the other half of analogy, nonetheless remains. Privileging both the freedom and challenges of fantasy, Tolkien also parenthetically suggests that fantasy is not detached from the Primary world at all: "That the images [of fantasy and the fantastic] are of things not in the primary world (if that indeed is possible) is a virtue not a vice" (67). Every image of fantasy, he implies, has an imaginative footing in the Primary World, a claim consistent with Tolkien's belief that long-enduring words can lead us back, in their etymology, to concepts that once existed but have since vanished (Shippey xiv). So Tolkien reveals that, while fantasy and realism of content are clearly distinguished by the worlds they treat (Secondary versus Primary), good fantasy answers its own demands for realism, and the Primary world is ever related by analogy and the referentiality of language itself.

The literary bias toward realism of content that Lewis recognized in the 1960s arguably endures in the early twenty-first century. As it was then, the bias is an academic rather than a popular one. In fact, both Joseph Pearce and Tom Shippey have outlined well the recent public polls that place The Lord of the Rings as the greatest book of the twentieth century.[4] Professional critics and university professors have responded quite differently, finding troubling implications in such popular adulation of a work of fantasy (Shippey xxi). Critic Germaine Greer's recent commentary on such popular polls sums up their dismay: "The books that come in Tolkien's train are more or less what you would expect; flight from reality is their dominating characteristic" (qtd. in Shippey xxii). In the 1930s Tolkien already knew well the scornful charge that fairy-stories, fantasy, science fiction, and their creators are—because they depart from realism of content—escapist by nature. Convinced that "Escape" was, in fact, sometimes the more practical or even heroic action in both art and literature, Tolkien suggests in "On Fairy-Stories" that critical denunciations of literary escapism are often fundamentally flawed, if not also disingenuous:

> Why should a man be scorned, if, finding himself in prison, he tries to get out and go home? Or if, when he cannot do so, he thinks and talks about other topics than jailers and prison-walls? The world outside has not become less real because the prisoner cannot see it. In using Escape in this way, the critics have chosen the wrong word, and, what is more, they are confusing, not always by sincere

> error, the Escape of the Prisoner with the Flight of the Deserter. ("On Fairy-Stories" 76)

Aesthetically, realism of content proved a prison for Tolkien, and he found his way of escape in fantasy, much as Greene found his in global wanderlust and the realistic works that grew out of it. To distinguish among kinds of escape (from what, into what?) might be a good antidote against unquestioned literary biases. As it is, realism of content remains a litmus test for literary worth in much of the academy, certainly when it comes to literature written since the end of the nineteenth century. The attendant denigration of fantasy is regrettable, for the more interesting literary picture involves both fantasy and realism and their mutual relations, relations Greene and Tolkien recognized in their common respect for myth. In a 1963 interview with Frank Kermode, Greene himself situates The Power and the Glory in the realms of myth:

> My own wish always is to produce a central figure who represents some idea of reasonable simplicity, a mythical figure, if you like. And the simplicity often gets damaged by plot making . . . I would like to ascend into myth, but find my boots so often muddy with plot. My own feeling is that the nearest I came to hitting the mythical element was in The Power and the Glory, where I feel the plot was sufficiently simple for the main purpose of this story to remain clear throughout. (qtd. in Cassis 157)

Greene's whisky priest achieves a mythic dimension in a journey shadowed by impending capture and death. He reveals his ultimate integrity and achieves a kind of redemptive efficacy for others only when he rejects escape to the comfortable complacency that priestly life outside of Tabasco would mean, only when he accepts self-sacrifice for the sake of a criminal and his own vocation. Frodo

Baggins must likewise leave the deceptive security of the Shire, just as, when he has accepted the burden of being ring-bearer, he must eventually leave Rivendell and Lothlorien and, finally, the reclaimed Shire as well. He, too, journeys under the shadow of death and moves toward a doom that is paradoxically his and his world's only hope. As Jane Chance has noted well, Frodo goes not to obtain knowledge or gifts but "to divest himself (and the world) of this power" of the Ring (32).

On their journeys, both Frodo and the whisky priest discover who they are and what they live for, and the dramatic effect of both journeys suggests the kind of disclosure that David Tracy associates with religious classics—"that how we ought to live is grounded in reality itself" (164). In particular, mercy and self-sacrifice resonate with the very nature of Providence ("the power of the whole" and the ground of reality) implied in both works, suggesting, as many critics have already noted, the Christian dimensions of both works.

In disclaiming both topical and allegorical dimensions to his trilogy in the "Foreword to the Second Edition" of The Lord of the Rings, Tolkien places his aesthetic priority on freedom for the reader, versus what he saw as the author's "purposeful domination" through allegory (xvii). His aesthetic is consonant with the dramatic effect of The Lord of the Rings, in which domination of others through the use of power emerges as the epitome of evil (the same could be said of Greene, for whom treachery was also a definitive aspect of evil). In speaking of myth in a 1951 letter to publisher Milton Waldman, Tolkien emphasizes a similar need for care in writing modern myths: "Myth and fairy-story must, as all art, reflect and contain in solution elements of moral and religious truth (or error), but not explicit, not in the known form of the primary `real' world" (Letters 144). Describing The Lord of the Rings as "coming down from myth and legend to the earth"

(Letters 160), Tolkien also recognized it as an essentially religious story. As his now famous 1953 letter to Robert Murray, S.J. attests:

> The Lord of the Rings is of course a fundamentally religious and Catholic work; unconsciously so at first, but consciously so in the revision. That is why I have not put in, or have cut out, practically all references to anything like 'religion,' to cults or practices, in the imaginary world. For the religious element is absorbed into the story and the symbolism. However that is very clumsily put, and sounds more self-important than I feel. (Letters 172)

While Greene's novel explicitly treats Christian mysteries, any particularly Christian elements of myth are only implied in The Lord of the Rings, for Tolkien's represented world is indeed pre-Christian, though its genesis obviously is not. Frodo's journey certainly reveals the presence of a governing, if inscrutable, loving Providence and the privileging of mercy indicative of the Christian myth. Gandalf helps to shape Frodo's later behavior toward Gollum by his early admonition:

> I have not much hope that Gollum can be cured before he dies, but there is a chance of it. And he is bound up with the fate of the Ring. My heart tells me that he has some part to play yet, for good or for ill, before the end; and when that comes, the pity of Bilbo may rule the fate of many—yours not the least. (58)

Pity and mercy are bound up with "fate" and Providence in the wisdom of Gandalf, and so, too, is the notion of Gollum's possible if unlikely "cure." Gandalf implies that Elrond's later words are true, that nothing begins as evil, so that Gandalf's advice "not to strike without need" is consistent with his view of the Power that governs the world. Likewise, Greene's whisky priest, recognizing the mestizo as "Judas," must also admit that

> at the centre of his own faith there always stood the convincing mystery—that we were made in God's image. God was parent, but He was also the policeman, the criminal, the priest, the maniac, the judge . . . and God's image shook now up and down on the mule's back, with the yellow teeth sticking out over the lower lip. (101)

The mestizo, too, he believes against belief, was made in the image and likeness of God, and even when he is actually being betrayed, the priest pities the betrayer for the sin he commits: "It was really shocking bad luck for the poor devil that he was to be burdened with a sin of such magnitude . . . Poor man, the priest thought, he isn't really bad enough . . ." (184). Mercy and pity are consonant with the Christian imperatives that the whisky priest accepts and that Greene's overall narrative suggests as true. Not only imagining but acting on mysteriously motivated mercy, the whisky priest, against his own self-recognition as the worst of sinners, follows the pattern of Christ. Placing the whisky priest in the picaresque tradition as "the rogue . . . on his undignified flights from and toward the forces of destruction," R.W.B. Lewis was one of the earliest to recognize the nature of Greene's success at capturing the "paradoxes of sainthood" (249). The whisky priest's mythical association with Christ—a servant of the poor, betrayed by a Judas figure into the hands of authorities and executed as a criminal, whose death suggests halting elements of redemption and resurrection—might have betrayed the artistic integrity of the novel for the sake of the pattern, a danger that Tolkien connected with allegory. But, as R.W.B. Lewis suggests, while the pattern here is mythic in its movement, perhaps bordering on allegory, "it is nevertheless artistically redeemed by a full awareness of the grotesque disproportion between the model and its re-enactment" (258). While for Tolkien the mythic dimension of The Lord of the Rings, a modern fantasy, demanded for its integrity a distancing from any explicit religious elements, for Greene the mythic dimension of The Power and the Glory, a work of modern Christian realism,[5] demanded a different kind of distance—a represented distance between the myth and what is, between Christ and followers of Christ; in effect, realism of content.

Indeed, in the early scene in the novel in which the pious woman reads modern stories of saints' lives to her children, she bristles at the thought that the "whisky priest," whom the family briefly harbored, could ever be a holy martyr like those in the stories She worries to her husband:

> ". . . the boy—he asks such questions—about that whisky priest. I wish we had never had him in the house."
>
> "They would have caught him if we hadn't, and then he would have been one of your martyrs. They would write a book about him and you would read it to the children."
>
> "That man—never."
>
> "Well, after all," her husband said, "he carries on. I don't believe all that they write in these books. We are all human." (28)

The husband proves more accurate in his reading of characters and stories insofar as the whisky priest does become a martyr, and, to their son, a more believable one. To the husband, the sanitized stories his wife reads are unrealistic; to the boy they are boring and inaccessible.

The whisky priest simply does not fit the pattern, and here lies both his credibility as a character and his paradoxical efficacy as a mythical figure. Frodo, on the other hand, has no Christian pattern to follow or against which to be measured. When he agonizes to Gandalf, "I am not made for perilous quests. I wish I had never seen the Ring! Why did it come to me? Why was I chosen?" Gandalf can only reply, "Such questions cannot be answered . . . You may be sure that it was not for any merit that others do not possess: not for power or wisdom, at any rate. But you have been chosen, and you must therefore use such strength and heart and wits as you have" (60). Frodo is an unlikely figure for such a "perilous quest," but he must mark out a new path. He is called, and called evidently by the same power Gandalf alludes to in connection with Bilbo's discovery of the Ring: "Behind that there was something else at work, beyond any design of the Ring-maker. I can put it no plainer than by saying that Bilbo was meant to find the Ring, and not by its maker. In which case you also were meant to have it. And that may be an encouraging thought" (55). Bilbo's journey led him to adventures and treasures, including the Ring; Frodo's journey takes on a completely different focus. Frodo speaks the truth when he accepts the quest to destroy the Ring: "I will take the Ring . . . though I do not know the way" (264).

As Gandalf anticipates, the Enemy can imagine only his own self-serving pattern: "the only measure that he knows is desire, desire for power; and so he judges all hearts. Into his heart the thought will not enter that any will refuse it, that having the Ring we may seek to destroy it. If we seek this, we shall put him out of reckoning" (262). In concurring, Elrond notes the inscrutability of the road ahead and suggests that the ring-bearer cannot rely on the usual creaturely powers in the face of such peril:

> "The road must be trod, but it will be very hard. And neither strength nor wisdom will carry us far upon it. This quest may be attempted by the weak with as much hope as the strong. Yet such is oft the course of deeds that move the wheels of the world: small hands do them because they must, while the eyes of the great are elsewhere" (262).

Elrond's observation about the "small" anticipates the Christian paradox of strength in weakness that both Frodo and the whisky priest prove true. But, rejecting the notion that Frodo is a "type" of Christ, Tom Shippey rightly notes that Frodo has "no supernatural dimension at all" and promises no soul-salvation (209). The evocative power of Frodo's journey, Shippey admits, offers, as does the trilogy as a whole, "hints of the Christian message" but the overall narrative "refuses just to repeat" that message (210). In refusing to impose the Christian pattern (or any mythic pattern) and in dramatically revealing the gap between creaturely efforts and Providential power, Tolkien suggests an aesthetic and moral impulse surprisingly similar to Greene's, considering their crucial differences. For both writers, the integrity of realism and myth demanded such distance and difference. Indeed, the debate over what constitutes reality drives the dramatic action of Greene's novel. The whisky priest's belief in the power of the sacraments, particularly the Eucharist, remains unwavering, despite his sense of his own moral failure: "Now that he no longer despaired it didn't mean, of course, that he wasn't damned—it was simply that after a time the mystery became too great, a damned man putting God into the mouths of men: an odd sort of servant, that, for the devil" (60). And when he does seem to despair even over the Eucharist, it is despair over the capacity of the beleaguered faith to endure among the people. Witnessing the anger and hopelessness of Maria, the mother of his daughter Brigitta, "[he] was aware of faith dying out between the bed and the door—the Mass would soon mean no more to anyone than a black cat crossing the path. He was risking all their lives for the sake of spilt salt or a crossed finger" (80). What he imagines here is the kind of spiritual desolation that the lieutenant wishes to achieve, one that accurately reflects the quagmire of human suffering in Mexico. The lieutenant's view is purely political and physical:

> It infuriated him to think that there were still people in the state who believed in a loving and merciful God. There are mystics who are said to have experienced God directly. He was a mystic, too, and what he had experienced was vacancy—a complete certainty in the existence of a dying, cooling world, of human beings who had evolved from animals for no purpose at all. He knew. (24-25)

Convinced that the Church is perpetuating fantastic lies about human existence and driven by a hatred of priestly power and hypocrisy originating in his childhood, the lieutenant demonstrates a religious intensity in his nihilism as he considers the poor village children:[6]

> [I]t was for these he was fighting. He would eliminate from their childhood everything which had made him miserable, all that was poor, superstitious, and corrupt. They deserved nothing less than the truth—a vacant universe and a cooling world, the right to be happy in any way they chose. He was quite prepared to make a massacre for their sakes—first the Church and then the foreigner and then the politician—even his own chief would one day have to go. He wanted to begin the world again with them, in a desert. (58)

The visions of the lieutenant and the whisky priest differ essentially in their view of what reality is. The lieutenant's vision is atheistic, nihilistic, and, in its insistence on "a cooling world" and on "human beings who had evolved from animals for no purpose at all," naturalistic.[7] To the lieutenant, Christianity is a destructive fantasy propped up by a self-interested priesthood. The whisky priest, on the other hand, still believes in spiritual imperatives and eternal consequences. In an essay written during the late 1930s, Greene criticizes Somerset Maugham for his shallow characters, attributing their failure to Maugham's agnosticism. Aligning his aesthetics and religious belief, Greene asserts: "Rob human beings of their heavenly and their infernal importance, and you rob your characters of their individuality" (154). Greene's own realism, particularly before 1952, explicitly reflects this larger spiritual scope that includes but extends beyond what Virginia Woolf referred to as "the dark places of psychology" (152), and what Greene insisted were the real details—physical, social, political—of place. And so, in the famous prison scene that marks the center of The Power and the Glory, the whisky priest's consciousness and words reflect his conviction that the world, epitomized in his mind by the prison itself, "overcrowded with lust and crime and unhappy love" is nonetheless loved by God:

> He was moved by an irrational affection for the inhabitants of this prison. A phrase came to him: "God so loved the world . . . "He said, "My children, you must never think the holy martyrs are like me. You have a name for me. Oh, I've heard you use it before now. I am a whisky priest" (127).

Stripped bare of all pretension, he "had a sense of companionship which he had never experienced in the old days when pious people came kissing his black cotton glove" (128). Characteristically, Greene's representation of faith is credible because it comes to us through his character's troubled perceptions, uncertainties, and longings. The conversation between the whisky priest and the lieutenant near the end of the novel is perhaps the most telling illustration of what is at stake in Greene's realism and how that realism opens into mystery. When the lieutenant argues that religious people rationalize about suffering and suggests that the suffering in the world negates any claim he might make that "God is love," the whisky priest answers, "Oh . . . that's another thing altogether—God is love. I don't say the heart doesn't feel a taste of it, but what a taste. The smallest glass of love mixed with a pint pot of ditch-water. We wouldn't recognize that love. It might even look like hate" (200). If he emphasizes elsewhere the immanence of God among the suffering people, the whisky priest here stresses the difference between human love and God's love—the lieutenant, he suggests, errs in believing that God's love shows clearly in the people around him. The priest goes on, "It would be enough to scare us—God's love. It set fire to a bush in the desert, didn't it, and smashed open graves and set the dead walking in the dark. Oh, a man like me would run a mile to get away if he felt that love around" (200). The priest's rendering of salvation history suggests the poignant description of mythology that C.S. Lewis's hero Ransom apprehends at the end of the novel Perelandra: "gleams of celestial strength and beauty falling on a jungle of filth and imbecility" (201). The priest underscores the otherness of that love which he believes paradoxically entered the mire of human experience in the person of Christ, becoming radically immanent.

It is a love that demands human decision, and so the whisky priest earnestly explains to the lieutenant,

> I'm not as dishonest as you think I am. Why do you think I tell people out of the pulpit that they're in danger of damnation if death catches them unawares? I'm not telling them fairy stories I don't believe myself. I don't know how awful the human heart looks to Him. But I do know this—that if

> there's ever been a single man in this state damned, then I'll be damned too . . . I wouldn't want it to be any different. I just want justice, that's all. (200)

Suggesting that some fairy stories indeed call for belief and reveal, as Tolkien argues, truth, the whisky priest imagines himself as the lowest of sinners and demands his own damnation as an act of justice should anyone else in the ravaged state be damned. He has already prayed a similar prayer for his daughter on the rubbish heap: "O God, give me any kind of death—without contrition, in a state of sin—only save this child" (82). While his offering of his soul as a sacrifice for others resembles that of Greene's later and pitiful character of Scobie in The Heart of the Matter, it also echoes the mystery of Christ's suffering and death. The whisky priest follows the pattern of Christ in his self-sacrifice for others, even as his moral transgressions and ruthless self-awareness keep him from ever imagining himself a holy martyr, let alone a modern figure of Christ. Though A.A. DeVitis has argued that the whisky priest finally emerges less as a Catholic hero and more as a champion of the individual, "an important figure in contemporary mythology" (Bloom 84) in a novel that is "a consistent allegory on the theme of Everyman" (DeVitis 77), the culmination of the narrative points toward the Christian myth as the more fundamental context for interpretation, a context that ultimately includes "Everyman." DeVitis, contending that Greene's whisky priest, as an Everyman, helps the novel transcend "its narrowly Roman Catholic" identification, responds to the notion that Roman Catholic belief narrows experience for both reader and writer. But considered both aesthetically and ontologically, Greene's effected vision implies just the opposite. Flannery O'Connor makes the point well: "the chief difference between the novelist who is an orthodox Christian and the novelist who is merely a naturalist is that the Christian novelist lives in a larger universe. He believes that the natural world contains the supernatural.

And this doesn't mean that his obligation to portray the natural is less; it means it is greater" (M&M 175). Greene's realism, reflected in the whisky priest and counter to the realism of the lieutenant, has the wider scope, for it suggests the influence of the unseen on the seen and reveals the potent mercy of Christ, in word, in sacrament, in acts of mercy and self-sacrifice, amid the wreckage of human weakness and egotism, as a haunting, living imperative and hope. All this, however, emerges through character, consciousness and nature; Greene's realism, naturally colored by his own conviction that human nature "is not black and white but black and grey" (CE 17), is not heavy-handed in its effected revelation. The Power and the Glory reveals grace working through nature, so that every hint of the supernatural has a natural explanation.

Tom Shippey, claiming that metaphorical or analogical power is equally the province of fantastic and realistic fiction, argues well that even realists (and Greene could certainly be counted among them) express patterns in their stories, including the "kind of Providential interlacing" found in The Lord of the Rings. But such realists do not see this authorial patterning as untrue, although one could dismissively say, as some critics say of fantasy, that it is "just made-up" (327-328). Though Flannery O'Connor, like Greene, has apparently left no recorded comments about contemporary J.R.R. Tolkien, she, too, understood the crucial relations of fantasy to realism and the truth that could be found in both:

> Fiction is an art that calls for the strictest attention to the real—whether the writer is writing a naturalistic story or a fantasy. I mean that we always begin with what is or with what has an eminent possibility of truth in it. Even when one writes a fantasy, reality is the proper basis of it. A thing is fantastic because it is so real, so real that it is fantastic. Graham Greene has said that he

> can't write, "I stood over a bottomless pit" because that couldn't be true, or "Running down the stairs I jumped into a taxi," because that couldn't be true either. (M&M 97)

Echoing Tolkien's own emphasis in "On Fairy Stories" O'Connor adds, "I would even go as far as to say that the person writing a fantasy has to be even more strictly attentive to the concrete detail than someone writing in a naturalistic vein in because the greater the story's strain on credulity, the more convincing the properties in it have to be" (M&M 97). O'Connor is really the perfect mediator between Tolkien and Greene because, Catholic like them, she wrote what she called romances in the tradition of Hawthorne (Habit 407)—she set her stories securely in the Primary World of the Southern United States, but she freely includes distortions, fantastic scenarios, and irony, effecting what she describes as "the action of grace in territory held largely by the devil" (M&M 118). Her work stands, then, in terms of its primary tonality (which, as Northrop Frye suggests, usually involves multiple modes), between Tolkien's fantasy in The Lord of the Rings and Greene's realism in The Power and the Glory. The aesthetic challenge common to all three was to make the fantastic believable in their fiction, and the fantastic included a religious vision of reality in an increasingly secular age.

When the whisky priest, with his own death imminent, tells the lieutenant, "I'm not telling them fairy stories I don't believe myself," he defends himself against the charge of hypocrisy. He also recognizes the fantastic nature of his Christian faith: without diminution, he defends the Gospel as a "fairy story," but one in which he believes, and one for which he is willing to die. Greene unwittingly echoes Tolkien's claim in "On Fairy-Stories" that "[t]he Gospels contain a fairy-story, or a story of a larger kind which embraces all the essence of fairy stories" (32). At the culmination of their excruciating journey to the Crack of Doom, Frodo and Sam experience what Tolkien calls in "On Fairy-Stories" a eucata-strophe, which is the essence of the "Consolation of the Happy Ending" of fairy stories:

> In its fairy-tale—or otherworld—setting it is a sudden and miraculous grace: never to be counted on to recur. It does not deny the existence of dyscatastrophe, of sorrow and failure: the possibility of these is necessary to the joy of deliverance; it denies (in the face of much evidence, if you will) universal final defeat and in so far is evangelium, giving a fleeting glimpse of Joy, Joy beyond the walls of the world, poignant as grief. (81)

The central moment of eucatastrophe in Frodo's journey with Sam in The Lord of the Rings occurs when Gollum takes the Ring, finger and all, away from Frodo, and accomplishes what Frodo finally could not do:

> "Precious, precious, precious!" Gollum cried. "My Precious! O my Precious!" And with that, even as his eyes were lifted up to gloat on his prize, he stepped too far, toppled, wavered for a moment on the brink, and then with a shriek he fell. Out of the depths came his last wail Precious, and he was gone. (925)

Sam's reaction is completely appropriate in terms of a eucatastrophic moment: "'Master!' cried Sam, and fell upon his knees. In all that ruin of the world for the moment he felt only joy, great joy. The burden was gone. His master had been saved; he was himself again, he was free" (926). Frodo recognizes the significance of the moment as well:

> [D]o you remember Gandalf's words: Even Gollum may have something yet to do? But for him, Sam, I could not have destroyed the Ring. The Quest would

> have been in vain, even at the bitter end. So let us forgive him! For the Quest is achieved, and now all is over. I am glad you are here with me. Here at the end of all things, Sam. (926)

From the beginning, the task of destroying the Ring has seemed both essential and nearly hopeless; its final destruction and the undoing of Sauron is the central eucatastrophe of the story, although it is not the only one. Sam registers this reality when he awakes following their rescue by the Eagles: "Gandalf! I thought you were dead! But then I thought I was dead myself. Is everything sad going to come untrue? What's happened to the world?" (930) It is in Tolkien's notion of eucatastrophe that Greene's novel and Tolkien's fantasy are finally and most profoundly bound. While the victory over Sauron with the destruction of the Ring is momentous and definitive in The Lord of the Rings, much damage has still been done and much sacrifice lies ahead for those in Middle-Earth. The Shire must be reclaimed. Samman must be vanquished. The elves, fading in their glory in Middle-Earth, depart West to their Deathless world across the Sea. Frodo is never the same and finally departs with Bilbo and the elves for healing in the mysterious West. He tells the grieving Sam,

> "I have been too deeply hurt, Sam. I tried to save the Shire, and it has been saved, but not for me. It must often be so, Sam, when things are in danger: some one has to give them up, lose them, so that others may keep them. But you are my heir: all that I had and might have had I leave to you." (1006)

The Consolation of the Happy Ending is not, for Tolkien, a matter of cheap grace. His trilogy ends with hope, but it is a hope bound up with sacrifice, sorrow, and uncertainties. Much the same can be said of the ending of The Power and the Glory. Once the whisky priest chooses to go with the mestizo, his Judas-figure, he is resolved to give up his life. He goes for the sake of the dying American criminal whose last moments seem to the priest to represent a mutual failure: "At the best, it was only one criminal trying to aid the escape of another—whichever way you looked, there wasn't much merit in either of them" (190). And from the perspective of the whisky priest on the morning of his execution, he is again a complete failure:

> He felt only an immense disappointment because he had to go to God empty-handed, with nothing done at all. It seemed to him, at that moment, that it would have been quite easy to have been a saint. It would only have needed a little self-restraint and a lime courage. He felt like someone who has missed happiness by seconds. He knew now that at the end there was only one thing that counted—to be a saint. (210)

His last moments starkly contrast those of the pious and recollected martyr Juan in the story that the devout mother reads to her children. And unlike Frodo and Sam, the whisky priest finds no rescue from death. The power which Frodo finally relinquishes lies in the Ring; the priest, of course, gives up his life. The view of the execution from Mr. Tench's perspective rings with defeat: "he saw the officer stuffing his gun back into his holster, and the little man was a routine heap beside the wall—something unimportant which had to be cleared away" (216). If there is anything like a eucatastrophe in Greene's novel, it comes subtly and in connection with the "fairy story" that the whisky priest earlier defended. We learn in the closing chapter that the whisky priest has, in fact, been somehow efficacious, both in his life and in his death. Coral Fellows, the young unbelieving girl who sheltered him earlier, has died, but the father, wondering if the condemned priest was the same priest they had hidden, hints that Coral was changed by her encounter: "But the odd thing is—the way she went on afterwards—as if he'd told her things" (214). The pious woman, speaking to her children, now defends the whisky priest and re-imagines him as "one of the martyrs of the Church" and perhaps "one of the saints" (219). The lieutenant is left feeling empty—"the dynamic love which used to move his trigger-finger felt flat and dead. Of course, he told himself, it will come back. It was like love of a woman and went in cycles: he had satisfied himself that morning, that was all. This was satiety" (220). But onto his emptiness is heaped the rejection of the pious woman's son, who had once admired the lieutenant. Greeting the boy from the street below the boy's window, the lieutenant anticipates a kind recognition, but instead, "the boy crinkled up his face and spat through the window bars, accurately, so that a little blob of spittle lay on the revolver-butt" (220). Finally, the young boy, moved by the story of the whisky priest's death, greets with eagerness and awe another priest who suddenly appears at his door that night seeking refuge. His mother had earlier said of the martyred whisky priest, "Of course, before we know he is a saint, there will have to be miracles" (219), and in the scope of Greene's novel, this short litany of transformations indeed constitute the miraculous.[8]

This turn of events hardly resembles, in its subtler dramatic intensity, the eucatastrophe in Tolkien's trilogy, but this brings us back once more to the mysterious relations of realism and fantasy. In his epilogue to "On Fairy-Stories," Tolkien claims:

> The peculiar quality of the "joy" in successful Fantasy can thus be explained as a sudden glimpse of the underlying reality or truth. It is not only a "consolation" for the sorrow of this world, but a satisfaction, and an answer to that question "Is it true?" The answer to this question that I gave at first was (quite rightly): "If you have built your little world well, yes: it is true in that world." That

> is enough for the artist (or the artist part of the artist). But in the "eucatastrophe" we see in a brief vision that the answer may be greater—it may be a far-off gleam or echo of evangelium in the real world. (83)

Writing this well before the completion of The Lord of the Rings, Tolkien imagines for good fairy-stories the kind of power that David Tracy ascribes to religious classics, and particularly, to Christian classics. Provocatively linking his aesthetics to his faith, and fantasy to history, Tolkien asserts:

> The Birth of Christ is the eucatastrophe of Man's history. The Resurrection is the eucatastrophe of the story of the Incarnation. This story begins and ends in joy. It has pre-eminently the "inner consistency of reality." There is no tale ever told that men would rather find was true, and none which so many skeptical men have accepted as true on its own merits. (83-84)[9]

The Power and the Glory is not a fairy-tale in the way that The Lord of the Rings is, but the two works converge in their different evocations of myth and mystery, particularly the mystery of Christ. The whisky priest's life and death and the ripple of transforming effects that emerge from them are invested with mystery and power because they explicitly evoke and participate in the eucatastrophe of Christ's Incarnation and Resurrection. While the integrity of Tolkien's mythic dimension, like Greene's, demanded distance between his belief and his representations, he nonetheless recognized that his belief ennobled and gave meaning to his art. Referring to the Gospel of Christ and emphasizing the charmed analogical relations of art and life, of God and human being, Tolkien might have spoken for the albeit more skeptical Graham

Greene, too, when he wrote in his poignant Epilogue to "On Fairy-Stories",

> Redeemed Man is still man. Story, fantasy, still go on, and should go on. The Evangelium has not abrogated legends; it has hallowed them, especially the "happy ending" . . . All tales may come true; and yet, at the last, redeemed, they may be as like and as unlike the forms that we give them as Man, finally redeemed, will be like and unlike the fallen that we know. (84)

Christian hope, with its companion respect for mystery, informs and finally unites the aesthetics of both Tolkien and Greene, for their respective works of fantasy and realism both reach haltingly toward such an ultimate future.

NOTES

1. Tracy, of course, speaks here of the reader disposed to religious interpretation, but he does not limit the experience of a religious classic's mystery to the "religious self": "even if the religious character of the classical religious expressions is denied, the event character of true disclosure and concealment implied in its classical status will yet endure . . . as any secular person can and ordinarily does experience, with or without the aid of Henry Adams, in experiencing the event of Chartres" (172).
2. One notable exception, one which Greene regretted and subsequently revised, is in *The End of the Affair*, where miraculous healings occur in connection with Sarah Miles. Greene notes in Ways of Escape, "every so-called miracle, like the curing of Parkis's boy, ought to have had a completely natural explanation" (116).
3. Tom Shippey has painstakingly explored Tolkien's governing interest in linguistics and philology and the ways in which this shaped and drove his major works of

fantasy. See both The Road to Middle Earth (1982) and his most recent J.R.R. Tolkien: Author of the Century (2000).

4. The controversy initially began with the 1996 poll jointly commissioned by British booksellers Waterstone's and the BBC program, Book Choice, to determine the five books readers considered the "greatest of the century." *The Lord of the Rings* was a consistent first place in almost every store branch in Britain (some 105 of them). Later polls confirmed this popular opinion. See Shippey, xx-xxi, for a concise summary and Pearce, 1-10.

5. Its theological dimension considered, Greene's work, particularly between 1938 and 1952, also registers the reality of a world informed by modern psychology, devastated by modern warfare, and confronted by modern literature that revealed and sometimes reveled in lost or abandoned faith in traditional religious beliefs. His realism of content in The Power and the Glory immediately distinguishes itself from other "realisms" by an effected belief in things seen and unseen, natural and supernatural.

6. See Greene's prologue to *The Lawless Roads* for a brief historical overview of Mexico during the religious persecutions of the 1920s and 1930s, as well as Judith Adamson's chapter "Greene's Mexico" in *Graham Greene: The Dangerous Edge* (1990). In Volume I of his biography of Greene, Norman Sherry gives a characteristically thorough historical overview and a particularly helpful description of the historical prototype for Greene's lieutenant, Garrido Canabal (see especially 705-78).

7. Cates Baldridge has recently suggested that in *The Power and the Glory* the lieutenant and the whisky priest are each half right about the world, that the universe is "not vacant, for the merciful God of the whisky priest exists; but the world is cooling, and so is the God who created it" (70). Granted Greene's rich ambiguities, the redemptive transformations in the end, it seems to me, qualify such a notion that the lieutenant's vision is finally as truthful in the novel as the whisky priest's.

8. Greene's subtle transformations here belie Flannery O'Connor's comment about Greene (perhaps referring to *The End of the Affair*), "What he does, I think, is try to make religion respectable to the modern unbeliever by making it seedy. He succeeds so well in making it seedy that then he has to save it by the miracle" (*Habit of Being* 201).

9. In *God in the Dock*, C.S. Lewis similarly claims that in Christianity "myth became fact" (63-67).

REFERENCES

Adamson, Judith. *Graham Greene: The Dangerous Edge: Where Art and Politics Meet*. New York: St. Martin's, 1990.

Baldridge, Cates. *Graham Greene's Fictions: The Virtues of Extremity*. Columbia: U of Missouri P, 2000.

Bloom, Harold, ed. *Graham Greene: Modern Critical Views*. New York: Chelsea House, 1987.

Cassis, A.F. *Graham Greene: Man of Paradox*. Chicago: Loyola UP, 1994.

Chance, Jane. *The Lord of the Rings: The Mythology of Power*. Revised Edition. UP of Kentucky, 2001.

DeVitis, A.A. *Graham Greene*. Revised Edition. Boston: Twayne, 1986.

Frye, Northrop. *Anatomy of Criticism*. 1957. Reprint. Princeton: Princeton UP, 1971.

Greene, Graham. *Collected Essays*. New York: Penguin, 1970.

——. *The Lawless Roads*. 3rd Edition. New York: Penguin, 1982.

——. *The Power and the Glory*. New York: Penguin, 1991.

——. *Ways of Escape*. Canada: Lester and Orpen Dennys, 1980.

Lewis, C.S. *An Experiment in Criticism*. Canto Edition. Cambridge: Cambridge UP, 1992.

——. *God in the Dock: Essays on Theology and Ethics*. Ed. Walter Hooper. Grand Rapids: William B. Eerdmans Publishing, 1970.

——. *Perelandra*. New York: Scribner, 1996.

Lewis, R.W.B. *The Picaresque Saint: Representative Figures in Contemporary Fiction*. Keystone Edition. Philadelphia: J.B. Lippincott, 1961.

O'Connor, Flannery. *The Habit of Being*. Ed. Sally Fitzgerald. New York: Noonday, 1988.

——. *Mystery and Manners: Occasional Prose*. Eds. Sally and Robert Fitzgerald. New York: Noonday, 1961.

Pearce, Joseph. *Tolkien: Man and Myth*. San Francisco: Ignatius Press, 1998.

Shippey, T.A. *J.R.R. Tolkien: Author of the Century*. Boston: Houghton Mifflin, 2001.

Sherry, Norman. *The Life of Graham Greene*. Volume I, 1904-1939. New York: Penguin, 1990.

Tolkien, J.R.R. *The Letters of J.R.R. Tolkien*. Ed. Humphrey Carpenter. Boston: Houghton Mifflin, 2000.

——. *The Lord of the Rings*. Boston: Houghton Mifflin, 1994.

——. "On Fairy-Stories." *Essays Presented to Charles Williams*. Reprint Edition. Freeport, NY: Books for Libraries, 1972.

Tracy, David. *The Analogical Imagination: Christian Theology and the Culture of Pluralism*. New York: Crossroad, 1981.

5

Scobie Reconsidered: A Casualty of Catholicism or Conscience?

—Lisa Crumley Bierman

Graham Greene's novel The Heart of the Matter is typically viewed as a "Catholic" novel, and understandably so. Scobie, the protagonist of the novel, is a Catholic convert. The role of his religion is an overarching theme in the text. As the story unfolds, he faces numerous moral obstacles that he attempts to surmount by adhering to his religious beliefs. However, a detailed examination of the work reveals that Scobie has tailored and customized his adopted religion to fit into his own generally skewed view of the world, in which his primary goal is preserving the happiness of those around him, despite the cost to himself. In the end, he does not turn to God for assistance in resolving his problems; he instead takes matters into his own hands. It may reasonably be argued that if Scobie had followed the prescriptions for living essential to his Catholic faith, he could have repented and been forgiven.

However, in his invented version of Catholicism, these options do not exist. In fact, the work is less a specifically

"Catholic" novel than an investigation of Scobie's world, as it exists within his own mind, and his psychological motivation for his actions within his world. Traditional Catholic beliefs are only one factor in Scobie's interpretation of his world. He is not constrained or condemned by any kind of religious imposition as much as he is a victim of his own conscience, which includes but is not limited to traditional elements of Catholicism. His sense of obligation to others, particularly his often self-imposed obligations of duty, justice, and responsibility, ultimately leaves him with no other option than to take his own life.

As discussed in "Scobie the Just: A Reassessment of The Heart of the Matter" by Teresita Fay and Michael Yetman, Scobie is a typical anti-hero. As the authors explain, "the modern anti-hero's differs from the traditional hero's ethos where goodness and truth are absolute values. He lives in an existentialist milieu in which good and evil, virtue and sin are bafflingly intermixed, indeed inseparable from one another" (144). Scobie is constantly presented with problems that (in his mind) have no clear, distinctively right or wrong answers. Although the Catholic Church, to which he looks for guidance and structure, outlines for him which actions are sinful, his religion ultimately fails to save him. Initially, the reader might sympathize with Scobie because it seems that he commits his sins with good intentions.

Consider his dilemma when he has an affair with Helen. Is it right to commit adultery? Absolutely not, his religious beliefs tell him. Is it right to comfort and bring happiness to a young widowed woman? Those same beliefs would suggest that of course it is right to do so. Scobie repeatedly confuses his good intentions with good actions, although strict Catholicism insists that "a good motive cannot make a bad action good (i.e., evil must not be done that good may come of it)" (Attwater 334). Despite how Catholic doctrine advises Scobie about the wrongfulness of his actions; that is, adultery is sinful regardless of the motive, Scobie improperly justifies his actions by focusing on his worthwhile intentions. These religious inconsistencies between how Scobie behaves and how his religion instructs him to behave serve as a flag to readers, warning them that Scobie's viewpoints must not always be taken at face value.

Scobie serves as both the protagonist and the antagonist of this novel. He is his own worst enemy. In his relationships with other people, he invariably takes on responsibility for their well-being whether or not he would be reasonably expected to do so. He seems to think that his pessimistic, gloomy outlook on life is simply a realistic one. At times he appears disgruntled because others do not share his views. He thinks to himself, "What an absurd thing it was to expect happiness in a world so full of misery [. . .] Point me out the happy man and I will point you out either extreme egotism, evil—or else an absolute ignorance" (123). Clearly he has no understanding of or sympathy for content individuals.

Because this work is primarily a psychological novel—that is, much of the development of the novel takes place in Scobie's thoughts—it is imperative to examine how Scobie perceives his external environment and his role in that environment, and how he relates to others around him. First, consider the external setting that constitutes Scobie's world. Although he is a British citizen, he is removed from his native soil. Instead, he lives in a bleak, barren country, a wasteland. The text is peppered with references to the constant heat, but there are very few, if any, references to true beauty. Scobie's world is a sort of Hell on earth. Images of death and decay surround him. As he drives down the road one evening, he swerves to avoid a dead pye-dog (35). Prisoners and policemen, individuals with whom Scobie deals on a regular basis, smell of "a zoo, of sawdust, excrement, ammonia, and lack of liberty"

(15). The bathroom of his home, which is the only room that his wife did not decorate, and the only room he seems fond of, is drab and dingy, and occasionally populated by rats. While sitting in the bathroom he muses, "He was happy here, sitting where the rat had sat, in his own world" (41). At times, Scobie is asked what he likes about the war-torn West African country where he lives. He responds, "It's pretty in the evening" (17). Scobie's comment represents one of the only positive remarks he makes about the exterior world. Most of his observations about the world and the people who occupy it are negative and disparaging.

Moreover, there are no means of release or relief in Scobie's mind. From outside Scobie's thoughts, the narrator observes that Scobie built his home by a "process of reduction" (15). As R. H. Miller suggests, "Scobie is a man without a country, without a culture, without most significantly, a philosophical and intellectual framework" (140). It is important to remember that these deficiencies in his world—lack of a country, culture, or philosophical and intellectual structure—are self-imposed. Scobie has chosen to stay in West Africa; he is not interested in retiring from his position as Deputy Commissioner of Police. He criticizes the social gatherings his wife enjoys, and he makes no attempt to develop an interest in literature. He adopts Catholicism when he marries Louise, yet he accepts just enough of it to compound his overwhelming sense of guilt about whatever happens to anyone, but not enough to trust that God can handle his troubles and provide relief. He claims that he desires peace, but he creates for himself a world in which peace is not possible.

Examining Scobie's views of duty and responsibility reveals how seriously he takes himself and how vital he believes he is to those around him. He views himself as a caretaker for individuals he considers in need of assistance. In a conversation with Wilson, a civilian clerk whose social status Scobie recognizes as lower than his own, Scobie asks how Wilson came to West Africa. Wilson replies, "One drifts into things." Scobie then responds and says, "I don't [. . .] I've always been a planner. You see, I even plan for other people" (73). Later, when describing his job, Scobie matter-of-factly thinks that, "I am the Deputy Commissioner of Police [...] I am the responsible man. It is my job to look after the others" (224). During the entire novel, Scobie spends his time planning for others and assuming responsibility for their happiness, no matter what the price. One particular emotion that produces this almost unnatural obsession with responsibility is pity. He repeatedly feels responsibility for any person who arouses pity in him, and particularly for the women in his life.

For Scobie, love and pity are inextricably connected. On one occasion, he asks himself if what he is feeling is love, or if it is "Only this automatic pity that goes out to any human need—and makes it worse?" (206) Later, he admits that despair does not last, and love does not last, but he surmises that despair remains after love ends. In the final days of his life, Scobie ponders his own definition of love. He reaches the following conclusion:

> When he was young, he had thought love had something to do with understanding, but with age he knew that no human being understood another. Love was the wish to understand, and presently with constant failure the wish died, and love died too perhaps or changed into this painful affection, loyalty, pity . . . (253)

Scobie's warped associations of responsibility, love, and pity render him incapable of having relationships based on mutual respect. Because he feels he must assume responsibility for those around him, he cannot view them as equals. Whether consciously or not, Scobie lives with the perspective that he is somehow superior to the people in his life. Why does Scobie perceive others around him as people to be pitied, as people for whom he must be responsible? He expresses frustration that "It sometimes seemed to him that he was the only one who recognized his responsibility" (122). Critic D.S. Savage, in his article, "Graham Greene and Belief," has suggested that this acceptance of responsibility for others gives Scobie an imagined sense of spiritual superiority (210). Indeed, there are times in the novel when Scobie visualizes himself as an equal to God. In "confessions" shortly before his suicide, he states "O God, [. . .] if instead I should abandon you, punish me but let the others get some happiness" (220). Later he wonders, "How was he to hate this God who of His own accord was surrendering Himself into his power?" (223). The pronoun use alone makes the sentence ambiguous, but the author-supplied capitalization implies that Scobie perceives God submitting Himself to Scobie. He ignores traditional beliefs in Catholic hierarchy—God, Pope, priests, laity—that allow for mediation of "grace and truth" (Hornsby-Smith 31).

BY placing himself on the same level as God, Scobie removes all possibility of hope for himself, and institutes a world that is devoid of compassionate love, peace, and meaning. As he tells himself, "This isn't a climate for emotion. It's a climate for meanness, malice, snobbery, but anything like hate or love drives a man off his head" (31). Perhaps it is this belief, perpetuated by his environment, that partly contributes to Scobie's inability to feel affection and love as separate from despair. Or perhaps his psychological state was always (even before he moved to West Africa) such that he was unable to experience love or affection for other human beings close to him. He also contemplates the idea of peace:

> The lights inside would have given an extraordinary impression of peace if one hadn't known, just as the stars on this clear night gave also an impression

> of remoteness, security, freedom. If one knew, he wondered, the facts, would one have to feel pity for even the planets? if one reached what they called the heart of the matter? (124)

Quotes such as these remind the reader of Scobie's arrogant and pessimistic nature. It is difficult to establish whether his external world determines his pessimistic nature, or if it is because of his nature that he feels comfortable in his desolate environment. At the beginning of the novel, he has already resided in West Africa for fifteen years, so it is possible, even likely, that the external environment of this country has shaped him. Regardless of which came first, his pessimistic nature or his relocating to a desolate environment, it is Scobie's internalization of his external world that informs his thoughts and deeds.

Considering the ways that Scobie relates to and perceives others in the novel provides concrete examples of Scobie's thought processes in action. First, contemplate his relationship with his wife, Louise. It can hardly be characterized as a happy, loving one. In the first few pages of the text, Scobie thinks about Louise, reflecting, "The experience that had come to her was the experience selected by himself. He had formed her face" (16). When imagining that others might perceive her critically, he becomes angry, thinking, "What right have you . . . to criticize her? This is my doing. This is what I've made of her" (32). He feels responsible for shaping Louise. When recalling their wedding vows, Scobie explains that he had promised to make her happy. He does not say anything about the traditional vows of "to have and to hold," "in sickness and in health," and so on. Based on his thoughts and actions, he does not view marriage as Pope Leo XIII outlined in his 1880 papal encyclical on the topic; that is, "a great sacrament; honorable in all, holy, pure, and to be reverenced as a type and symbol of most high mysteries" (31). Moreover, Catholic doctrine on marriage would remain essentially unchanged until the latter half of the twentieth century and Vatican II, and although the Catholic Church became more liberal after Vatican II, it still reveres marriage as a sacred institution.

Nor does Scobie seem to share the Catholic view of compassionate marriage characterized by mutual respect. He prefers only to care for Louise in sickness, not health. He pities her when she is weak and unattractive; he hates her when she is strong. He provides for her, but it is difficult to believe that he feels any kind of real affection for her. On occasion, he says that he loves her, but any actions he takes that may be perceived as beneficial to her seem motivated by his sense of duty rather than by his love for her.

For example, when Louise expresses a desire to travel to South Africa to take a vacation, Scobie arranges the trip. He promises her that he will take care of everything, even though he knows they do not have the money for her to travel. In one of their conversations about the trip, he explains that he wants her to be happy. She asks him to say that he loves her, and he responds by saying, "Of course I love you, darling. And I'll fix that passage. You'll see" (60). The paragraph immediately following this resolution is especially telling of Scobie's mindset:

> He would still have made the promise even if he could have foreseen all that would come of it. He had always been prepared to accept the responsibility for his actions, and he had always been half-aware, too, from the time he made his terrible private vow that she should be happy, how far this action might carry him. Despair is the price one pays for setting oneself an impossible aim. It is, one is told, the unforgivable sin, but it is a sin the corrupt or evil man never practices. He always has hope. He never reaches the freezing-

> point of knowing absolute failure. Only the man of goodwill always carries in his heart this capacity for damnation. (60)

His concept of love is tied invariably to his sense of duty and responsibility. He compromises his ideals of honesty and borrows money from a shady Syrian trader, Yusef, because he believes that going to South Africa will make Louise happy. If Louise were portrayed entirely through Scobie's eyes, it would be tempting to conclude that she is a weak, helpless woman, who needs Scobie for her happiness. He could then be perceived as caring and sympathetic. However, when Louise interacts with other characters, such as Wilson, she is depicted as a much more independent woman than Scobie chooses to believe. Furthermore, Louise sees through his promises of duty and obligation and does not mistake them for love. As she and Scobie lie in bed discussing her trip to South Africa, he says he will work out something, and she perceptively asks, "This isn't just two in the morning comfort, Ticki, is it?" (44). Later, admitting that she believes Scobie does not actually love her, she tells Wilson that Scobie will "do anything for me [. . .] he has a terrible sense of responsibility" (79). Despite Scobie's best effort to appear in control, Louise knows that he is not happy (55). Hence, it is primarily in his own mind that she is fragile and helpless.

Scobie's relationship with Helen is also unhealthy; it is formed in pity and steeped in guilt and responsibility. She enters his life via a shipwreck during the time that his wife is away in South Africa. When he first sees her, he sees a face "ugly with exhaustion" and her skin "looked as though it were about to crack over the cheek-bones" (121). This is not an image that typically would evoke love at first sight, but Scobie, true to his character, undoubtedly feels pity for Helen during their first encounter.

Their relationship begins as a casual one. Helen moves into a Nissen hut down the road from his home, and he offers to assist her in any way he can. For a few pages they both seem content with each other's company. At first, the relationship seems safe and secure. They like each other, but in Scobie's mind there is a gorge between them that will prevent them from becoming uncomfortably close. This gap is created by their acknowledgement that he is married, that she is recently widowed, that there exists a considerable age difference between them, and that her father is a clergyman.

However, despite any initially perceived hindrances to such a relationship, Scobie has an affair with Helen. They attempt to keep the affair secret, since Scobie is married and holds a prominent position in the government. This attempt fails, though, as evidenced by the fact that Wilson knows about it and Louise returns home from South Africa earlier than planned because she learns of it. Yet Scobie mistakenly assumes that they have kept their secret, and unfortunately for him, this mistake results in a series of bad decisions and attempts at concealment that eventually lead him to hide the truth by taking his own life.

Even before they consummate their relationship, Helen remarks to him, "I have a feeling that you'd never let me down" (160). To Scobie, these words are like "a command he would have to obey however difficult" (160). Theirs does not appear to be an enjoyable affair. It brings Scobie much more guilt and concern than joy. Immediately after it begins, he contemplates the consequences. There is no wild, carefree, intermediary period of lust and passionate sex; rather, there is a notable lack of concupiscence. Without delay, he assumes responsibility for both of them. The following passage outlines his initial reaction to the situation:

> In the future—that was where the sadness lay [. . .] human beings were condemned to consequences. The responsibility as well as the guilt was his [. . .] He had sworn to preserve Louise's happiness, and now he had accepted another and contradictory responsibility. He felt tired by all the lies he would some time have to tell; he felt the wounds of the victims who had not yet bled. (161-62)

This passage is particularly harrowing when considered in the context of the entire work. Who are the victims of whom he speaks? He will be the final one, but the penultimate victim of his guilt-ridden conscience is his "boy," Ali. Throughout most of the text, Ali is Scobie's most trusted servant. In fact, he is one of the few individuals who Scobie repeatedly claims to love. However, after Scobie takes money from Yusef, and after he begins his affair with Helen, his world enters a downward spiral from which he can see no escape. His conscience torments him; his sense of guilt and responsibility overwhelms him. David Hesla, in his article "Theological Ambiguity in the `Catholic Novels,'" generalizes Greene's central characters as individuals who, "Driven by an uncontrollable passion or need [. . .] produce extreme unrest and turbulence of spirit" (100). In this sense, Scobie is no different from certain other of Greene's protagonists. The "extreme unrest" he experiences eventually leads him to distrust Ali. At no point in the novel does he possess solid evidence that Ali has betrayed him, but because he is living a life mired in lies, his suspicion of the actions of those close to him is heightened.

In an ironic twist, Scobie consults with Yusef about this concern. Throughout most of the work, Scobie scoffs at the idea of turning to Yusef for help. Yusef is viewed by most of the characters as someone not to be trusted. However, as Scobie sinks deeper into despair, he believes he cannot trust anyone close to him, not even God. Again, he ignores Pre-Vatican II theology that God is "remote, unchanging and perfect," and perfectly capable of dispensing hope (Hornsby-Smith 32). When he meets with Yusef, Yusef explains that he can remedy Scobie's situation. He does not outline the details of his solution, but Scobie instinctively questions Yusef's methods. Nonetheless, Scobie does not insist that Yusef elaborate on his plan. Instead, he mostly keeps his concerns to himself. He drinks with Yusef and allows his senses to be dulled by alcohol.

After he leaves Yusef's home, he discovers that Ali has been murdered. Although it is never proven, he has a sense that Yusef and one of his servants contributed to the murder. Ultimately, though, the responsibility for Ali's death is Scobie's alone. While it should be noted that it would be completely out of character for Scobie to have a clear conscience by this point in the text, considering his affair and all the lies he has told, he could have kept his concerns about Ali to himself. If he felt he had to tell Yusef, he could have insisted on knowing the details of Yusef's solution. His failure to act led directly to the murder of his most favored servant. On this occasion, the guilt and responsibility Scobie assumes are absolutely justified.

For most of the work, the reader is given clues instead of concrete answers as to what makes Scobie the way that he is. His thoughts are manifested in his actions, but where do his thoughts originate? At the end, just before he takes his life, he says he does not trust God, because He made "This feeling of responsibility that I've always carried about like a sack of bricks" (259). Contrary to conventional Catholic beliefs, passages from this work contain overtones of fatalism and pre-determination. Although Scobie is given free will to commit adultery, that sin could be forgiven if he could forsake Helen and return to his wife. However, since he feels such an overwhelming responsibility for Helen's happiness (a trait given to him supposedly by God), leaving Helen is not an option for him. Leaving Louise is not an option, either. This sense of responsibility generally leads him to feel guilty, and his strong feelings of guilt lead almost directly to Ali's murder. If pity, too, is tied into this sense of responsibility that Scobie believes is imparted to him by God, then how is the reader to view Scobie? The final question is, will he be redeemed?

Numerous critics have addressed this question. Irma Maini, in an article entitled "The Theme of Grace in The Heart of the Matter," contends that Scobie's sense of pity "redeems him, ennobles him in our eyes" (56). However, the portrait painted of the pitying Scobie is more pathetic than sympathetic. As described by Savage, Scobie is a typical Greene protagonist whose world comprises "tedious adventure, joyless pleasure, lustful love, heroic suicide and saving damnation" (220). It is difficult to accept him as a noble character. After all, he is a grown man incapable of feeling or expressing real love, and unable to accept that God's grace can ultimately redeem him. He cannot imagine that others can be happy without him making them so, and he arrogantly assumes that he must bear responsibility for the well-being of those around him. While Scobie may perceive his intentions as noble, his actions may easily be interpreted as much less honorable than that.

Maini's article implies that Scobie will be redeemed after his suicide because his suicide was a form of self-sacrifice. In taking his own life, Scobie's goal is to make both Louise and Helen happy. But an examination of the text reveals that Scobie likely died in vain, because there are many clues that suggest that both Louise and Helen could live contentedly without Scobie. That is not to say that neither woman cared about him, but rather that they could have managed without him. For example, consider Louise's treatment of Scobie when she returns home, after learning of his affair. She does not appear to be a jealous, bitter woman. She almost seems complacent. She does not insist that Scobie tell her the truth about his affair, nor does she threaten to leave him. She is willing to ignore it and move on with their lives. After she returns from South Africa, she appears stronger and more self-assured than before she went. Had Scobie's actions played as prominent a role in determining her happiness as he imagines, she likely would have reacted differently. If she depended on him for happiness, she would have felt threatened and insecure at the thought of him being involved with another woman. Instead of obsessing about the affair, she briefly discusses the situation with Wilson in a casual manner.

Additionally, after Scobie's death, Louise states, "I did love him, but now he seems so very very gone" (268). Very little of the text is devoted to Louise's grieving over her husband's death. While it saddens her, she does not act as if her sole source of joy has been destroyed. Unfortunately for Scobie, his self-sacrifice for Louise is not acknowledged or appreciated as such.

Of the two women in his life, Helen seems more distraught about Scobie's suicide than Louise does. However, it must be recalled that Helen was planning to end her affair with Scobie prior to his suicide. In their final conversation, she tells him, "`You know,' she said, this is the end for us. I can't go on ruining you anymore' [. . .] `Don't worry about me. I'll be all right'" (250-51). But Scobie refuses to let her end the relationship. He assures her that they can continue to see each other. Her willingness to take responsibility for her own happiness, end the relationship and move away shows that she is a strong, independent woman. Although it seems to be a difficult decision for her, it is one she is capable of making.

It is reasonable to presume that Helen would be able to continue her life and find happiness without Scobie. Blinded by his pride, Scobie cannot see this, and he feels that ending his life is the only way to bring her happiness. Sadly (for Scobie), although understandably, Helen does not perceive his suicide as some kind of grand, noble gesture any more than Louise does. Her emotions range from anger to apathy, but do not appear to include overwhelming sorrow or pride. She thinks to herself, "There's nobody in the world I love, and out of it doesn't count, so why not let them have their prangs (it was Bagster's phrase) if they want them enough" (270). Then she tells Bagster, her would-be suitor, "I don't love anyone [. . .] You can't love the dead, can you? They don't exist, do they? It would be like loving the dodo, wouldn't it?" (270).

To further support the notion that Scobie is redeemed in the end, despite his suicide, Maini argues that Scobie is a traditional Greene protagonist in the sense that he "must first fall before he can rise" (58). She holds out hope that since Scobie clearly falls, he will ultimately rise, i.e., he will be redeemed. Nonetheless, Scobie's redemption is at best questionable. The belief that there is no grace without sin does not automatically guarantee his redemption. To complicate matters, Scobie consistently rejects grace throughout the text. One of his last internal conversations with God is especially revealing of his mindset. Scobie explains that he will "damn himself" (258). The voice in his head that he interprets as God responds as follows:

> Can't you trust me as you'd trust a faithful dog? I have been faithful to you for two thousand years. All you have to do now is ring a bell, go into a box, confess . . . the repentance is already there, straining at your heart. It's not the repentance that you lack, just a few simple actions: to go up to the Nissen hut and say goodbye. Or if you must, continue

> rejecting me but without lies any more. Go to your house and say good-bye to your wife and live with your mistress. If you live you will come back to me sooner or later. One of them will suffer, but can't you trust me to see that the suffering isn't too great? (259)

Historically, a significant difference between Protestants and Catholics is that Protestants are instructed to speak directly to God or Jesus in prayer, while Catholics are encouraged to use an intermediary—a priest or Mary, for example—in supplication. The conventional hierarchy of the Catholic Church is God, Pope, priest, then laity. However, in the above passage, Scobie violates traditional Catholic hierarchy and converses directly with God. This action implies a break with convention, and could be considered more Protestant than Catholic in nature. However, such a break with tradition may be forgiven if not for his penultimate rejection of God and grace, which occurs when he replies to the above question by thinking, "No. I don't trust you. I've never trusted you" (259). He proceeds to blame God for making him the person he is, the person who feels responsibility for everything that happens to those around him. As a Catholic, Scobie's rejection of God's grace coupled with his final commission of a mortal sin allow for little chance of redemption. Perhaps the only semblance of hope lies in Father Rank's reassurance to Louise that no one can really understand the scope of God's mercy, and that the Church "doesn't know what goes on in a single human heart" (271). Yet Father Rank's opinion may be biased, because he never suspected Scobie was capable of serious error. Throughout the work, he holds Scobie in high esteem. Considering that Father Rank is essentially a minor character in the work, and that his credibility is barely established, his final observations are not convincing enough to ensure the reader of Scobie's redemption.

Another source that may shed light on the question of Scobie's redemption is Greene himself. One of his primary goals in creating this work was to show how excessive pity can be as dangerous to the destruction of one's character as pride. As Richard Freis points out, "Greene portrays Scobie here as a man who, in his obsessive attachments to an autonomous and controlling pity, has become enmeshed in spiritual pride" (70). W.H. Auden further explores the correlation between pity and pride. In a discussion of Greene's characters, he states the following:

> To feel compassion for someone is to make oneself their equal; to pity them is to regard oneself as their superior and from that eminence the step to the torture chamber and the corrective labor camp is shorter than one thinks. (Freis 62)

Auden's insightful comments, although not specifically about Scobie, reflect the path that Scobie follows to his ultimate damnation. It has been suggested that Scobie's downfall is a byproduct of his imprisoned "Roman Catholic conscience" (Fay 151). However, since Scobie lives according to his own seemingly unorthodox form of Roman Catholicism, his being Catholic is only one factor that imprisons his conscience. The religion he practices may be unrecognizable to devout Catholics. He complains that God is too accessible, he has an affair, he lies, he takes bribes, he does not have faith in God's grace, and he ultimately commits suicide, which is "a mortal sin against the fifth commandment" (Attwater 479-80). This is not to say that all Catholics except Scobie are perfect. But it seems that he focuses as much or more attention on his sense of responsibility, duty and pity, i.e., his own actions, as he does on his religion, i.e., his own faith. Hence, it is not just his religion that imprisons his conscience. His decision to go so far as to take his own life in a gesture of self-sacrifice, through which he believes he can bring happiness to Louise, Helen and God, shows that he is a victim of his conscience, a conscience imprisoned by more than just the Catholic religion. After all, he imagines God to say that he can be forgiven. God offers him hope, but he stubbornly rejects it.

In one sense, this novel is a reflection of Greene's attitude toward being called a Catholic writer. According to Bernard Swift, Greene complained that "Many times since Brighton Rock I have been forced to declare myself not a Catholic writer but a writer who happens to be Catholic" (111). The Heart of the Matter may be considered not a specifically Catholic text but a text that happens to contain a Catholic protagonist. The theological limitations that Greene worried would be associated with him if he were labeled a Catholic writer are the same constraints that would be placed on Scobie if he limited his beliefs to those that are conventionally Catholic. Instead, Scobie invents his own version of Catholicism, and in his imagined world, his actions are not limited by traditional Catholic values. In the same way, the scope of Greene's writing is not limited by strictly Catholic views.

Had Scobie chosen to adhere to the principles of the religion he claims for his own, redemption could have been possible for him. The pride that clouds his mind also taints his judgment, rendering him a victim of his own conscience. Will his good intentions redeem him in the end, despite his actions? Perhaps God's mercy is so infinite that there is hope for Scobie regardless of his final sin. But if he is judged according to conventional Catholic standards, his prospects seem rather dim.

REFERENCES

Attwater, Donald, ed. *A Catholic Dictionary*. 2nd edition. New York: Macmillan, 1949.

Carlen, Claudia. *The Papal Encyclicals, 1878-1903*. Pierian Press, 1990.

Greene, Graham. *The Heart of the Matter. 1948, 1971.* Reprint. New York: Penguin, 1978.

Fay, Teresita, and Michael G. Yetman. "Scobie the Just: A Reassessment of The Heart of the Matter." *Renascence* 29 (1977): 142-156.

Freis, Richard. "Scobie's World." *Religion and Literature* 24.3 (1992): 57-78.

Hesla, David J. "Theological Ambiguity in the `Catholic Novels.'" *Graham Greene: Some Critical Considerations.* Ed. Robert O. Evans. Lexington: U of Kentucky P, 1967. 96-111.

Hornsby-Smith, Michael P. *Roman Catholics in England.* Cambridge: Cambridge UP, 1987.

Maini, Irma. "The Theme of Grace in The Heart of the Matter." *The Literary Criterion* XVII (1982): 51-59.

Miller, R.H. "Graham Greene and His `Saddest Story.'" *Renascence* 49 (1999): 133-43.

Savage, D.S. "Graham Greene and Belief." *Dalhousie Review* 58 (1978): 205-229.

Swift, Bernard C. "`The Dangerous Edge of Things:' Mauriac, Greene and the Idea of the Catholic Novel." *Journal of European Studies* 22 (1992): 111-126.

6

Graham Greene's "Saddest Story"

—R.H. Miller

Readers familiar with Ford Madox Ford's The Good Soldier will recognize his earlier title for the novel, "The Saddest Story," which he was forced to change at the insistence of his publisher (Ford xi).[1] It requires no stretch of the imagination to apply that abandoned title to Graham Greene's The Heart of the Matter, perhaps his most poignant and moving novel. Although there has been considerable notice given to Greene's debt to Ford, up to this time no one has taken note of the several close material parallels and narratological differences between these two novels.[2] I hope to show that Greene found the frame of his idea for The Heart of the Matter in The Good Soldier but rejected for the time Ford's inspired narrative strategy, to employ it later in The End of the Affair. In preferring a more conventional mode of narrative, a limited third-person point of view, he created a story quite different from Ford's. Instead of aiming for Ford's sense of epistemic play and the multifaceted effect of his narration, Greene opted for a story anchored in the psyche of his protagonist, Major Henry Scobie, and for the emotional links that such a strategy might hope to achieve with his readers. Thus he identifies his readers more closely with Scobie and with Greene himself and matters closer to his own heart, to the failure of his own marriage and his affairs with Dorothy Glover and Catherine Walston, both of which are documented extensively throughout the second volume of Norman Sherry's biography. In his introduction to the novel Greene says, with what must be taken now as a large measure of bluster, that "Scobie was based on nothing but my own unconscious" (HM xv), knowing what we know now about Greene's love affairs.

Given also the close similarities between these novels, it is likely that Greene found Ford's story pressing more and more insistently into his consciousness, even though he may not or seems not to have realized his indebtedness to his master. What Greene created from Ford's novel is not so much a post-Victorian tale of passion at war with outmoded mores as it is a sad story indeed of a good man lost, directionless, in a nihilistic world. Perhaps the saddest of all outcomes to this effort is that Greene's novel, for all its artistry, does not make the subtle but devastating impact that The Good Soldier continues to make on its readership to this day. It was not Greene's intention to outdo Ford, but it was perhaps his undoing that Scobie would pale in stature by comparison to his model, Captain Edward Ashburnham, and that Scobie's wife Louise would likewise never rival in the depth of her character the brilliantly portrayed Leonora Ashburnham.

About Ford Madox Ford, Greene says that two of his works, the Tietjens series and The Good Soldier, "stand as high as any fiction written since the death of James."[3] A little over a week after Ford's death, Greene published a moving tribute to him in The Spectator, which was later included in his first collection of essays, The Lost Childhood and Other Essays. In 1962-1963 Greene provided two lengthy introductions to the newly published Bodley Head Ford Madox Ford, the former being an appreciation of the artistry of The Good Soldier. These were combined with Greene's earlier piece from The Lost Childhood to constitute the longer essay, "Ford Madox Ford," published most recently in his Collected Essays in 1969. Of special note is Part 2 of the essay, the discussion of The Good Soldier.

In that section Greene expresses almost boundless admiration for The Good Soldier. He mentions coming back often to the novel in over forty years of reading it (167). Equally significant is the affinity Greene felt for Ford as both writer and person. Of the former role Greene remarks on Ford's need to move far afield to find his material: "How seldom a novelist chooses the material nearest to his hand; it is almost as if he were driven to earn experience the hard way" (162). For "novelist" here, read not just "Ford" but "Greene" as well, for over the years Greene too has found his stories in distant places.

Both writers draw in some part on the personal tragedies of their own marriages for material, which provide the framework for the failed marriages of the Ashburnhams and the Scobies. Ford's Catholic marriage to Elsie Martindale, like Greene's to Vivien Dayrell-Browning, began satisfactorily enough, in spite of her family's misgivings, but eventually the couple grew estranged, and Ford had to console himself with long-term relationships and/or marriages de facto with Violet Hunt, Stella Bowen (for whom he changed his last name from Hueffer to Ford), and Janice Biala. Elsie Hueffer, as Vivien Greene seems to have done also, never had any intention of giving Ford a divorce, and managed to survive him by ten years. Mrs. Greene continues to reside in Oxford, now six years beyond her husband's death. Greene also sought to find solace in less permanent relationships than those of Ford, but still ones that fired his creative energies through the writing of The Heart of the Matter and The End of the Affair, both novels drawing heavily from the two early affairs of his life. His affair with Dorothy Glover had begun before the war and continued for a short time after. The sequent affair, with Lady Walston, Greene had initiated in late 1946, as he was beginning work on The Heart of the Matter.

Of Ford's anguish over his failed Catholic marriage, from which there seemed for him to be no release, Greene comments, "A novelist is not a vegetable absorbing nourishment mechanically from soil and air: material is not easily gained, and one cannot help wondering what agonies of frustration and error lay behind The Saddest Story" (167). Concomitantly, we can see both the autobiographical element of The Heart of the Matter and what similar agonies lay behind it. Greene hints darkly at them in his introduction to the novel (xii-xiii), but, as he also says in his comment on Ford, "The private life cannot be escaped and death does not come when it is most required" (171), that is, unless, as our two protagonists choose to do, one hastens that death by taking the matter into one's own hands. Greene was convinced that he would not live through the war, but he survived it by many years. Thus it occurs in the making of these two novels that we have two writers, drawing on like personal experiences, the one ineluctably drawn to create a story remarkably like the other's, but with a difference, of course.

Further, Greene shows a sure understanding of Ford's masterpiece, for he recognizes that the subject of the novel is both Edward Ashburnham and Dowell, that Dowell as a narrator is both a means to an end and an end in himself. To Greene The Good Soldier was not an epistemic puzzle but an account of personal and domestic tragedy if finally not a tragedy of a whole culture, whose poignancy is heightened by the use of Dowell as narrator, a flawed yet credible one. Greene's choice not to follow Ford's technique of the fallible narrator shows, first of all, that Greene probably did not feel that he was, as a craftsman, ready to take on such a demanding task. Secondly, and most obviously, it makes all the difference in the world between his novel and Ford's, in tone, in the motivation and ethical stature of the two protagonists, Scobie and Ashburnham, and in the larger "moral" implications of the two books. Even when he did accept the challenge in The End of the Affair, Greene found the crafting of that novel a daunting task: "Many a time I regretted pursuing `I' along his dismal road and contemplated beginning The End of the Affair all over again with Bendrix seen from the outside in the third person" (The End of the Affair viii).

Similar as Ford's and Greene's novels may be, a crucial difference between them is that the heightened conflict of The Good Soldier is purportedly distanced and externalized, residing as it does in the narrational perspective provided by Dowell and in the relationships between the members of the triangle, while in The Heart of the Matter, the conflict resides to a large extent in Scobie, and the result is that the narrative is focused mainly on and within him. The effect he achieves is to intensify and perhaps sentimentalize our experience with Scobie by restricting the dramatic possibilities of the narrative, a result Greene was well aware of, but one, given the narrative strategy he chose, that concentrates almost all our attention on Scobie.

A knowledge of the basic lines of Ford's novel is instructive in understanding The Heart of the Matter. The story is told by the American, John Dowell of Philadelphia, a well-meaning but at times confused narrator, and concerns a retired English military officer who has made a bad marriage to a devout Anglo-Irish Catholic girl, Leonora Powys. In spite of his efforts to maintain the highest code of conduct, Ashburnham carries on a number of affairs, accumulates devastating gambling debts from which his wife rescues him, shows himself to be an incompetent although compassionate businessman, and finally brings his tragic life to a crisis by falling hopelessly in love with their young ward, Nancy Rufford.

This final quasi-incestuous disaster prompts him to take what he thinks to be the only way out of the situation, knowing that he cannot live without Nancy's love, and he kills himself. Leonora remarries after his death, has a family, and lives quite happily. Nancy, however, goes mad.

With some variations, the story of The Heart of the Matter has obvious parallels: Major Henry Scobie, a professional military man based in Sierra Leone, is in a loveless marriage to Louise, of fourteen years' duration. She is Catholic by birth, he a convert by marriage. They had one child, who died in England some three years earlier. While Louise is away on holiday in South Africa, a ship is sunk by enemy action, and Scobie falls in love with Helen Rolt, one of the survivors. Louise hears of these developments and returns to Freetown. Scobie, in an effort to resolve his dilemma, secure peace for himself, Helen, and Louise, commits suicide by poisoning in an effort to simulate a heart attack. His ruse is rather easily uncovered. Louise seemingly picks up her life with little difficulty. Only Helen is left truly bereft and disillusioned.

The parallels between the two novels and their love triangles are apparent. Leonora, Nancy, and Captain Ashburnham stand in relation to each other as do Louise, Helen Rolt, and Major Scobie. Louise's rigid Catholicism parallels that of Leonora Ashburnham, but in other ways they are totally unlike. Leonora as a character is a grand achievement, perhaps one of the most powerful woman figures in modern fiction. She shows herself more than equal to the task of coping with Edward's failings, while he lives in the past and in his emotions. Ford created in Leonora, through the fumbling but incrementally revealing awarenesses of Dowell, a figure of great complexity. Louise, in spite of Greene's later efforts to present her in a more favorable light, is far less independent.[4] Like Louise Scobie, Leonora harbors a view of her faith that is at once rigid and simplistic, as Dowell speaks of her "English Catholic conscience, her rigid principles, her coldness, even her very patience" (GS 60). These are qualities evident also in Louise when she torments Scobie by constantly asking him to attend mass, knowing he will refuse communion because of his sinful state. When she seeks to understand his death within the confines of narrow dogma she sees it, perhaps correctly, as a sign of Scobie's weakness but she sees it also in terms of traditional dogma, in spite of Father Rank's effort to give her a broader perspective. Her dependence on Scobie, on men generally, is as much a function of her sense of alienation, as she sees it, in Freetown, as it is in her feelings of alienation from the English colonial community. She has too often been seen in simplistic terms as a fishwife, whining, parasitical, where Greene intended her to be rather more guileful.

The connection between Helen Rolt and Nancy Rufford is perhaps more tenuous, but it is a firm one nonetheless. They are fairly close in age, Helen aged nineteen but seeming much older, Nancy at the close of the novel, twenty-two. Both are alone in the world. Nancy has been abandoned by her mother and placed in the care of the Ashburnhams by her father. Helen is now widowed, having lost her husband in the ship disaster: Her father lives on in Bury St. Edmunds, an Anglican clergyman. Her mother died when she was young. Of course, Helen comes to occupy the role of adultress, which Nancy does not, in spite of her one mad effort to sacrifice herself to Edward to save him from a painful, waning death. Greene chooses to bring Scobie and Helen together in a consummated affair, while Ford creates the tension in the forbidden desire Edward feels for Nancy and the consequent horror all three experience as his feelings become known. Helen has an independent but somewhat sacrificial quality about her, whereas Ford has invested Nancy with genuine, self-destructive, Brontean passion. She is the dutiful convent-school ward, but underneath she is as caught up in the destructive drama as are Edward and Leonora.

The illuminating parallels occur, of course, between Ashburnham and Scobie. They are somewhat close in age. Ashburnham, at the time of his death, is forty-two, Scobie, just fifty. Both are known to their wives by similar nicknames; Ashburnham is "Teddy," Scobie, "Ticki." Both share a life of competent, and in Edward's case, distinguished military service in the provinces, the one a captain in India, from whence he retires to his country estate in Hampshire, the other a colonial officer in Sierra Leone. Both are professional military men and have a keenly developed sense of professionalism. Ashburnham is described as

> the cleanest looking sort of chap; an excellent magistrate, a first-rate soldier . . . To the poor and to hopeless drunkards, as I myself have witnessed, he was like a painstaking guardian. And he never more than once or twice in all the nine years of my knowing him told a story that couldn't have gone into the columns of the Field. (GS 11)

Scobie's associates call him "Scobie the Just," a mocking allusion to the classical Aristides the Just, out of respect for Scobie's reputation for being rigorously fair. Scobie is not retired but is contemplating retirement. Both, in their conversation, meet our expectations, given their military backgrounds; their speech is brief, sensible, to the point. Both are decidedly anti-intellectual, but where Scobie has no interest in literature whatever, Ashburnham is a fan of sentimental novels and reads them incessantly and tearfully: ". . . he would pass hours lost in novels of a sentimental type—novels in which typewriter girls married marquises and governesses earls" (GS 27). Scobie rarely reads books, owns almost none, dislikes poetry or any literature that reveals human emotion. Joseph Hynes calls him the least intellectual of all of Greene's characters (717). Both his speech and his diary show him to be almost incapable of expressing his true feelings. Both, of course, have made socially acceptable but disastrous marriages. Edward marries Leonora in a dutiful act of acquiescence to Victorian familial tradition. Out of concern for the future of his seven daughters, Colonel Powys writes Colonel Ashburnham and suggests that his son Edward marry one of their daughters, and that if one marries, then the others might get the same idea. A photograph of the girls, specially taken for the occasion, is sent to the Ashburnhams, and in it Leonora's face is obscured by a shadow from a tree branch (GS 138). While the Ashburnhams are visiting the Powyses, by some mysterious agreement between parents and son, Leonora is chosen ("And then, one evening, Mrs. Ashburnham had with her boy one of those conversations that English mothers have with English sons" [GS 139]). Scobie's marriage to Louise is also shrouded in mystery, but we know it was more an act of duty than of love. As Scobie describes it: "No man could guarantee love forever, but he had sworn fourteen years ago, at Ealing, silently, during the horrible little elegant ceremony among the lace and candles, that he would at least always see to it that she was happy" (60). Edward has the greatest admiration for Leonora but no real passion. As Dowell describes it: "She had not for him a touch of magnetism. I suppose, really, he did not love her because she was never mournful; what really made him feel good in life was to comfort somebody who would be darkly and mysteriously mournful" (GS 140). In parallel fashion, one can almost read into that description Scobie's own reaction to Louise, and that he found Helen appealing because of her vulnerability, her total aloneness. Edward Ashburnham's twisted love of the mournful Greene converts into Henry Scobie's often appalling sense of pity. Both marriages are now childless, the Ashburnhams' barren from the start, due no doubt to Edward's being sterile, as we can surmise from Leonora's child-blessed second marriage, the Scobies' so by the death of their daughter Catherine. Their respective affairs occur under similar circumstances.

Ashburnham, unlike Scobie, has a history of sexual dalliances; but their crucial affairs occur in their lives like bolts of lightning. Both are immediately and absolutely overwhelmed by their feelings for their young loves. Both end their lives by suicide.

Both of them, Othello-like, show themselves unskilled in the subtleties of the civilian world and blind to the strengths of the women they seek to protect from the harsh realities of life. Most significantly, both have an almost astonishing capacity to misjudge women generally. Ashburnham's sentimentalism is commented upon at length by Dowell:

> You see, along with the passion of the chase went a frame of mind that made him be extraordinarily ashamed of himself. You may not believe it, but he really had such a sort of respect for the chastity of Leonora's imagination that he hated—he was positively revolted—at the thought that she should know that the sort of thing that he did existed in the world. (GS 57)

Scobie believes that Louise must be protected from the truth of his affair at all costs, while in fact she receives news of it from her gossipy friend back in Freetown almost as soon as it begins and, when she returns, uses the information to play out her little drama of irony before the reader's eyes. This is the woman Scobie feels he should guard from realities. Where Edward foolishly believes that he has to "look after" Leonora, who is fully capable of looking after both herself and her husband, Scobie, too, foolishly believes that he and he alone can make Louise's and Helen's lives endurable. He thinks at one point, "The less he needed Louise the more conscious he became of his responsibility for her happiness" (HM 13). That impulse is Scobie's undoing, just as much as Edward's failure to see how incompetent he is, is his. Dowell says of Edward that "he was the normal man, but there was too much of the sentimentalist about him and society does not need too many sentimentalists" (GS 238). Likewise Scobie, Greene states, was intended to show that "pity can be the expression of an almost monstrous pride" (HM xiv). Ashburnham is known to us, as are all the characters in Ford's novel, through the narrator Dowell, who tries in his limited way by misdirection and indirection to help us understand this honorable man driven by a forbidden passion he cannot control, that scorches his very soul and ultimately drives him to suicide. Ashburnham is driven by a desire to maintain the code of the gentleman and an outward show of respect for the rigid Catholicism of his wife. This he finds he cannot do without overwhelming torment. Once Nancy is gone, he is so overcome with grief that he kills himself to resolve his dilemma and to free both women from his shameful passion. In that sense he and Scobie share the deadly sin of pride, because they are both unable to reveal the extent to which they harbor weakness and the extent to which they are ashamed of that fact. Dowell says of Ashburnham, almost as if he is speaking as well of Scobie,

> In all matrimonial associations there is, I believe, one constant factor—a desire to deceive the person with whom one lives as to some weak spot in one's character or in one's career. For it is intolerable to live constantly with one human being who perceives one's small meannesses. It is really death to do so—that is why so many marriages turn out unhappily. (GS 117)

Wrapped in his code of honor, rather simply conceived, Edward Ashburnham represents the death of squirearchy as England had come to know it. There is no subtlety, no sophistication to his world-view. He has adopted a code of values and sticks by it. Remarkably, though, his passing strikes one as heroic, "more an antique Roman," as Horatio says, and he confirms that judgment by quoting Swinburne translating Julian the Apostate (251). Edward's death is not drawn out in the face of an adopted religious creed; it comes about spontaneously in response to the loss of the one person who gave him a reason to live. Ashburnham's solution to his dilemma is in his eyes perhaps the only one honorable both to the women and to the code of the gentleman. It releases Leonora from an intolerable situation and frees her to marry Rodney Bayham and have the family she always desired. Its effect on Nancy, however, is destructive. Its tragedy of course lies in its senselessness, but in his own way Edward manages to retain, in his belief in the rightness of his actions, an outward dignity. His act is one of resolution, not of escape, as Scobie's tends to be interpreted. As one who lives life lacking any meaningful code whatever, Scobie is tormented by doubts. He has become a Catholic and he tries valiantly to understand his moral quandary through its tenets. He posits existentially the world of values he inhabits; it is the tottery certitude of the Catholic faith he has adopted as a convert that anchors him. Scobie is a man without a country, without a culture, without, most significantly, a philosophical and intellectual framework. Early in the novel Greene describes him as a man who constructs his living space, and one might add his view of the world, through a systematic "process of reduction," of shedding (6). He feels no commitment to the traditions that the English community cling to so pathetically in The Heart of the Matter. His allegiance to the professional code erodes in the course of the novel. In an effort to overcome that rootlessness of which Greene has often spoken, Scobie finds structure in the teaching of the Church (Allain 20). He turns to that structure, which presents him with a seemingly inflexible moral code that pushes him to extremes of guilt and pity, and it inevitably fails him.

His flaw is his inability to realize a concept of self out of the cultural void he inhabits and thus is tortured by the fiery cloak of his Catholicism, from which suicide comes as a release from suffering. Conversely, Edward never doubts who he is or what he stands for, antiquated and corroded as that code might be. The net effect of Scobie's anguish is to make what has been viewed as one of the most religious of Greene's novels to be far more a secular one, with its failure of a stultified faith to minister to the needs of a new age and the disillusionment that awaits those who believe they can cope with the world through it. Scobie does fail, true, but the faith he turned to, as he understood that faith, failed him as well. Greene eloquently if sadly comments about Scobie that "somewhere between the Nissen hut and home he had mislaid his joy" (HM 185). One can only hope that in the life beyond death Scobie can realize his dream of an earthly paradise, in which he and Ali walk through "a wide cool meadow" with birds overhead, and where, when he reclines on the grass, a small green snake slithers harmlessly over his arm and touches "his cheek with a cold, friendly, remote tongue" (91). One can almost hear him speak Edward's muttered line from Swinburne, "Thou hast conquered, O pale Galilean" (GS 251), although Edward's meaning would be much closer to Julian the Apostate's putative dying words, "Vicisti Galilaee." Edward's own dying statement to Dowell is more prosaic: "So long, old man, I must have a bit of rest, you know" (GS 256), as is one of Scobie's last remarks: "I just want to stop giving pain," a sentiment that could just as well come from Edward (HM 295). Their manner of deaths, too, bespeak their natures. Edward deftly slits his throat with a penknife he takes out and toys with in Dowell's presence. No fuss, no pretense. Scobie's suicide is less direct, in fact is compromised. He poisons himself with the drug Evipan (reminiscent of Florence Dowell's suicide by prussic acid) in an effort to fake a heart attack, and manages to fool no one.

Looking at both novels, it is easy for us to see how Greene set a difficult task for himself in recasting Ford's "tale of passion" for a new age. Ford's novel has come to be one of the classics of modern fiction; while much admired, Greene's has not achieved that stature. When Ford took what was by his testimony an episode from life (xx) and found in it both the elements of his own personal loss and a manifestation of the impending tragedy of Western war, he knew that the key to the fiction he was about to create lay in the narrational perspective that was the genius of his novel. It gave him his structural tour-de-force and a novel of philosophical-historical dimensions. Greene must have realized he could not simply replicate the narrative technique of The Good Soldier, nor did he feel ready as a narrativist to do so. And yet it is clear that Ford had the greater success precisely because he saw both the narrational and compellingly emotive effect that Dowell would bring to the story. Greene takes us into the heart of the matter, into Scobie, and it is an almost embarrassing sight, to see such an anguished man turned inside out, as it were. On the other hand, Dowell provides a "scrim" between us and Ashburnham that proves to be the perfect narrational convention, because it allows us to live with our inferences rather than "troths," to sympathize and yet judge.

NOTES

1. This article extends a discussion that first appeared in my book, *Understanding Graham Greene*, 78-81, where, because of editorial constrictions, I was able only to suggest my argument in brief.
2. In her extended study of the relationship between Greene and Ford, Radell misses the parallels between Ashburnham and Scobie, discussed below. Her comments on the importance of Eliot to Greene, which echo those of several other critics, are very much to the point, as are those of Richard Creese and others who anatomize

the various narrative techniques Greene practiced in *The End of the Affair*, most of which come from *The Good Soldier*.

3. Greene, *Collected Essays* 161; all subsequent quotations from "Ford Madox Ford" are taken from this edition and are cited by page in the text.

4. In the 1971 text of *The Heart of the Matter*, Greene included an additional scene between Louise and Wilson that had been cut from the 1948 edition (HM xii, and Higdon and Stratford).

REFERENCES

Allain, Marie-Francoise. *The Other Man: Conversations with Graham Greene*. New York: Simon and Schuster, 1983.

Ford, Ford Madox. *The Good Soldier: A Tale of Passion*. 1915; rpt. New York: Vintage, 1955.

Greene, Graham. "Ford Madox Ford." *Spectator* 163 (7 July 1939): 11.

——. "Ford Madox Ford." *The Lost Childhood and Other Essays*. London: Eyre & Spottiswoode, 1951, 89-91.

——. "Ford Madox Ford." *Collected Essays*. New York: Viking, 1969, 159-171.

——. *The Heart of the Matter*. 1948; rpt. London: Heinemann and Bodley Head, 1971.

——. *Introductions in The Bodley Head Ford Madox Ford*. London: Bodley Head, 1962-1963, I: 7-12, III: 5-8.

Higdon, David Leon. "Graham Greene's Second Thoughts: The Text of The Heart of the Matter." *SB* 30 (1977): 24-56.

Hynes, Joseph. "The `Facts' at The Heart of the Matter." *TSLL* 13 (1972): 711-26.

Miller, R.H. *Understanding Graham Greene*. Columbia SC: U of South Carolina P, 1990.

Radell, Karen Marguerite. *Affirmation in a Moral Wasteland: A Comparison of Ford Madox Ford and Graham Greene*. New York: Peter Lang, 1987.

Sherry, Norman. *The Life of Graham Greene.* 2 vols. New York: Viking, 1989, 1994.

Stratford, Philip. "Second Thoughts on Graham Greene's `Second Thoughts': The Five Texts of The Heart of the Matter." *SB* 31 (1978): 263-66.

7

The Pursuit of Justice: Graham Greene's Refiguring of the Detective Story in 'It's a Battlefield'

—Brian Diemert

Graham Greene remarked towards the end of his life that "in the twenties and thirties I was much interested in the detective story" ("Last Word" viii). These decades are routinely referred to as the golden age of the detective story by the genre's historians;[1] however, the classical British detective story familiarly presented to us in the work of Christie or Sayers failed to meet Greene's demands that the story express both a sense of realism, and social and political concern. Aiming his attack at Sayers's novels particularly, he recalls in Ways of Escape that classical detective stories were, "[w]ith all their carefully documented references to Bradshaw's timetable or to the technique of campanology or to the geography- complete with plan- of a country house . . . lacking in realism. There were too many suspects and the criminal never belonged to what used to be called the criminal class" (73). Instead, Greene preferred the "blood" or the thriller as the form best able to deal with the modern world:

> There never was a school of popular English bloods. We have been damned from the start by middle-class virtues, by gentlemen cracksmen and stolen plans and Mr. Wu's. We have to go farther back than this, dive below the polite level, to something nearer the common life. (Reflections 65-66)

Although Greene is discussing the popular cinema here, the idea of going further back to the thrillers of Buchan, Childers, or Wallace, to name just three authors Greene enjoyed reading, inspired attempts in his own early fiction to adapt the detective story and the thriller to the political and social concerns of the day by recreating and restructuring these forms to produce a new kind of thriller not steeped in the jingoistic, even fascistic, ideology of the pre-World War I thrillers. This endeavour is most clearly seen in those texts Greene chose to call "entertainments," but is not exclusive to them. It's a Battlefield (1934), which he described as "his first overtly political novel" (Allain 87), was never considered an "entertainment," but it is, nonetheless, a text that marks the beginnings of Greene's attempts to rework the formula of the thriller in order to challenge the form's implied ideology and to bring political, social and economic concerns into popularwriting so as to make it the vehicle of both entertainment and "serious" purpose.

Considered one of his best novels in the thirties (Calder-Marshall 373), It's a Battlefield follows its textual precursor, Conrad's The Secret Agent, in using the thriller as it derives from the detective story to interrogate received and accepted ways of interpreting or reading the world and, by implication, texts. Detective fiction is a particularly apt genre for this purpose since, as Todorov and others have pointed out, the classical detective story is itself a story of reading.[2] Most clearly, the detective is a figure for the reader in the text, since the detective must read a text that is written by a criminal or murderer in the clues that he or she finds. However, the murderer attempts to keep this story hidden from the detective by creating a fiction, an alibi, which will conceal the true story of the crime. That is, the murderer is the author of a palimpsestic account of the murder, with the story of the crime as it really happened lying beneath a story of the crime claiming to be the truth of what happened. The detective is forced to interpret one text, the alibi, in such a way that he or she is able to uncover the hidden story that is the true account of events, for showing through the fictional account of the crime are indications of what actually happened. The detective story ends with the detective producing a new narrative, which is the explanation and interpretation of the criminal's fiction. In this way, "[d]etective fiction, particularly of the classical formula, . . . thematizes narrativity itself as a problem, a procedure, and an achievement" (Huhn 451).

Structurally, the detective story is made up of layered narratives. Aside from the various accounts of the crime- the testimonies of witnesses, the murderer's fiction, the detective's explanation, and the often implicit story of events as they really happened- there is a larger structural layering that subsumes and reflects the interpretive relationships among these competing accounts. As Todorov observes, the detective story tells two basic stories: the first is the story of the investigation, which is foregrounded and present for the reader of the text, and the second is the story of the crime which ends before the first story begins and so is largely absent for the reader. This hidden story is intermittently revealed in the clues that the investigator uncovers as he or she retraces the path of the murderer. At the end of the narrative the hidden story is fully made present in the primary story when the detective retells the story of the crime and reveals the murderer's identity. The detective's final explanation unravels the text's enigmas and closes the gap between the two stories of the crime and of the investigation; the narrative resolves itself and the text consequently ends. Hence, as Peter Brooks notes, the interpretive dynamics of the classical detective story's structure lay bare the structure of all narrative (25).

In the thriller, however, although it remains the investigator's task to uncover the origins of the crime for those around him or her, the story of the crime is not hidden from the reader. Instead, it is foregrounded and vitalized while the story of the investigation is largely suppressed. This structure removes the question of "whodunit?" from the reader's mind, but renders the metaphor of reading more complicated as the investigator still seeks to read the story of the crime while, correspondingly, the criminal seeks to read the story of the investigation in order to prevent his or her own story from being read. Both the investigator and the criminal attempt to plot their actions in response to each other, and in this sense, each constructs an interpretation of the other's plot.

Traditionally, in the classical detective story, the detective's final explanation is presented as the correct reading of events, triumphing over the false or deceitful interpretations offered by other characters such as the police or the criminal himself, and so the detective is a figure of absolute interpretative authority: he or she is a kind of Nietzschean superman standing above and beyond the law whose vision reaches into the heart of mysteries that perplex his or her more human rivals such as friends, the police, or the reader.[3] The detective's mission is "to dispel magic and mystery, to make everything explicit, accountable subject to scientific analysis" (Belsey 111). In the thirties, with the rise of fascism in Europe and a growing sense of crisis in British affairs, the interpretive authority usually accorded the detective was viewed with increasing suspicion as "the assumption, strong in English fiction, that we live in an intelligible and generally benevolent universe, that crime is the aberration, peace and tranquillity the norm, and that the proper occupation of man is the bringing of order to chaos" collapsed (James 639). Equally damaging for the detective's authority in the thirties was an awareness that the structure of totalitarianism is present in the genre insofar as the criminal is often made the scapegoat for society's ills while the detective's own extralegal position allows him or her to employ extraordinary measures not possible within conventionally ordered society (Aydelotte 93-94).[4]

Consequently, in Greene's novels the investigators, unlike detectives of the classical detective story such as Holmes and Poirot, usually, fail in their endeavours or, when they do achieve their ends, do so almost in spite of their methods of reading. Hence, in Greene, a text's authoritative, univocal reading cannot be determined given the overwhelming complexity of society, the world, and language. Rationality or intellect, the traditional power of the classical detective that leads to the correct reading of events, is not enough for Greene's investigators and is frequently undermined by the efficacy of irrational practices or coincidence or by society itself. For example, extrasensory impressions lead Raven to rescue Anne from her entombment in the chimney in A Gun for Sale, and Ida consults a ouija board in Brighton Rock. Similarly, in The Confidential Agent, D., who fails both in his mission to buy coal and then in his attempt to persuade the miners not to go back to work, is surprised to learn that his enemy, L., has been refused the coal as well. In It's a Battlefield the Assistant Commissioner's skill is rendered sterile by the restrictive and authoritarian society, in which he operates.

Greene's sense of the limitations of his investigators helps to align his thrillers with the hard-boiled detective fiction first produced by American authors such as Dashiell Hammett and Ravmond Chandler in the twenties and thirties. Whereas the classical detective story, typified by the work of Poe, Doyle, and Christie among others,[5] presupposed the certainty of a correct reading, the hard-boiled detective story is "caught up in the uncertainties of the activity of interpretation itself, for which a final and valid result may be imagined but can never be confidently predicted" (Most 350). As Štephen Marcus explains in a discussion of Hammett's work, the problem of interpretation is never resolved in this kind of fiction:

> What he [Hammett's early detective, the Continental Op] soon discovers [in any of his investigations] is that the "reality" that anyone involved will swear to is . . . itself a construction, a fabrication, a fiction, a faked and alternate reality—and that it has been gotten together before he ever arrived on the scene. And the Op's work therefore is to deconstruct or reconstruct out of it a true fiction, that is, an account of what "really" happened . . . [However], the story, account, or chain of events that the Op winds up with as "reality" is no more plausible and no less ambiguous than the stories that he meets with at the outset and later. (201-02)

In Hammett's fiction, the work of the detective is clearly a fiction-making activity, and the detective knows it. For example, in The Dain Curse (1929) the Op concludes a lengthy interpretation of Joseph Haldorn's activities by affirming that none of it happened: "I hope you're [Fitzstephan, the murderer though the Op is not aware of this at the time] not trying to keep all this nonsense straight in your mind. You know damned well all this didn't happen"(103). More to the point, Fitzstephan accuses the

Op of never being satisfied "until you've got two buts and an if attached to everything" (63).

In It's a Battlefield there is a similar uncertainty about the interpretive project. Ultimately, Greene's text shows how reading and interpretation are always problematic activities, and one of the ways it does this is to undermine conventional reading strategies by challenging the traditional, largely conservative, ideology of both the detective story and the pre-World War I thrillers such as those by Buchan or Wallace.

That It's a Battlefield was conceived at least partially as a response to the ethos of the detective story is surely made clear in Greene's statements about the book's conception. In Ways of Escape, he records "a piece of rough verse" written in his diary on 21 November 1932:[6]

> This the analysis of blood-stain—on woollen beret of a common make'; the experts complain that the fingers left no mark On the park chair or the young breast; microscopic stare at uncertain past, Grass inspected, note-book entry, 'torn bodice and lace'; Over the body the solitary sentry of her certain peace. (27)

Similarly, in A Sort of Life Greene quotes from his diary (19 August 1932) his description of the initial idea for It's a Battlefield: "A large inclusive picture of a city, the connecting link the conviction of a man for the murder of a policeman. Is it politic to hang him? And the detectives go out through the city listening . . ." (152-53). Both of these entries (and a number of others outlining dreams that Greene had in late 1932 and early 1933, mentioned in Sherry's biography [457-581) explicitly link It's a Battlefield with the detective novel and, particularly, with the idea of detection as surveillance, which, following the thought of Foucault, acts in the novel as an expression of political power and as a metaphor for both reading and narrative itself.

Greene described It's a Battlefield as "a panoramic novel of London" (Sherry 456) that traces the actions of a number of characters throughout the city. The narrator's gaze plays over these characters- none of whom singly dominates the narrative's plot in the role of a protagonist. In this regard, the city itself comes to dominate the narrative, and within its bounds class differences are sharply contrasted as the narrative moves between the world of the upper classes and the world of the lower classes. The first is characterized by Caroline Bury's literary salon, Surrogate's bourgeois bedroom, and the Berkeley hotel where Beale's private secretary meets with the Assistant Commissioner; and the second is typified by the basement flat Milly and Kay share, the match factory where Kay works, and the prison where Jim Drover awaits his execution. Between these two worlds lies the battlefield of London.

The emphasis It's a Battlefield places on the city itself, while displaying the fascination with the urban landscape that is widely reflected in the literature of the modern period, also recalls comments by G.K. Chesterton, who saw the detective story as unique in expressing "some sense of the poetry of modern [which is to say, urban] life" ("Defence of Detective Stories" 158). For Chesterton, author of detective stories featuring Father Brown and the thriller The Man Who Was Thursday, the detective story offers the "realization of the poetry of London" because for the detective the city, indeed the world, is seen as a mysterious, even occult, text that demands interpretation:

> there is no stone in the street and no brick in the wall that is not actually a deliberate symbol- a message from some man, as much as if it were a telegram or a post card. The narrowest street

> possesses, in every crook and twist of its intention, the soul of the man who built it, perhaps long in his grave. Every brick has as human a hieroglyph as if it were a graven brick of Babylon; every slate on the roof is as educational a document as if it were a slate covered with addition and subtraction sums. (159)

Such a vision of the world is certainly that of Sherlock Holmes, whose "Book of Life" asserts that "By a man's finger-nails, by his coat-sleeve, by his boots, by his trouser knees . . . [his] calling is plainly revealed" (Doyle 23); and, though doubts about the classical detective's ability to read these signs correctly appear in later detective fiction, this vision of the world as text remains in most detective fiction and in Greene's thrillers.

Chesterton also goes on to remark that detective fiction "tends to remind us that we live in an armed camp, making war with a chaotic world, and that the criminals, the children of chaos, are nothing but traitors within our gates" (161). This conception of the detective story translates itself into the traditional thriller's emphasis on a clear division between opposing forces, between an "us" and a "them" as Auden puts it (147). It's a Battlefield highlights both of the qualities Chesterton describes: the second through the Assistant Commissioner's conception of the city as a battlefield, and the first through a vision, derived from Greene's precursor text, Conrad's The Secret Agent, of the city as a textual field wherein language circulates.

On one level, the sense of the city as text is conveyed through the repeated mentioning of street names, particularly as the paths of characters are traced and retraced. Not only does this naming lend a geographic realism to the book's setting, but it also transforms the city's streets into a metaphor for a restrictive and governing social structure since the city and the society are imaged as an interlocking web that is linked to the circles of hell by an allusion to Dante (22-23). In one sense the cartography of the city of London is laid over the novel as a container for the narrative, but in another sense the network of streets becomes the concrete and asphalt image of the invisible "wires" of influence (64) that govern the lives of the book's characters and bind separate and seemingly unrelated elements in the novel's plot. Compatible with this is the title's implication, supported by the epigraph from Kinglake's The Invasion of the Crimea, of individual and seemingly unrelated battles taking place under the direction of remote and invisible high-ranking commanders whose orders travel along a chain of command.

However, the suggestion that the city is a site where language circulates is also confirmed in the novel by the frequent inclusion of newspaper headlines (some of which deal with real political events at the time of the book's composition), by the repeated allusions to the "Sale. Premises damaged by fire" sign (55, 61, 155), and, perhaps more importantly, by the recurring mention of "the pram on top of the taxi" (10, 16, 60, 113, 155, 193), first overheard by the Assistant Commissioner while with the private secretary. Each of these repetitions suggests the circulation of language within the text and functions, like the city itself, as a unifying force in the novel. For example, since the "pram on a taxi" recurs in the thoughts of Conrad Drover and the Assistant Commissioner, the phrase links the two characters. However, the phrase itself is a fragment of another narrative which is never told in It's a Battlefield. What happens is that a second suppressed narrative intrudes into the discourse of the primary narrative though, unlike the criminal's story in the more conventional detective story, the pram and taxi story remains enigmatic. In this respect, the puzzlingly surreal quality of the image suggests the chaos of the modern city, but, more significantly, it demands interpretation from those who encounter the fragment. For the Assistant Commissioner it is nothing more than a bizarre joke emblematic of the chaos he guards against; but, for Drover, it becomes representative of the mocking provocation of the establishment tied to a particular concept of the rule of law and justice (60, 193). Ultimately, the "pram on the taxi" is a narrative fragment, like the stories alluded to by the fire-sale sign or the recurring mention of the Streatham murder case, whose repetition allegorizes the circulation of texts within a textual field wherein individual texts intersect, run parallel, and repeat each other. (Conder, the newspaper man, is perhaps dimly aware of this textual property: "He gave the impression that all human stories were often repeated and that it was his unfortunate fate to listen to every repetition" [103].) In this sense, the city's street grid images the linguistic field in which texts are found, that is to say, detected. Similarly, the "battlefield" of the title identifies this space as a site of struggle where a number of narratives, roughly corresponding to the number of characters but also including things like the pram on the taxi narrative, compete for dominance both within the novel and within interpretations of the novel. In the text, no one narrative emerges as central and so the conflict of narratives continues throughout.

My point is well illustrated by Surrogate's telling of the story of Jim Drover to Caroline Bury:

> He told her all he knew, humbly, a little grudgingly, watching the wheels of a fine intellect beginning to turn. He was jealous. Beneath Drover's story, buried only just beneath the succeeding words, "policeman- wife- Hyde Park- appeal", buried so shallowly that between the phrases scraps of old bones showed plain ("It reminds me . . . by the way . . . you remember"), lay his own tale, the first example he knew of Caroline Bury's passion to help. (88)

Here, two narratives struggle for dominance within Surrogate's report with Surrogate's own story about himself penetrating his telling of Drover's story. The passage illustrates a general quality of narrative in that any narrative has other narratives behind it and within it and so is intertextually related to these other narratives. Similarly, any narrative is in some ways a repetition or reinterpretation of previous narratives (Todorov 244). On another level, if one takes "Surrogate" in its sense of "deputy" or "substitute," we can see in the passage a reference to Greene's own telling of Drover's story and its effects on the characters of It's a Battlefield. The implication is that behind the literal story of the novel there are other stories- at least one of which is the story of its telling, inspired by the condition of England in the early thirties, but another of which is surely Conrad's The Secret Agent.[7]

It's a Battlefield, however, is not a detective story in the sense of having a detective who works to uncover the story of the crime in the conventional manner. Rather, it is a novel that begins after the crime has been solved, and, in this respect, differs markedly from both the classical detective story and the thriller. Conventionally, the classical detective story ends with the discovery of the criminal's identity and an accompanying explanation of the crime. The criminal's punishment is generally not made a part of the story; the murderer is occasionally left to commit suicide (as is the case with Dr. Sheppard in Agatha Christie's The Murder of Roger Ackroyd or Matthew Cayley in A. A. Milne's The Red House Mystery) or is handed over to the authorities (as in many of the Sherlock Holmes's stories) or, if the workings of justice are to be presented, is summarily dealt with (as in Greene's own short story "Murder for the Wrong Reason"). In this way, neither the reader nor the detective is forced to witness the execution of justice. As Foucault would argue, this development in the history of literature dealing with crime, from the

Newgate Calender for instance to Christie's work, indicates a shift in the way society is disciplined as the explicit emphasis on the manner of punishment is replaced by the coercive force of surveillance (Foucault 67-69).

However, since the criminal is often presented as a double of the detective, as we see in the pairings of Holmes and Moriarty in some of Doyle's stories or Dupin and the Minister D_____ in Poe's "The Purloined Letter," the fact that punishment takes place outside the narrative demonstrates a moral aporia that paradoxically preserves the rigidity of the classical detective story's moral structure. The force of law, of the good, is seen to triumph over the force of disorder, of evil, but the moral ambiguity inherent in the expiation of evil by a process that involves the repetition of the initial crime is suppressed in the interest of preserving the sense of the criminal as "other," despite his or her kinship with the detective and with other members of the society. By placing punishment outside the bounds of the narrative, the illusion of localized guilt and the assumption of moral superiority on the part of other characters and the reader is maintained. Crime, in the classical detective story, is rooted in the individual; it is an aberration and not a response to social conditions or the expression of a shared and innate tendency towards violence.

This kind of literature places enormous trust in the mechanisms of justice which are assumed to be impervious to the vagaries of the everyday world's political squabbles and individual preferences. However, when this trust disappears, or when these same mechanisms of law and order show themselves to be unworthy of the public trust, a new kind of literature emerges that realigns the matrix of criminal, detective, judge and jury. In the thrillers of Hammett or Chandler, for example, the instruments of justice are perceived as ineffectual or corrupt and so the detective, as is partly the case with Conrad Drover in It's a Battlefield, takes on their functions with limited or, perhaps, no success.[8]

It's a Battlefield both formally and thematically challenges the conservative moral absolutism of the classical detective story by employing techniques similar to those used by the American writers of hard-boiled thrillers. In making "the injustice of men's justice" his main theme (Ways of Escape 28), Greene explicitly focuses on that part which is either treated perfunctorily or ignored altogether in the classical detective story. In terms of genre, Greene's novel leaves the classical detective story behind for the thriller's ambiguous world of corruption and indeterminacy. In It's a Battlefield, Jim Drover awaits execution for his murder of a London police officer, but the novel works against the Assistant Commissioner's confident assertion that "we got the man" (11). Circumstances surrounding the crime blur the issue of Drover's guilt and extend culpability to those charged with enforcing the laws and administering justice. Indeed, the whole question of what defines a murderer is brought into the text. Ultimately, blame is shown to rest with the society itself and, more particularly, with the dominant ideology that directs sociopolitical life.

In It's a Battlefield political power is exercised and maintained by means of surveillance, which, as Foucault argues, acts as a technique of coercion by making the visible subject the principle of his own subjection (202-203) and by incorporating him or her into a panoptic schema whose aim is to strengthen existing social forces (208). In the novel, surveillance occurs at every level of what is shown to be a disciplinary society. Of course, there are the police throughout the city reporting on the expected political reaction to Drover's execution (as Greene describes in his diary), but at least half a dozen other incidents of overt or covert surveillance are also apparent: Conder, a reporter with the Evening Watch, tells the detective

Patmore of events at a Communist party meeting in exchange for an exclusive on the Paddington trunk murderer's arrest (a bargain that suggests police control of an always vigilant press); the offices in Scotland Yard and in the insurance company where Conrad Drover works are partitioned with glass; overseers in the prison and the factory observe their inmates; a pair of watchers keep their eyes on Jim Drover in prison; the Assistant Commissioner is unable to keep out of the way of his men; and Conrad Drover stalks the Assistant Commissioner through the city. Each of these incidents stresses the controlling nature of observation in the city, for surveillance is used as a means of exercising power over individuals because it inspires fear — a point best seen in Conrad Drover's paranoid belief that he is being watched (I 72) and in Conder's and Bennett's responses to their mutual suspicion that each is being followed by the other (137-38). The gaze of others establishes a totalitarian control, as in Bentham's Panopticon, because it constitutes a network of obser-vation that links and subdues disparate elements within the city (Foucault 202-203).

In this way, the skills of detection possessed by the police and particularly by the Assistant Commissioner are tied to the maintenance of an oppressive "existing order" (19), which is capitalist and authoritarian.

As a character, the Assistant Commissioner is a type derived from both the classical detective and, perhaps more specifically, Conrad's character of the same name in The Secret Agent. Greene's Assistant Commissioner possesses a passion for accuracy (13) and Holmesian skill in the reading of minute detail: "But turning over in his mind the woollen beret, noting the texture of the wool, the pattern of the crochet, he understood more than the most sensitive artist, noticed more than the most inquisitive woman" (13). As well, he makes his work the sole focus of his life. (He fears retirement [81] while the pleasures of detection can move him to ecstasy [202].) However, because his concentration on detail at the expense of the larger vision is shown to be inadequate given the need for social change in the thirties, the novel questions the detective's authority. Unlike earlier detectives such as Holmes or Poirot, the Assistant Commissioner cannot put everything right at the end of It's a Battlefield- indeed, his report on Drover is ignored by the government that commissioned it — because the problems are ones to which he contributes by continuing to work "to preserve the existing order" (19). In this sense, the Assistant Commissioner is implicated in Drover's crime because not only is he the supervisor of a force that attacked demonstrators, including women and children, with clubs (Drover is defending his wife when he stabs the policeman Coney), but he also works for and helps to perpetuate a regime that exploits workers to the point where they demonstrate en masse. In this way, he resembles Chandler's Marlowe at the end of The Big Sleep who, unable to bring the racketeer Eddie Mars to justice, makes himself a party, to the crime by lying to General Sternwood- an act of deception which protects the network of corruption Marlowe has uncovered.

The duality of the Assistant Commissioner's position is reflected in his own conceptions of himself as a "general" (128) and, alternatively, as "a mercenary soldier" (129) or a "private soldier fighting in a fog" (166) in "a civil war" (165) in which the demonstration is only one struggle. For him the urban landscape is a battlefield: "the front line was only a hundred yards away, where the trams screamed down the Embankment and the buses circled Trafalgar Square . . ." (129).

> . . . [H]is enemies were not only the brutal and the depraved, but the very men he pitied, the men he wanted to help; if he had done his duty the unemployed man would have been arrested for begging. The buildings seemed to him then to lose a little of their dignity; the peace of

Sunday in Pall Mall was like the peace which follows a massacre, a war of elimination; poverty here had been successfully contested, driven back on the one side towards Notting Hill, on the other towards Vauxhall. (165-66)

As Peter Widdowson points out, this kind of martial imagery, typical of Greene's work in the thirties and forties, is at once a metaphor for both the violence of the modern world and the class war within society (Widdowson 154). In this "civil" war, the Assistant Commissioner is charged with the defence of the city against crime, which is explicitly tied to poverty, and, more crucially, against social upheaval: "His work was simply to preserve the existing order" (19), or, as he thinks to himself, "the State . . . employs me to keep order, to see that the unemployed beg and do not demand" (163).

This role, however, is not one that the Assistant Commissioner relishes, so he protects himself by taking refuge in comforting thoughts of doing one's duty (76) and by compartmentalizing his vision of the world in such a way that things like justice, morality, and politics are conceived of as independent and separate things:

> It was as well to be conventional when one fought so fierce and so indecisive a war; one's thoughts had to be canalized: Streatham, Paddington, wireless inventions, these principally had held the mind, so one bought a poppy and saved the time which might have been wasted on the dead; one raised a hat and forgot the done-with past; one wore one's school tie and dispensed with introductions; one touched wood and saved the harassing and useless thought: perhaps I am wrong. (170)

Although encouraged by the established order in the person of the private secretary, who twice assures the

Assistant Commissioner that he need only concern himself with "the poorer parts" of London (13,14), the Assistant Commissioner's compartmentalized vision fails because it ignores the undeniable connections — figured again by the city's streets — between things. The Assistant Commissioner may think his job has nothing to do with justice, but for Conrad Drover the Assistant Commissioner is the very embodiment of justice (161). Similarly, though the Assistant Commissioner insists on having nothing to do with politics, he is engaged in an explicitly political task- the writing of a report on the expected reaction to Jim Drover's execution. The Assistant Commissioner's vision of society is thus shown to be both naive and narrowly focused, yet its very limitations allow him to function within the society.

The problem is that, although he is the defender of the established order, he knows that "the laws were made by property owners in defence of property" (169), and so, personally, he is sympathetic to those who are marginalized or impoverished by these laws (16, 162-62). The result is a separation between his natural feelings of sympathy and his responsibilities to his employer, the State. This division produces a sense of alienation since it forces the Assistant Commissioner to adopt both a public and a private persona; he is compelled to act against his own inclinations to defend a system in which he does not believe: "His business was not justice; his business was only to catch the right man; but in private, in his secret life, he was troubled by the slightest deviation from the strictest justice" (162). In the face of this dilemma he dreams of "an organization which he could serve for higher reasons than pay" (130), but age and weariness have sapped both his faith in the possibility of a new social order and his will to help bring about such an order. Ultimately, his blinkered social vision protects both himself from the terror of "the demands which might be made on him" (166) and the social order from revolution because it allows the Assistant

Commissioner to continue doing his job. (On another level, as the Nuremberg trials demonstrated, this kind of social vision leads to extremist political forms like fascism or Stalinism, the crimes of the Nazis, and the abdication of personal morality and responsibility.) As with most characters in the book, then, the Assistant Commissioner's actions are largely directed by self-interest. "The truth is," he tells Caroline Bury, "nobody cares about anything but his own troubles. Everybody's too busy fighting his own little battle to think of . . . the next man" (188).

This meeting with Caroline Bury inspires the Assistant Commissioner to condemn himself for his own cowardice in not helping to create a new order. However, instead of taking the necessary action of resigning, he slips back into his old habit of mind, forgetting the drama of Drover and the chaplain and Conrad's attempt at murder, to focus his thoughts solely upon the Streatham case. The book ends with the Assistant Commissioner finding his moment of contentment, yet we cannot help wondering at the cost. Unlike other politically uncommitted figures in Greene's novels who for whatever reasons are compelled to take some action- Fowler in The Quiet American, Brown in The Comedians, Plarr in The Honorary Consul, and even Chase in Rumour at Nightfall, for instance- the Assistant Commissioner cannot regain "faith" (190) and act on his sense of social justice.

If the idea of the detective as the representative of a tradition of law, order and justice is questioned in It's a Battlefield, then so too is the conception of the murderer as an aberration within an otherwise stable and contented society. In large measure this is done through a consideration of Jim Drover, who is awaiting execution. Early in the novel, Kay confidently thinks, "They'll reprieve him. He isn't a murderer" (31), and later Conrad Drover, Jim's brother, considers the official judgment that one is a murderer meaningless:

> . . . I've seen through that; you can't shame me any longer with a word like murderer; I know what a murderer is- Jim is a murderer. The law told me that, impressed on me through three long days, counsel have made expensive speeches on the point; six shopkeepers, three Civil Servants, two doctors, and a well-known correspondent have discussed it together and come to that conclusion- Jim is a murderer, a murderer is Jim. Why shouldn't I be a murderer myself? Always, from the time I went to school, I have wanted to be like Jim. It's no good calling me a murderer. I've seen through that. (111)

Still later, he carries these thoughts further: "a murderer is strength, protection, love" (160). This conception sharply undermines the legal establishment's determination, by and large accepted by the public[9] (who are given their own part to play in the procedure), of a murderer as a disease in the body politic. However, for both Conrad and Kay, Jim is a murderer in name only; he is not, by his nature, murderous.

Conder's and the Assistant Commissioner's experiences of other murderers similarly intensify the questions that surround the figure of the murderer within detective fiction. Conder remembers "the man who drowned his wife at Shoreham, flushed and neat in the dock with a tiepin in the shape of a horse's head; the widow of the grocer who drew the Derby winner and who, dead drunk the same night, drove his car into the Thames, a widow with 20,000 [pound] of her own; she said, 'I've always been lucky at such things, raffles, I mean, and so on'" (135). While the case of the widow suggests her culpability in her husband's death, the first recalls the paradoxical nature of some murderers that the Assistant Commissioner also finds in Crippen and the Salvationist, who is arrested for the Paddington trunk murder. Although both have committed grisly crimes, Crippen and the Salvationist present themselves as respectable members of society: Crippen, a doctor, is forever neat and the Salvationist calls for the faithful to "Come to Jesus" (81). The inclusion in the narrative of the Salvationist's arrest not only reinforces the metaphor of the battlefield, since the murderer is a member of the Salvation Army, but also subverts the dominant ideology by dramatizing the disparity between the actions of the speaker and the rhetoric of the established order which, in this case, is exemplified by religious teaching. As the analysis of Conrad's remorse after his sexual encounter with Milly shows, this kind of rhetoric is part of the panoptic schema of the disciplinary society in that it reinforces the individual's own conscious self-surveillance: the development of Conrad's sense of remorse demonstrates how he is made the principle of his own subjection:

> It had been difficult to believe in the wrong during the commission . . . but afterwards . . . he had pasted the proper labels on his memory of it. 'A mortal sin.' 'The bitter wrong. "A broken commandment.' But the labels were not his; he had taken them from others; others had made the rules by which he suffered; it was unfair that they should leave him so alone and yet make the rules which governed him. It was as if a man marooned must still order his life according to the regulations of his ship. (159)

Of course, this is not to imply that Conrad is entirely innocent of wrongdoing (he has, after all, slept with Milly and betrayed both Jim and his own sense of honour), yet the remorse he feels is reinforced by the limiting mores of a social order from which he is excluded. He is co-opted and made a part of the panoptic mechanism.

The contradiction between accepted rhetoric and actual behaviour is similarly exposed in the Assistant Commissioner's reflections on his career among criminals:

> he thought of innumerable clerics rising in innumerable pulpits to talk of cleanliness as next to godliness . . . praising the clean body as an indication of a clean mind. He thought of Crippen shaving carefull everyday of his trial, particular about small things. It was these contradictions, the moral maxims which did not apply, that made it impossible for a man to found his life on any higher motive than doing his job. A life spent with criminals would never fail to strip the maxims of priests and teachers from the underlying chaos. (80-81)

As the passage makes clear, the mere fact of the murderer undercuts the myth of social and political harmony underpin- the classical detective story, and so the passage reflects a social vision more akin to that of the authors of the hard-boiled school of detective fiction. Greene presents crime and murder as stemming from deep fissures within the structure of society between the wealthy and the powerful, who control the established institutions within the society, and the great mass of people who subscribe to a sociopolitical ideology that fails to recognize them as equals. The result is that, despite the prevailing establishment's rhetoric, social, political and economic chaos results from clashes between the powerful elite and the divided majority.

It's a Battlefield, like The Secret Agent, exposes the chaos beneath the veneer of civilization, and Conrad's thoughts as he sees the Assistant Commissioner walk down the street aptly characterize the vision of Greene's novel:

> he came slowly, justice with a file of papers; he came, respectability, with bowler hat and umbrella; he came, assurance, eyes on the pavement, safe in London, safe in the capital city of the Empire, safe at the heart of civilization (I see no reason to reverse

the judge's decision'; the raised truncheon; the forbidden meeting; 'after one year we allow them to embrace'; reduced staffs, unemployment; the constant struggle with your fellow man to keep alone upon the raft, to let the other drown; desire; adultery; passion without tenderness or permanence); down the street the upholder of civilization, eves on the pavement, neat file under his arm. 161). As the parentheses suggest, at the heart of London exists the brutality and meanness that lie beneath the civilization of Empire and the capitalist ideology of imperialism. For Conrad and others who are marginalized by class, gender, or race, safety in London — even civilization itself — is a fiction: "'Them as knows what London is,' Mrs. Simpson [says], would not be surprised to find their nearest and dearest bleeding'" (182). Similarly, the maxims of law and justice within the society are exposed as fictions:

> Somewhere, at some time, in a newspaper or a book, Milly had read the words, "Judgement by your peers". She had thought it meant judgement by your lords and had been laughed at for thinking so, "It means judgement by your equals", but where, she asked now of Mrs. Coney, was a judge who was their equal, a man with three pounds a week, who lived as they lived? And the jury? Tradesmen and gentlemen. It wasn't fair . . . (97)

Given its vision of the central hypocrisy within the society of the 1930s, it is not surprising that It's a Battlefield blurs the images of detective and murderer alike while suggesting that true justice may be elusive. Unlike in the classical detective story, not even poetic justice operates in Greene's novel; instead, all forms of human justice are seen as inadequate in It's a Battlefield because, as the chaplain says, they are arbitrary and incomprehensible (199). Later Greene thrillers build on the equivocations in the roles of detective and murderer that emerge in It's a Battlefield and in his other early work. However, Greene's reshaping of the detective story as a thriller exposes the contradictions and the conservatism at the heart of what in the period was one of the most dominant forms of popular writing. With It's a Battlefield Greene made his first move towards a popular literature that could suggest moral values. By turning away from the models of his youth, Greene fashioned a new kind of thriller that, as the work of John Le Carre demonstrates, has been enormously influential.

NOTES

1. See, for example, works by Howard Haycraft (*Murder for Pleasure: The Life and Times of the Detective Story* [New York: Carroll, 1984])], A.E. Murch (*The Development of the Detective Novel* [London: Peter Owen, 1958]), and Julian Symons (*Bloody Murder: From the Detective Story to the Crime Novel* [New York: Viking, 1985]).

2. Tzvetan Todorov's essay "The Typology of Detective Fiction" (1966) is seminal in this regard (*The Poetics of Prose*, trans. Richard Howard [Ithaca: Cornell UP, 1977, esp. 42-52). Peter Brooks (*Reading for the Plot: Design and Intention in Narrative* [New York: Vintage, 1985]), Dennis Porter (*The Pursuit of Crime: Art and Ideology in Detective Fiction* [New Haven: Yale UP, 1981]), and Peter Huhn ("The Detective as Reader: Narrativity and Reading Concepts in Detective Fiction," [*Modern Fiction Studies* 33.3 (1987), 451- 466]) also offer important discussions of the relationship between the detective story and reading.

3. For an analysis of the detective along this line of inquiry see William O. Aydelotte's "The Detective Story as a Historical Source" (*The Yale Review*, 39 [1949]: 76-95).

4. Similarly, Michael Denning sees an "anti-fascist aesthetic" in the serious thrillers of the thirties (66).

5. For descriptions of those elements that make up the formulas of the classical detective novel and of the hard-boiled detective Novel see Dorothy Sayers's "Introduction to The Omnibus of Crime," George Grella's "The Formal Detective Novel" and "The Hard-Boiled Detective Novel," and John G. Cawelti's *Adventure, Mystery, and Romance*, chapters 4 and 6.

6. Dates for comments from Greene's diary are given in Sherry's biography. Those passages relevant to the genesis of It's a Battlefield are found on pages 457-58.

7. Greene's debt to Conrad's novel has been remarked upon and discussed by a number of critics, among them Kenneth Allott and Miriam Farris (87-89), Norman Sherry (457), and Lynne Cheney.

8. This tendency for the detective to assume the functions of judge and jury in hard-boiled fiction is clearly exemplified in the title of Mickey Spillane's first novel, I, the Jury; in this novel, though, Mike Hammer's pursuit of justice, like Conrad Drover's pursuit in It's a Battlefield, is clouded by a morally dubious desire for personal revenge. The hard-boiled detective's sense of impotence is well illustrated near the end of Hammett's *Red Harvest* (1929) by the Op's comments made to Willson, the wealthy publisher who hired the Op to rid Personville ("Poisonville") of the criminal gangs dominating municipal politics: You'll have your city back, all nice and clean and ready to go to the dogs again" (187). Similarly, the Op's comments at the end of "$106,000 Blood Money" also suggest his impotence: "I'm going to take a couple of weeks off,' I said from the door. I felt tired, washed out" (458).

9. For instance, the Assistant Commissioner's housekeeper, Mrs. Simpson, agrees with the courts: "'I'd like to see'em [murderers] all strung up and finished with'" (76-77).

REFERENCES

Allott, Kenneth, and Miriam Farris. *The Art of Graham Greene.* 1951. New York: Russell , 1963.

Allain, Marie-Francoise. *The Other Man: Conversations with Graham Greene by Marie-Francoise Allain.* 1981. Trans. Guido Walman. London: Bodley, 1983.

Auden, W.H. "The Guilty Vicarage." 1938. *The Dyer's Hand and Other Essays.* London: Faber, 1963. 146-58.

Aydelotte, William O. "The Detective Story as a Historical Source." *The Yale Review* 39 (1949): 76-95.

Belsey, Catherine. *Critical Practice.* New York: Methuen, 1980.

Brooks, Peter. *Reading for the Plot: Design and Intention in Narrative.* 1984. New York: Vintage, 1985.

Calder-Marshall, Arthur. "The Works of Graham Greene." *Horizon* 1 (1940): 367-75.

Cawelti, John G. *Adventure, Mystery, and Romance: Formula Stories as Art and Popular Culture.* Chicago: U of Chicago P, 1976.

Cheney, Lynne. "Joseph Conrad's The Secret Agent and Graham Greene's It's a Battlefield: A Study in Structural Meaning." *MFS* 16.2 (1970): 117-32.

Chesterton, G.K. "A Defence of Detective Stories." *The Defendant. London: Dent,* 1901. 157-162.

Denning, Michael. *Cover Stories: Narrative and Ideology in the British Spy Thriller.* New York: Routledge, 1987.

Doyle, Arthur Conan. *The Complete Sherlock Holmes.* 2 vols. Garden City: Doubleday, 1930.

Foucault, Michel. *Discipline and Punish: The Birth of the Prison.* 1975. Trans. Alan Sheridan. New York: Vintage, 1979.

Greene, Graham. *It's a Battlefield.* 1934. Harmonds worth: Penguin, 1980.

_____. "The Last Word" and Other Stories. Toronto: Lester, 1990.

_____. *Reflections.* Selected and introduced by Judith Adamson. Toronto: Lester, 1990.

_____. *A Sort of Life.* 1971. Harmondsworth: Penguin, 1974.

_____. *Ways of Escape.* 1980. Harmondsworth: Penguin, 1981.

Grella, George. "The Formal Detective Novel." *Winks* 84-102.

_____. "The Hard-Boiled Detective Novel." *Winks* 103-20.

Hammett, Dashiell. *The Dain Curse*. 1929. New York: Vintage, 1972.

_____. *Red Harvest*. 1929. New York: Vintage, 1972.

_____. "$106,000, Blood Money." *The Big Knockover: Selected Stories and Short Novels*. Ed. Lillian Hellman. New York: Vintage, 1972. 412-58.

Haycraft, Howard. *Murder for Pleasure: The Life and Times of the Detective Story*. 1941. New York: Carroll, 1984.

Huhn, Peter. "The Detective as Reader: Narrativity and Reading Concepts in Detective Fiction." *AMS* 33.3 (1987): 451-466.

James, P.D. "The Art of the Detective Novel." *Journal of the Royal Society of Arts* 133 (1985): 637-49.

Marcus, Stephen. "Dashiell Hammett." Eds. Glenn W. Most and William W. Stowe. 197-209.

Most, Glenn W. "The Hippocratic Smile: John Le Carre and the Traditions of the Detective Novel." Eds. Most and Stowe. 341-65.

_____ and William W. Stowe, eds. *The Poetics of Murder: Detective Fiction and Literary Theory*. San Diego: Harcourt, 1983.

Murch, A.E. *The Development of the Detective Novel*. London: Peter Owen, 1958.

Porter, Dennis. *The Pursuit of Crime: Art and Ideology in Detective Fiction*. New Haven: Yale UP, 1981.

Sayers, Dorothy L. "Introduction to The Omnibus of Crime." *Winks* 53-83.

Sherry, Norman. *The Life of Graham Greene 1904-1939*. Vol. 1. Toronto: Lester, 1989.

Symons, Julian. *Mortal Consequences*. New York: Harper, 1972. Rev. and updated as Bloody Murder: From the *Detective Story to the Crime Novel*. New York: Viking, 1985.

Todorov, Tzvetan. *The Poetics of Prose*. 1971. Trans. Richard Howard. Ithaca: Cornell UP, 1977.

Widdowson, Peter. "Between the Acts? English Fiction in the Thirties." *Culture and Crisis in Britain in the 30s*. Eds. Jon Clark et al. London: Lawrence, 1979. 133-164.

Winks, Robin, ed. *Detective Fiction: A Collection of Critical Essays*. Woodstock: Countryman Press-Foul Play Press, 1988.

8

Experimenting with the Genre: Greene and The Confidential Agent

—John Coates

His villains were almost always foreigners and foreigners, more often than not, were villains. Teutons, dagoes and Jews were the foreigners that The Breed particularly disliked. The Drummond books, right from the start, had foreign villains who were trying to smash England.[1]

Richard Usborne's deservedly well-known account of the world of John Buchan, Dornford Yates and "Sapper" (H.C. McNeile), the popular thriller writers of the 1920s and 1930s, offers a short route into one of the contexts for Graham Greene's The Confidential Agent (1939). It is worth knowing something of the thriller genre as Greene found it in order to understand the effects he produced by his variations of this popular form. However enjoyable, a wide reading of our recent thrillers would not be helpful. A great gulf divides the world of John Le Carre or Len Deighton from that of Yates and "Sapper." More than anyone else, Greene is responsible for that gulf. Writers of early twentieth century British thrillers largely catered to the expectations of their readers within familiar conventions. Most of these novels offered a simple moral framework. On the one side were decent upper-class Englishmen. On the other were their devious and alien adversaries, moral nihilists driven by loathing for the British Empire (Englishmen "should realize that foreigners will always, through jealousy, want to bring England to her knees"[2]). By and large, thrillers of the period celebrated the triumph of straightforward goodness over sophisticated evil. Such evil was externalised, since thriller heroes did not experience mixed motives or serious temptations. They were healthy-minded young men, like Richard Hannay in John Buchan's The Thirty Nine Steps (1915) or Leithen and Chapman in his The Power House (1913), athletic former public-school boys, possessed of private incomes. They knew the right people, belonged to the best clubs and had all the appropriate instincts.

Claud Cockburn, in his study of popular literature between 1900 and 1939, suggests that the prevalence in many of these books of "hypothetical anarchist plots" and exotic villains "wielding immense international power"[3] were a means to displace the anxieties readers felt at the industrial and political troubles of the times. Complex and disturbing issues might be tidied up into a manageable scheme in which decent English values and the right kind of people were able to triumph. Such a refusal of complexity, of difficult problems or issues that could not be readily comprehended, is certainly implied in one feature of the pre-1939 thriller. Suspicion of the intellect in itself is widespread in these novels. Leithen, the hero of Buchan's The Power House which so impressed the young Greene when it appeared in book form ("who will forget that first thrill in 1916?"[4]) has "never had the gift of the gab."[5] He feels there is a "morbid charm" in intellectual discussion "of which one is half-ashamed." On meeting the villain Lumley (a secret foreigner) he is struck by his "restless intelligence which was at once attractive and disquieting"

(32). Leithen really dislikes Lumley's "superior and Olympian" (40) smile as he talks of the vulnerability of civilization and Britain (virtually synonymous terms) to a vast international conspiracy of superior brains. Fortunately, Leithen's suspicions have already been aroused. Lumley's servant is "very unlike the conventional butler" (17) since his eyes are "quick with intelligence." At the end of a tortuous and exciting narrative Lumley is outmaneuvered. Reproached by the victor ("You fear nothing and you believe nothing . . . Man, you should never have been allowed to live" [100]), he reaffirms his own sinister creed: "I have my own worship. I venerate the intellect of man."

The dated, even absurd, features of these old thrillers are easy to see. It is more useful to understand what drew Greene to the form he revolutionized. His comments on Buchan's Sick Heart River (1940) offer a clue. In Greene's view, Buchan and those who imitated him realized "the enormous dramatic value of adventure in familiar surroundings happening to unadventurous men."[6] Murder in an atmosphere of "simplicity and stability" was far more unsettling than Gothic horrors, or romantic feuds. In this sense, Richard Hannay or Sir Edward Leithen were more striking than Stevenson's the master of Ballantrae. The conventional hero, shaken out of his comfortable life by an unexpected and terrifying assault, raises disturbing issues, moral, political or perhaps religious. Greene approvingly quotes Leithen's comment on his own ordeal.

> Now I saw how thin is the protection of civilization. An accident and a bogus ambulance—a false charge and a bogus arrest—there were a dozen ways of spiriting one out of this gay and bustling world.

The thriller could be used to explore the individual's moral relationship to society or the world in a particularly sharpened form. It could reveal the nature of his inner resources (if any) when all props were pulled away. It might show the nature of society itself when suddenly and forcibly viewed from another angle, through the eyes of one ejected from its protective or delusive conventions, hunted or on the run. A surprising number of novels deal with middle-class sexual and emotional entanglements and with the analyses by refined, well-off and physically secure people of their own and each others' emotional problems. One can sympathize with C.S Lewis's remark that popular fiction at its best is more serious than "what is generally called `serious' literature."[7] Such mass-readership material often deals with the mythic, with the "permanent and inevitable". while "an hour's shelling or perhaps a ten mile walk" would erase many of the dilemmas of characters in highbrow novels. Greene's own opinion was similar. In an essay on Francois Mauriac, he remarked that because of their lack of a religious sense and of religious concerns, Forster's and Woolf's creations "wandered like cardboard characters through a world that was paper-thin."[8] On the other hand, Buchan "prepared us in his thrillers better than he knew"[9] for the mass-destruction, harrowing danger and sudden deaths of the London Blitz. Terrible as was the cost, an "old dog-toothed civilization"[10] breaking like "a cracked cup put in boiling water" might open the eyes to spiritual truths that routine and comfort had disguised. For all the faults of its current and previous practitioners, thriller-writing had a power of prophecy and of opening the eyes.

Readers coming from "Sappers" Bulldog Drummond, a "huge, ugly, cheerful apparently brainless man, who slaps you on the back with a hand the size of a leg of mutton,"[11] or from Richard Hannay who thinks that "Albania was just the sort of place that might keep a man from yawning"[12] would be disconcerted by D, the central character of The Confidential Agent. Weary and depressive, D is a physically weak former university lecturer. The death of his wife, executed in error ("a mistake not an atrocity"[13]) shortly after civil war broke out in his country, has left him traumatized. In any case, his nerves are shattered by constant bombing and ever present physical danger: "He tried to stop his fingers shaking, but he was afraid of pain" (68). (Although unnamed, D's country would obviously be identified as Spain by contemporary readers).

The confidential agent of the book's title, D has been sent by his government to negotiate a supply of coal from a group of British businessmen. Without this coal, D's side is doomed to almost inevitable defeat. Shipped through a neutral state to evade government regulations, the coal will enable D's government to continue their struggle, at least for a time. D's credentials are stolen and he is unable to negotiate the coal contract. Betrayed by agents supposedly working for his own government, he is falsely accused of murdering a girl who worked at his lodgings and whom he innocently befriended. On the run, he tries his "last shot" by appealing to the left-wing or working-class solidarity the unemployed miners in a Northern town might feel for the oppressed in his own land. Although they stand to regain their livelihoods if the mine reopens to supply the other side in the civil war, D pleads for their support: "Do you want to dig coal to kill children with?" (169). His appeal falls on deaf ears ("'Aw, shut up,' a voice said"). The confidential agent's mission is only redeemed from complete failure by several lucky chances. Rose Cullen, the daughter of the mine-owner with whom he unsuccessfully negotiates, grows attached to him. Her love for D develops in spite of the fact his low-spiritedness includes a failure of sexual desire and of any capacity for romantic feeling. Once arrested on the spurious murder charge, he is provided with expensive legal representation, bail-money and the means of escape from England by a wealthy Jewish businessman, Mr. Forbes (alias Fort). Forbes does this because he is pursuing Rose, while, simultaneously, being in love with a working-class woman he is keeping as a mistress. When he finally chooses his mistress in preference to Rose, he saves D for the latter. This may be a sentimental "gesture" (206) as Rose herself dismissively characterizes it. Undeniably it is strikingly generous and the reflection of Forbes's basic decency. D's enemies are prevented from obtaining the coal he failed to get by the bad publicity caused when an explosion is set off by a group of juvenile delinquents into whose company D briefly fell. These hooligans are entirely apolitical. They help D to escape and cause the explosion merely out of a liking for anarchy and destruction.

A summary of the narrative of The Confidential Agent is useful since it brings out a striking feature of the novel. There is a marked severance between conscious motives, deliberate choice and willed action on the one side and the course events follow on the other. D's fate is largely determined by what at least appear to be mere chances, freakish accidents and unforeseen collocations of circumstance. The idiosyncratic emotional needs of Rose and Mr. Forbes or an accidental meeting with a gang of young tearaways do far more to shape the course of D's life than his own devices and desires. However one interprets it, this severance between chosen action and actual events is clearly crucial to the novel's meaning.

The severance also suggests that the use of the initial "D" to identify The Confidential Agent's main character has more than a casual or chance similarity to Kafka's "K" in The Castle. The atmosphere of The Confidential Agent has something of the Kafkaesque in the claustrophobia of its foggy London streets, its failed attempts to influence enigmatic, powerful people, its bizarre, unexpected encounters; but most of all in that sense of being in a story whose plot one has not devised and cannot grasp. The Castle was familiar to English readers in the 1930s through the translation by Willa and Edwin Muir. In an essay published in 1934, Muir interpreted Kafka as a "profound religious thinker" whose work was "a comedy of cross purposes on a grand scale" displaying the "incompatibility of the ways of Providence and the ways of man."[14] It is interesting, for the purposes of exploring The Confidential Agent that, of several possible interpretations of Kafka, this was probably the most influential one current in Britain during the 1930s.

However one estimates the degree or significance of reminiscences of Kafka in The Confidential Agent, there is no denying the deliberate and self-conscious manner in which Greene's novel repudiates whole swathes of the thriller's moral and social attitudes. This is particularly notable in the way in which The Confidential Agent handles the figure of the foreigner and the nature of violence.

From the outset, the reader is aware of Greene's subversion of the 1930s thriller's xenophobic assumptions. When Rose Cullen accidentally hits a man with a bun she throws away, he threatens to sue her. And when D takes her part, "a voice wailed in disgust through the fog like a wounded sea animal, `A foreigner.'" The doting mother of a boy "clothed hideously in corduroy shorts, a lemon yellow jumper and a school cap, all chocolate and mauve stripes" tells D magnanimously that she has "nothing against foreigners" (81). When D points out to the depressed porter, at a railway station on his way to plead with the miners, that a table in the waiting room is useless since the seats are fixed and cannot be moved towards it, the man replies, "I've been here twenty years an' never thought of that. You're a foreigner, ain't you? . . . They're always sharp, foreigners" (154). Examples might be multiplied, but perhaps the most telling is D's own reflections on the abused skivvy Else's devotion to him after he has spoken a few considerate words to her: "What a life when a child had to fix her love on an old foreigner" (54).

Buchan, Dornford Yates, "Sapper" and others had repeatedly celebrated the triumph of English fists and manly courage over the knives of sly Dagoes or the secret weapons of guttural Huns. When D is caught making off with Rose Cullen's car, out of necessity, Captain Currie announces, in the best "Sapper" tradition, "We'll treat you better than you deserve—give you a thrashing, man to man" (34). A couple driving past ask what is going on and Currie explains, "One of these foreigners . . . glib of tongue, you know" (35). What follows is a studied reversal of one of the most typical inter-war British thriller scenes in which alien figures are punished and humiliated. Perhaps, too, readers are asked to look at the implications of their own wish-fulfillment and violent fantasies. Instead of being presented, in celebratory terms, by the home-grown "hero," it is shown from the point of view of the foreigner, weak, in poor health, with little power of resistance ("D's hands were useless; he made no attempt to hit back" [36]) and attacked by a man twenty years younger. Nevertheless it is D who wins the moral victory. He is ready to accept death at his attackers' hands. If they kill him, it will result in an international incident ("That would be worth while" [36]). D even handles the situation with a certain panache, cheekily asking his English assailants for a lift to London when their brutal assault is over. They are nonplussed by his demeanor and have failed to steal his credentials ("He realized with surprise that the manager was embarrassed" [36]). He ends the episode as "a battered middle-aged figure who carried himself with an odd limping sprightliness" (38).

D is unlike the heroes of British 1930s thrillers in a more fundamental way. He has experienced conditions of which the English people among whom he moves are ignorant but which, as the novel implies, they are soon to know clearly. He grasps more of the possibilities of life than the English do, as yet. To him, their order, civility and social rituals are the product of a lucky seclusion.

The official who examines his passport, "a very gentle man" (12) is "polite and unhurried" (13). At home, "soldiers would have been called in: they would immediately have assumed that he was a spy, the questioning would have been loud and feverish and long drawn out" (13). The difference between this and the British manner is not due to some innate British moral superiority. The Dover official can (up to now) afford to be pleasant and easy-going because "this was an island" (13).

This protected island people are also nostalgic and escapist, averting their eyes from the ideologies, torture and mass-bombing of civilians D has known. On the wall of the waiting room of the Dover passport office is a "picture of King Edward VII" surrounded by "extraordinary period faces" (13) grinning over high collars. The waiting room at the "small unimportant junction" station where D halts before making his abortive appeal to the miners is decorated with a photograph of "a gentleman in a grey bowler and a Norfolk jacket" (154) and "a lady in a picture hat and white muslin" surrounded by a "perspective of parasols." When D stops to look in the window of a London bookshop, the "new books" offered include one entitled A Lady in Waiting at the Court of King Edward with "a stout woman in white silk with ostrich feathers" on the cover. English people, it seems, would rather think about bygone elegance and picturesque little scandals than about Fascism or Communism. D's reaction is one of amused incredulity ("What a country he thought again with affection" [48]).

Skillfully, Greene shows how D's first perceptions of English life change. The insistent death imagery of the novel's opening ("siren mourned . . . a whole wake lifted up their voices . . . [The ship] reminded D of a hearse . . . the driver careful not to shake the coffin . . . Hysterical women shrieked among the shrouds" [9]) emphasizes the odd angle from which the observer, D, views the world. In his eyes, the ship's deck is "like a map marked with trenches" (10). Shell bursts sound in his brain and "bombing planes took flight from between his eyes." The obvious inference is that, disturbed by his sufferings, the man sees the world not as it is but refracted through his own disordered mind. Gradually, however, The Confidential Agent strips away this comforting illusion. What D sees lies at the core of human life.

Rose, the rich young woman who is drawn to D, tells him that "it doesn't need a war to flatten things. Money, parents, lots of things are just as good as war" (19). Limited as her experience may have been compared to his, she speaks from a sharp perception of what she has known. There is more to her feelings than peevishness. D gradually looks outward at the physical details and the social relations of English life as well as inward at his own memories and physical sensations. He sees proof everywhere in a peaceful country that war lurks under the surface of its "ordinary" life, ready to dart out:

> The soap-box orators talked in the bitter cold at Marble Arch with their mackintoshes turned up around their Adam's apples, and all down the roads the cad cars waited for the night easy girls, and the cheap prostitutes sat hopelessly in the shadows, and the blackmailers kept an eye open on the grass where the deeds of darkness were quietly and unsatisfactorily accomplished. This was technically known as a city at peace. (136)

The furtive and joyless sexuality, linked with and partaking of the bitter cold, the empty political ranting, the blackmail, spying and treachery point to disorder existing outside the circle of D's own memories and experiences. What D sees is what Greene describes in an essay published a year after The Confidential Agent had appeared and amid the catastrophe the novel had prophesied, a civilization in which "violence comes to us more easily because it was so long expected—not only by the political sense but by the moral sense."[15] Greene imports into the thriller some of the sense of desolation and impending doom, on which the poetry of the 1920s and 1930s dwells. The presence of Eliot's The Waste Land is never far away. The vapid film D and Rose see at the cinema they visit (65) recalls C. Day Lewis's "Newsreel," and Captain Currie's mock Tudor road-house belongs with John Betjeman's "Slough" on which the "friendly bombs" are asked to fall. When D reaches the blighted town of Benditch, he discovers in the "horrifying simplicity" (161) of its "curiously empty streets" a confirmation the war is only a continuation and development of the savagery which permeates much of human life. The town's squalor "was like war, but without the spirit of defiance war usually raised" (161). It is the condition natural to man's existence if the trick or tour-de-force of civilization and the constant effort and self-confidence it requires break down: "Bombardment was a waste of time. You could attain your mined world as easily by just letting go" (160). Among the feral boys who rescue D from the police at Benditch "there was no enthusiasm anywhere—no wildness" (173). These youths with their "soft, unformed, anarchic faces" (172) offer no motive or justification for their eagerness to blow up the mine. The question does not arise for them. When D points out that their own fathers work there, they reply "That don't worry us" (174). A rewriting of sentimental portrayals of the urban dispossessed, such as Sherlock Holmes's Baker Street Irregulars, the sub-moral Benditch delinquents suggest that civilized consciousness (granted it even exists) can be sloughed off effortlessly: "Anarchy was just an absence of certain restraints" (174).

The Confidential Agent may be read in one of three ways. Most obviously, it may be enjoyed simply as a thriller, for its vivid incidents, rapid narrative, the unexpected twists and turns of its plot and for that sense (which we know Greene himself valued) of the individual slipping through the cracks of civilization. However, what account would such a reading give of reversal and undermining of so many features of the thriller genre as Greene found it?

A second way to explore the novel would be to take its declared structure as the guide to its meaning. The Confidential Agent is divided into four parts: "The Hunted," "The Hunter," "The Last Shot," and "The End." Such a disposition of the book's contents seems to indicate another version of a fairly common and satisfying narrative pattern. Repressed, apathetic and haunted by his memories, D is the passive victim of others' violence. (Indeed he is unable to resist an attack by his landlady [73-74]). Roused by the murder of Else, he becomes forceful and energetic, wins a limited victory over his enemies, avenges the murder and escapes with the woman who loves him. It would be easy to find examples of this scenario in many novels and films. Understandably so, since like the conventional thrillers Greene remolded, such a plot caters to audience wish-fulfillment. D's resolution that "they had pushed him around . . . it was his turn now" (140) is an almost universally appealing mantra.

While denying them to its readers, The Confidential Agent questions the very nature of such satisfactions. Consider the effect of the scene in which D, having compelled the wretched K to accompany him, forces himself to carry out his act of vengeance for Else's death. There is no concession to the pleasures of "justified" violence, no sense of release in getting one's own back vicariously. D finds that years of academic life "make one a good judge" not "a good executioner" (140). Through his habit, acquired in scholarly work of exploring "other people's pain, their lives, their individual despairs" (140), D is "damned like a creative writer to sympathy." The more he learns about K, the harder it is for him to maintain his own ruthless tough-guy posture. His victim, with only six months to live, has turned traitor to gain a "little comfort" and "respect" as a university lecturer in the time left to him. As he explains his yearning to escape from his poverty-stricken life as a teacher at the Entrenationo school, his broken phrases and yelps "of mourning like a dog" (141) carry the "awful impress" of the existence he has endured. D shoots at him wildly, missing by a foot, but precipitating the heart attack K's doctor had foretold. This absurd and pathetic episode makes it impossible to read The Confidential Agent as the revenge of the "hunter." The novel discovers its meaning as much by working against the expectations raised by its structure as it does by challenging those raised by its genre.

It is worth seeking that meaning in D's changing responses to people, incidents and conversational exchanges within The Confidential Agent. A novel of action, Greene's book is also subtle in its account of the inner life of its main character. Fragmentary, suggested rather than enforced, meaning lurks as a still, small voice heard in D's own mind, at the margins of his conscious beliefs, that "left wing materialism" which, as one critic remarks, Greene conveys with "great sympathy."[16] The agent of a Marxist government, D cannot maintain the belief system he ostensibly supports ("heresies crept in . . . there were aspects of economic materialism which, if he searched his heart, he did not accept" [10]). The movement to which D belongs has split, turning in on itself like Russian Communism in the 1930s or like Republican liquidation of the Anarchists Orwell recorded in Homage to Catalonia (1938). The result is an obsession with treachery and an endless and bloody inquisition in the name of purity and total commitment ("One friend was found with a holy medal under his shirt, another belonged to an organization with the wrong initial letters" [10]). Heresy-hunting feeds universal suspicion ("You could trust nobody but yourself" [10]). Worse still, as in D's case, it breaks down the individual's own personal and intellectual self-belief. Like the accused in Stalin's show-trials, or their fictional counterparts in Koestler's Darkness at Noon (1941), prepared to accuse themselves for the good of the Party, D "wasn't certain that it wasn't right for him to be watched" (10).

D is sustained not by his conscious political allegiances and beliefs but by his love for his dead wife and by his sympathy for the poor, seen as individuals. Subtly, Greene suggests a disparity between what D thinks is his attitude to the woman he has lost ("She had been a passion, and it is difficult to recall an emotion when it is dead" [14]) and the nature of his enduring love for her. One clue is the quotation from "an English poet of Italian origin" (39) he found somewhere and kept since it "expressed a mood connected with his own dead":

> the beat
> Following her daily of thy heart and feet
> How passionately and irretrievably
> In what fond flight, how many ways and days

The verse suggests a constant yearning for the lost love and a continuous search for her. A little later, the cries of an old clothes man and a wandering chair-mender bring back "the years before his marriage with intensity" (56). He and his wife had listened to such cries together. He feels that to live on after her is perjury. In the entire absence of religious belief such a daily quest for the dead and such a love beyond death, being incapable of satisfaction, is pointless and irrational. D's dreams are another anomaly. At night, his mind feeds on "peaceful images" from the past (37-38), of lecture rooms, of his dead wife, of food and wine, often of flowers. D himself notes and dismisses popular psychological explanations like "compensation" and "wish-fulfillment." Interestingly, when Rose discusses her love for D, she perfunctorily mentions another text-book possibility that for her he is a "father fixation" (67). The inference is that loves like hers for D, or D's for his dead wife, are routinely described in such terms. The psychological language is a way of closing down subjects that are difficult or embarrassing to discuss.

D's responses to the people around him and to the people he meets are shaped by two main features of his personality. He possesses an unusually sharp eye for the manifestations of human folly and falsehood and, at the same time, a characteristic gentleness, fairness and restraint in the presence of individual examples of human weakness. In the eyes of D, the novel's central consciousness, the world is colored by an almost ribald pessimism which embraces a wide range of human beliefs and activities. Left-wing politics and ideologies, Conservative ideas and attitudes, Liberal efforts at human understanding, big business and captains of industry, the sturdy, noble proletariat as portrayed in 1930s propaganda, the romantic illusions of the cinema and popular music, for him, are all aspects of a common appetite for self-delusion. For all his weariness, there is nothing merely slack or cynical in D's view of life as it is lived. He displays an active intelligence which pounces on the fundamental flaws in a belief or way of life, grasping those threads which only have to be pulled to see the whole fabric unravel.

If the Marxist regime and ideology he serves are collapsing into warring sects, heresy-hunting and treachery, D finds little to admire in the Conservative views of his rival agent L, whom he unexpectedly encounters on the boat at Dover. D recognizes L's cultivated manners and confident sense of himself ("Five hundred years of inbreeding had produced him" [28]). He sees his enemy as the understandable product of a privileged past, and is even ready to acknowledge L's patina of charm. He sees, too, that L is loyal to his own standards ("The man had integrity of a kind: he gave an impression of truth" [29]). Yet, at the same time, he grasps the human failure lurking beneath Us values. The aristocrat tries to win D over by several plausible arguments ("They'll never trust you—you are a bourgeois" [29]). L's lament for the beauty and culture the revolutionary government have destroyed strikes a chord with D ("It was like being tempted by a devil of admirable character and discrimination" [30]). Then L compares his own loss of a manuscript of St. Augustine's City of God to D's loss of his wife: "It was amazing he hadn't seen his mistake." The civilization L purports to defend is no living organism but "a world of preserved objects" (30) kept for their quaintness or their picturesque qualities. Appreciation and scholarship without faith or love "could kill the human heart," and the well-bred, articulate L quite clearly "hadn't the faintest conception of what it meant to love another human being" (30). Yet although D despises Us politics and ideal of "civilization," he neither hates nor despises the man himself. He notices pathetic details about L, such as the way this "thin tormented creature" (29) cuts his meat into tiny pieces since "his digestion must be rotten" (28). More significantly, he rejects the pleasure of vengeance on L as an oppressor, a class-enemy or someone to make life simpler by hating. He "wanted to be driven to shoot" (171), to believe that L had given orders for the girl Else's death, "to hate him, despise him and shoot." Yet he knows that the fragile aristocrat would never do such a thing. When L convinces him that Else was in fact killed by her employer, the crazy woman manager at the London bed and breakfast where D had stayed, D's reaction is significant: "He felt a sudden lightening of the heart" (171) and an easing of responsibility. He may see L all too clearly for what he is, but he also sees him with understanding, even with sympathy.

Perhaps the funniest single episode in The Confidential Agent, D's encounter with the Entrenationo Language Centre, is an exposure of the Liberal secular dogma that evil is due to lack of knowledge or misapprehension. In E.M. Forster's phrase, what we need to do is "only connect."

Dr. Bellows, the principal of the Centre intends Entrenationo (a fabricated language like Esperanto) to act as the medium of "love of all the world" (43). It will be the means to fulfill "a desire to be able to exchange ideas-with-everybody." If only everyone could speak the same language, there would be no wars since "they are all due to misunderstanding" (43). D is alert to all the inane and pathetic details of Dr. Bellows's and his secretary's appearance. He notes the woman's "wizened idealist's face" and her gestures of gushing friendliness intended to produce an instant close relationship ("I hope you will soon be quite an old friend" [42]). Dr. Bellows, a "rash unfortunate man who has tried to bring his dream to life," talks with an air of buoyant expansiveness belied by his "look of timid hope" and his "frightened smile" (43). As D senses, Bellows "seemed to shrink from innumerable rebuffs" (42). There is a contrast between Dr. Bellows's dreams of universal love and understanding and his "draughty waiting room" in Oxford Street. However, this is nothing to the disparity between his belief in "love of all the world" and his habit of creeping about in rubber-soled shoes in order to catch his ill-paid assistants not speaking in Entrenationo to their students and fining them half their daily wage for any infraction. (The fact that the deluded man has no idea that D and K are using the Entrenationo Centre as a safe place for their undercover meeting is an added absurdity.) Yet D, seeing all the nonsensical aspects of Bellows's refusal to face the complexity of life and the reality of evil "felt sorry for the old man" (43) to whom he speaks gently and politely.

In Green's opinion, thriller writers like Buchan had mistakenly romanticized the world of bankers, financiers and industrialists, seeing them as individuals of superior ability and will-power, linchpins holding the world on course. Buchan's excessive admiration for success and his "materialism" were a weakness in his work. The account of D's meeting with Lord Benditch and his cronies is clearly a riposte to other thriller writers' adulation of the wealthy and influential. D is unimpressed by Benditch's parade of his money in a "fantastic hall" (85) with its "huge expanse of fake paneling" and its reproductions of well-known paintings of royal mistresses. These are the "day-dreams" and "vicarious sensuality of a working-man's son" (86) rather than a glimpse of the higher world of the elite. D is neither envious nor angry. He remains quite detached since, unashamed of being poor, he "simply didn't mind his shabbiness" (86). Benditch's Buchanesque features, the "bullet head," "the jaw of an equestrian statue" and the "mannerism of using his hand like a signpost" are a dead language for someone "born without the sense of snobbery" (86). In observing Benditch and his partners, D is too clear-sighted for hatred.

He sees the weakness and absurdity of Bates, the Trade Union leader, in a similar ironic detail, tinged with pity. Looking at this man playing the role of Radical and tribune of the people, D recognizes a social climber, concerned to escape his own origins ("and the marks of his rising he had tucked away with shame" [169]). For all his proletarian rhetoric and posturing, Bates is a careerist and time-server ("He had a mannerism learned from his leaders of tossing back his unruly hair—it was the only unruly thing, D thought, about him" [170]).

One way to misread D's responses to the varied figures he meets would be to see it as misanthropy, a jaundiced cynicism spilling over into contempt for everyone and everything. It is more specific and intelligent than that, catching in a popular novel something of the challenge presented by Bunyan's Vanity Fair, or the first section of Pascal's Pensees, the vision of life without spiritual dimension. What D has grasped about the world is the extraordinary prevalence within it of the self-deceiving and the dishonest. The words of the popular song he listens to with Rose and which, he supposes, represented the "spirit of the age, whatever that meant" (26), suggests facile emotions, self-pity, promises without commitment, almost words without meaning. The Confidential Agent is peopled by those who, making empty gestures to deceive others, also deceive themselves. Captain Currie's monocle, his retaining of his military rank in peace-time, his feverish desire to know the right people ("Excuse me. I think I see Monty Crookham" [21]) are of a piece with Bates's "Radical" way of tossing his hair back. The film D watches with Rose, an affair of "gelatine tears" in which "everybody behaved nobly and made a lot of money" (65), belongs to the same order (or disorder) of morals and emotion as the "gentle and spurious world" (150) of the Oxford Groupers or Buchmanites. Mr. Fortescue, the "old young man" (148) who interrupts Rose and D after K's death, mentions the help he gains from cosy Buchmanite support sessions ("there's nothing clears the air like sharing . . . the other fellows are always sympathetic" [149]).

Behind the novel's various satirical sketches and linking them together is the vision of a society which has lost a sense of value and meaning. It is the fact that D possesses such a sense that explains his attraction for Rose Cullen. Rose, who has "known so much fraud" (20) (as D himself recognizes), is drawn to his honesty and lack of pretense. She tests and probes his integrity suspiciously ("Don't be melodramatic . . . Do you want to impress me?" [19]) and finds that his low-key sincerity rings true. There is no sexual charge and almost no sexual attraction in their relationship. He feels "an immense tenderness for her because she might have been his daughter" (145) while she "made no demands on him for passionate love." Rose is clear enough about the reason she is attracted to D: "Go on being honest. That's why I love you" Among so many given over to lying to themselves and to others or displaying the "credulity and also mistrust inherent in human beings" (39), D tries to see and to tell the truth.

It is significant that his research, in his earlier life as a medieval scholar, involved demythologising a key text of European literature. The "Berne MS" of The Song of Roland, which he is supposed to have discovered, offers an alternative version in which Oliver, instead of giving Roland an accidental blow, "strikes down his friend in full knowledge" (62) for wasting the lives of his men by refusing to blow his horn. This lost version of the great epic poem was imposed on their own and succeeding generations by those, like the medieval nobles ("quite capable of being Rolands in a small way" [62]) who were unable to face the truth. D's refusal of false ideals in his own life is of a piece with his work as a scholar. He does (fictionally) with the codes and values of the epic what Greene does with those of the thriller.

In D, Greene offers a picture of how far natural virtue and intellectual honesty can take a man. Without religious beliefs or supernatural sanctions for his personal conduct, D sees truthfulness and morality as necessary if social life is to have meaning or even to be possible. "All over the world," he believes, "there were people like himself who didn't believe in being corrupted—simply because it made life impossible—as when a man or woman cannot tell the truth about anything" (32). In his view, life cannot be anything other than moral, a conscious choice to live by the best that one knows. As D tells Rose, "You've got to choose some line of action and live by it. Otherwise nothing matters at all" (60).

Having no religious belief, D chooses the pursuit of justice as his faith. Looking at Else's dead body, he reflects that "if you believed in God, you could also believe that it had been saved from much misery" (117). Since for him this is impossible, then the alternative must be the righting of wrongs in the life we know: "Unless people received their deserts, the world to him was chaos, he was faced with despair" (117).

A passive faith which leaves all to God and offers the consolation that wrongs will be remedied in a better life has (quite correctly and very often) been condemned. The goal of justice here and now, the imperative demand that "people received their deserts" has, generally, been seen as both desirable and possible. One effect of The Confidential Agent is to invite thought about this ideal of justice, to demur and suggest reservations about it, rather than to score points. D is treated sympathetically, but the complexities and divagations of his role as "the hunter" raise doubts about his choice of justice instead of faith. Undeniably, religious belief has its difficulties but secular justice, too, is problematic. Can it, in fact, be a workable, clear-cut alternative to the religion D has refused? Our knowledge may be limited or wrong like D's. Like his, our actions may be diverted from their aim.

The Confidential Agent portrays a man brought to the verge of another range of perceptions which complete and make sense of what he already understands. Curiously (and this is central to the novel's meaning) D is haunted by the God he consciously rejects. God is present at the margins of the novel. As has been suggested, the constant images of happiness in sleep and the persistent, questing love of the dead woman point to needs, experiences, even confidences daily life does not sustain but cannot erase. More than this, D is explicitly aware of a dimension which is missing. Contemplating Dr. Baines's unending idealism, he reflects that "there was something of a saint about him, but saints are successful" (43). There was a context in Baines's energy and good intentions that might have moved mountains, but it was not that of secular Liberalism. Explaining his choice of a moral life to Rose, D adds, "I suppose if I believed in a god it would be simpler" (60). If he possessed it, religious belief would make it easier for him to live a good or even a bearable life. Interestingly, D notices scraps of religious sentiment when they fall in his way. They hint of ways of thinking and feeling he does not share but which have the poignance of a road not taken. Just after his botched attempt to murder the traitor K, D glimpses a verse in an open book lying on the sofa in the flat into which he has intruded:

> God is in the candlelight
> Waiting in your home. (141)

His reaction to the sentimental lines is striking: "The absurd poem was like a wax impress on his brain. He didn't believe in God, he had no home: it was like the incantation of a savage tribe which had an effect on even the most civilized beholder" (141-2). Even in such a feeble and tarnished medium, the message is potent. D is aware of a loss and bleakness in his own life and of the appeal to deeper parts of his nature of what he consciously rejects. Rose shares his feeling of a lack in her own life. Fearing for his safety, she adds, "We're unlucky. We don't believe in God. So it's no use praying" (155). The God to whom one might turn in moments of crisis or peril would also have defined the otherwise fragmented, almost incomprehensible battles of the modern world. Reflecting on the political straggle in which he has been engaged, D contrasts it with wars in the medieval civilization he used to study: "Fighting was better in the old days . . . Men were united in a common belief" (56). In the light of his experiences, D has come to doubt the humanist, secular premise that crimes or faults in the individual or in society are caused essentially by ignorance, economic injustice or social oppression. For him, human nature is intrinsically wounded. Else's life, in routine contact with her friend's prostitution, reminds him of "the guilt which clings to all of us without our knowing it" (49). He sees suspiciousness, too, as universal: "It was as if the whole world lay in the shadow of abandonment" (64). Yet, although he accepts the facts for which the doctrine of original sin provides the readiest explanation, D can see no evidence of meaning or purpose in the "crazy mixture" (156) of life. For him, it is impossible to understand how, looking at the "monstrous world," there should "be people who talked of a superintending design" (156). Rejecting prayer as "a passive part" he is "anxious to express himself in action" (115). Yet, as the course of the novel demonstrates, action does not provide the clear-cut alternative D desires and expects. He cannot impose the order he wishes on the mysterious and fluctuating medium of life.

D is rescued from danger by factors which have nothing to do with his own plans. His escape and reunion with Rose are brought about by the character and choices of the Jewish businessman, Mr. Forbes. Like the rest of Lord Benditch's circle, Forbes is devious in his business activities. His pursuit of Rose while simultaneously keeping a young mistress ("She's not a bad girl . . . I think she's really fond of me" [192]) can hardly be defended on the grounds he himself alleges that "a man must live." Yet Forbes is very far from being the anti-semitic caricature some critics have called him.[17] As Forbes listens to D's account of the attack made on him, "he looked older and more Jewish." In fact, his ancestral inheritance is a gift of priceless value in the morally dishonest world The Confidential Agent portrays:

> Very far back in the past was the desert, the dead salt sea, the desolate mountains and the violence on the road from Jericho. (95)

The implication is obvious. Whatever his personal failings, Forbes is capable of the motives and actions of the good Samaritan. He has a "basis of belief" (95), a phrase which carries more weight than that he could believe D's story. Forbes had a capacity for sympathy with another's predicament, for compassion towards a stranger. Forbes's arranging of D's escape may be a sentimental gesture (in Rose's dismissive view), but it is also proof that he retains enough of a moral scheme to make disinterested kindness possible, perhaps mandatory. Obviously, The Confidential

Agent is not one of Greene's great novels, but it does display his agile and creative re-making of a popular form. He retains the thriller's adventure and heightened sense of insecurity when the fragile crust of ordinary habits (which pass for civilization) is broken. At the same time, and often hilariously, he undermines British thriller conventions current in 1939 and the moral expectations which accompanied them. He did not set out to write a thriller as the vehicle of a religious message, but he was aware that heightened personal danger and wider disintegration on which the form thrived created an open space in which it was both possible and necessary to ask fundamental questions.

NOTES

1. Richard Usborne, (1953 rpt., London: Hutchinson, 1974), pp. 146-147.
2. Usborne, 147.
3. Claud Cockburn, *Bestseller*, (1972 rpt., Harmondsworth: Penguin, 1975), p. 134.
4. Graham Greene, "The Last Buchan," (1940 rpt. *The Lost Childhood*, Harmondsworth: Penguin, 1962), p. 119.
5. John Buchan, *The Power House*, (1913 rpt. London: B and W Publishing, 1999), p. 36 Subsequent references in parenthesis are to this edition.
6. Greene, *The Lost Childhood*, p. 119.
7. C.S. Lewis, *Of This and Other Worlds*, (1982 rpt. London: Collins, 1984), p. 132.
8. Greene, *The Lost Childhood*, p. 76.
9. Greene, *The Lost Childhood*, p. 121.
10. Greene, "At Home" (1940 rpt. *The Lost Childhood*), p. 223.
11. Usborne, p. 150.

12. John Buchan, *The Thirty-Nine Steps*, (1915 rpt. London: B and W Publishing, 1999), p. 112.
13. Graham Greene, *The Confidential Agent*, (1939 rpt. Harmondsworth: Penguin, 1971), p. 13. Subsequent references in parenthesis are to this edition.
14. Edwin Muir, "Franz Kafka," (1934 rpt. Kafka, *A Collection of Critical Essays*, Englewood Cliffs: Prentice Hall, 1962), p. 33.
15. Greene, *The Lost Childhood*, p. 221.
16. Graham Smith, *The Achievement of Graham Greene*, (Brighton: Harvester, 1986), p. 34.
17. Michael Shelden, *Graham Greene: The Enemy Within*, (New York: Random House, 1994), pp. 124-126 for example.

REFERENCES

Buchan, John. *The Power House*. 1913. Reprint. London: B&W Publishing, 1999.

——. *The Thirty-Nine Steps*. 1915. Reprint. London: B&W Publishing, 1999.

Cockburn, Claud. *Bestseller*. 1962. Reprint. Harmondsworth: Penguin, 1972.

Greene, Graham. *The Confidential Agent*. 1939. Reprint. Harmondsworth: Penguin, 1971.

——. *The Lost Childhood*. 1940. Reprint. Harmondsworth: Penguin, 1962.

Lewis, C.S. *Of This and Other Worlds*. 1982. Reprint. London: Collins, 1984.

Muir, Edwin. "Franz Kafka." *Kafka: A Collection of Critical Essays*. Englewood Cliffs: Prentice Hall, 1962.

Shelden, Michael. *Graham Greene: The Enemy Within*. New York: Random House, 1994.

Smith, Graham. *The Achievement of Graham Greene*. Brighton: Harvester, 1986.

Usborne, Richard. *Clubland Heroes: A Nostalgic Study of Some Recurrent Characters in the Romantic Fiction of Dornford, Yates, John Buchan and Sapper*. 1950 Reprint. London: Hutchinson, 1974.

Index

□□□